THE AND

THE AND

Learning to trust God's sovereignty and grace

through life's heartache

Erin Reichman

THE AND
Learning to trust God's sovereignty and grace through
life's heartache

Reichman Publishing
Printing and distribution by CreateSpace

Unless otherwise noted, all Scripture quotations are taken from The
Holy Bible, New International Version (NIV) Study Bible, copyright
© 1995 by Zondervan Corp.

ISBN 978-0-9967594-0-3
eISBN 978-0-9967594-1-0

The Team: Chaya Chavez (editor)
Chloe Scheffe, Graphic Design, etc. (cover design)

Printed in the United States of America
First Edition 2015

For my incredible children, Adeline and Isaac,
You have brought so much love, laughter, and happiness into my life.

For Rachel, no words are enough to thank you for blessing my life in
such a profound way.

For my beautiful friend, Cindy.
I love you, I miss you, and I look forward to an eternity together.

For my remarkable father, Paul, who never finished writing his own
story, I pray I represented your thoughts and feelings well.

And most importantly, for God, who gave me a heart that
aches for Him

Acknowledgements

A huge thank you to my editor and awesome sister Chaya. She is not only an incredible sister and friend, but also a talented writer and thoughtful critic. Her tireless hours and selfless love is beyond measure. Just as essential to the completion of this book is my husband Ryan. He was always there to encourage me when self-doubt and frustration threatened to topple me. His love is unending and I am grateful to have him always by my side, during the good and not-so-good. Finally, a big shout out to my many friends, those mentioned in the book and even more that weren't. You have been so supportive during this endeavor, offering words of encouragement and helping with my faulty memory. Thank you!

PROLOGUE

Kindergarten is an amazing year of discovery, and hopefully for most students, it is also a time when your dreams and abilities appear limitless. I certainly felt powerful stepping onto that school bus with all of the older kids, ready to tackle the great big world that I was itching to explore. Having been enrolled by my parents in a specialty Montessori program in the Minneapolis Public School District, I still thought all learning was play, and some of it was tremendously captivating. In addition to the structures I built with blocks and houses I drew on paper, I started to explore the beautiful world of communication with words and writing. Although I had already proclaimed my career choice as an architect, I had no issue envisioning being a writer as well. You can do it all, right?

As motivation for me to write more, my teacher, Ms. Mobley prepared a folder of my current "works" (all about three to five sentences long) and a bunch of extra pieces of paper. On several pages she had written titles such as "Circus" or "My Home" that gave me a subject to spark my creativity, but many sheets had been left blank. In anticipation of my upcoming stories and before I even had a title on the page or any content at all, I first made sure that each empty piece contained what I thought was the proper conclusion. So at the bottom of each paper I wrote in capital letters "THE AND." After handing in the folder full of newly-written stories, the teacher sweetly praised each piece, without ever correcting my spelling, and told me she couldn't wait to see more.

The world was my oyster and I was in control of my own destiny. In my mind, if I set a goal and worked hard, there was nothing I couldn't achieve. Although some of my naiveté was squashed by the trials of middle school and the intrinsic maturation process, my perception was still that life was a boat, and I held the rudder and the throttle. God was there to make sure I didn't capsize by stupidity; and if I stayed smart and well behaved, I'd be sure to stay afloat.

Even by my senior year of high school, the reality of lacking real control over my life had not manifested in a dramatic way. So when the school newsletter posted a list of all of the graduating seniors' plans at the end of the year, my presumptiveness was painfully apparent. My post read: "I will attend college to study architecture, travel the world, get my licensure, and work in a medium-sized firm. After a few years I will start a family and then begin work for a small-sized firm." Wow, I had it all planned out, without much thought for life's interruptions, and certainly without asking God what His will was for me.

While almost everything has come to pass, nothing in this cookie cutter expectation happened as smoothly or in the manner I had imagined. Years of having my life weave in and out of chaos and calm, I have finally come to realize that the signature ending I wrote on all of my kindergarten stories was much truer to life than I could have ever imagined. First of all, there is no end to God's relationship with His people that have been redeemed by Christ; they live in the hope of eternal life. Secondly, only God can write the conclusion of our chapters, or the finale of our story in advance. It is impossible to count the times that I thought I knew what the outcome of my current circumstances would be, only to be sent on an even wilder adventure, filled with brand new situations and a fresh set of emotions. The transitions to the next season of life are rarely smooth and without pain, but in hindsight, almost always mind-boggling and purposeful.

The sovereign God I pray to and profess to follow leads me down paths only He could imagine and create, in a determined fashion that not even my obstinate maneuvering can adjust. His great plan can never be thwarted, as He seeks to mold me into the likeness of Jesus, which is the true source of joy and peace. So next time it feels like a door is closing on a chapter of your life or even life itself, consider that "The End" for people that live with the hope Christ provides, is actually "THE AND." With all hope secured in our salvation through Christ, our job is to live every moment to its fullest, furiously hanging on for the ride, and praising God for His loving dominion

.

Life should NOT be a journey to the grave with the intention of safely arriving in an attractive and well-preserved body, but rather to skid in sideways, champagne in one hand – strawberries in the other, body thoroughly used up, totally worn out and screaming, 'Woo Hoo – What a Ride.
Hunter S. Thompson. (Quote found buried amidst medical records of my father, Paul)

I

The morning was racing along, my mind absorbed in resolving a current set of architectural design issues and coordinating the engineering on a school renovation project. Lost in problem-solving mode, with my eyes glued to the computer screen, and my left hand scribbling notes on the latest set of drawings sprawled before me, significant time had passed since I had moved from my chair. Reeling around, I attempted to reach for an earlier drawing set that was laying on the right side of the desk. In a frightful shock, I was jarred out my trance. My right arm, which had been resting on the desk, flopped into my lap like a package of meat. It no longer held any life, entirely detached from sensation.

Not sure exactly when my arm had gone limp, I gingerly lifted my right arm with my left hand and tried to poke life back until it. It was not asleep, and provided no reassuring "pins and needles." I felt nothing. I had no ability to move it; it was dead weight from the shoulder down. Immediately, an intense panic kicked in.

It was Monday morning, August 29, 2005, the last full week of work before the Labor Day holiday (the day before my 29th birthday). Anticipating a hectic week, I had arrived at work before 7 a.m., slightly earlier than normal. The previous six months I had been working an excessive number of hours, and I knew this week would be no exception, since the project owners wanted an updated progress set to review before the three-day weekend. As a senior project manager in my architecture firm, I was responsible for the design and implementation of millions of construction dollars, which brought a lot of responsibility, and therefore an equal amount of stress. Fortunately, so far this morning, the phone calls had been limited, and the day looked promisingly productive. I was hoping to get a good jump start on the most pressing tasks while the day was still quiet.

Cautiously I stood up, making sure that I was steady on my feet. I looked around the sea of desks in our open office layout, realizing that no one had noticed how startled and uneasy I must have appeared with sweat beads on my forehead and eyeballs like saucers. Wrapped up in their own morning agendas, everyone was oblivious that my life had just been turned upside down. The world had become silent and still, and I was suspended in time. Reaching slowly into my purse with my left hand, I pulled out my wallet which contained my doctors' contact numbers.

Having a genetic heart condition, I was a frequent flyer with a group of cardiologists at University of Washington Medical Center, but I had not had a heart "episode" for at least six months. Slowly, I shuffled to the conference room, the closest enclosed room on my side of the office, and a quiet place for conversation, uninterrupted by the hum of background noise. Hoping for privacy, I shut the door behind me, not wanting to draw attention to myself. I pulled out the business card for the nurse of my electrophysiologist and dialed the number carefully. Miraculously, she answered the phone call on the third ring. Out of the numerous calls I had placed to her in the past, this was the first time I wasn't forwarded to her voicemail. Knowing the direness of my situation, I'm so thankful that I didn't need to wait for a return call.

When she answered the phone, I made another startling realization. As I opened my mouth to speak, nothing came out. I couldn't form words, and though they were so clear in my head, they were mysteriously disconnected from my tongue. Through a garbled mess of sounds, the nurse must have understood enough to recognize the seriousness of the situation. She told me that she didn't understand fully what I was saying but that I needed to get to a hospital right away. Slightly compromised mentally with a dangerous mix of my eternal optimism, I assumed it would pass and require only a follow-up office visit. The nurse's urgent direction threw a healthy dose of reality into my obscured thinking. I hung up the phone and sat there for a moment composing myself. I was on the verge of tears, but I was determined to stay stoic and calm. Rather absurdly, I wanted to remain professional, but it really had more to do with showing my weakness and vulnerability to people whom I respected and wanted to be respected by.

Rising from the desk, I walked the few hundred feet to the other side of the office and to the desk of the office manager, Shannon. I told her, in as few words as possible, that I needed to go the hospital. My words came this time, but were quivering and uncertain. She called Linda, one of the project administrators, on the phone, and she quickly came to her desk. Shannon explained the situation as fully as she could understand, graciously allowing me to remain silent, and Linda and I left immediately for the parking garage, where the company cars were parked. Moving excruciatingly slow, I was fearful that something worse would happen if I hurried. At this point, I wasn't sure if this incident had anything to do with my heart and I didn't want to set it into a bad rhythm.

Finally reaching the car, I slid in and buckled up instinctually, almost as if that would save me from what I was experiencing. Linda was visibly shaken by the situation she found herself in and remained silent. As she backed out of the stall guardedly, inch by inch past the imposing columns, I asked her to take me to UW, though there were several hospitals to choose from in close proximity to the office. Only later would I learn that she didn't drive much and it wasn't just my emergency that made her uneasy.

The company cars were located three floors underground, which forced us to maneuver around a tight maze of cars, columns, and thick concrete walls. After now almost ten minutes of terror, I sat quietly, continuing to poke and prod at my right hand, which was starting to regain some sensation. I squeezed my right hand vigorously with my left, meticulously massaging each finger in an attempt to elicit some response and grip. Thankfully, I could now move my arm at the shoulder, and my words were becoming clearer; whatever had seized my arm and tongue was starting to retreat. At the start of my episode, I was intentionally limiting the conversation, but as my tongue loosened, I tried unsuccessfully to lighten the mood a bit with some nervous humor. However, I was getting quite agitated by the speed at which we were moving around the garage. Even in my current condition, I could have walked faster. The garage was dimly lit and the tight corners, combined with the low ceilings and deep beams, were beginning to close in on me. Claustrophobia was not a feeling I had experienced before, and it was starting to induce a panic that accentuated an already bad situation. Respectfully, I asked if she could move a bit faster, to which she responded that she would try, but results did not materialize. Finally, we emerged from the crushing prison of the parking garage into the bright sunshine and my soul sang.

The rest of the trip (only about five miles) took an ungodly amount of time, or so it felt. As she pulled into the ER turnaround, I leaped out of the car and moved as quickly as possible to the triage desk. After explaining my symptoms, the nurse brought me immediately to a patient room, where a doctor came to evaluate me a few minutes later. He started a battery of tests on my right arm, and the reflexes and function of my other limbs. He checked my pupils and listened to my speech, which to my untrained ear was mostly back to normal. I was able to grip his hand with my right hand and I felt my strength returning. A CT scan was done on my head, but an MRI, that is also standard procedure, could not be done due to my pacemaker (magnetic properties of the machine could shut off the device). Afterward, I was left to wait in the ER patient room for the results; a severe headache was taking the place of my earlier symptoms that were now waning.

Ryan, my husband of six years, arrived shortly after my neurological evaluation, as Shannon had called him the moment I left for the parking garage. Currently working in a structural engineering office only blocks away from my firm, he was able to be with me at the hospital quickly. Throwing both my functioning arms around him, the tears that I held back so successfully were let loose like a dam. He always had a way of making me feel so safe and secure. It was such a relief to have him there, I was now free to abandon the stoic act and rely on his gentle, calming presence.

The cardiologist on duty in the ER came into the room in fairly short order which, from my experience, is not the norm unless you have been put on the "priority" list. He explained to us that it appeared that I had had a TIA (transient ischemic attack), essentially a mini-stroke, most likely brought on by a blood clot that originated in my inefficient and significantly thickened heart. He assured us that the TIA looked to have done no lasting damage, but that immediate measures needed to be taken to make sure we didn't have a repeat, and more dramatic performance. Their plan was to admit me into the hospital where they would start administering a blood thinner intravenously.

Additionally, he stated that after I achieved a "therapeutic" level on the blood thinner, I would be discharged from the hospital and put on a monitoring regiment to keep me stabilized. This would hopefully ensure that my heart didn't create any more clots to wreak havoc. In a rather casual tone, he informed us that the blood thinner I would be on was most likely permanent and was not conducive to pregnancy, as it was known to cause significant birth defects. Consequently, we should not try for children while on this medication. Unbeknownst to him, this final bit of news was enough to take our breath away.

Four short months previous, Ryan and I spent a romantic weekend away together on the beautiful, rainy Washington coast considering what the future held for us. While strolling down the wet sand beach, we had decided that after six years of honeymooning without children, getting rid of our student debt, and building two blossoming careers, it was now time to actively start trying for a family. While we were scared about how it would affect my heart, I had been relatively stable the past few years, and pregnancy, we speculated, would only affect it temporarily. Starting a family was always part of our marriage plan and we felt optimistic that we could accomplish it with a little medication, observation, and potentially some minor intervention. Although we knew that my condition could be passed down, we felt confident that our children, even if they inherited the gene, could live full, happy lives just as my father (who also had the condition) and I had.

To our surprise and disappointment, through no lack of effort, pregnancy didn't happened right away for us. As part of public school's attempt at encouraging responsible family planning, the teachers reiterate ad nauseam that having unprotected sex is the leading cause of children (or other worse fates). We believed them full heartedly and were quite disappointed to discover that it normally takes couples, without any fertility issues, six to seven months to conceive. We were starting to wonder if there was something wrong with one or both of us, and were recently considering seeking profession help.

To be told that children couldn't happen while I was on a blood thinning medication, which would be permanent, was devastating. Questions swirled in my throbbing brain, threatening to consume me. Does this mean I can never be pregnant? How will the TIA affect my heart condition and future prognosis? What are the chances that this will happen again, but with more severe results? My hope for carrying a child was beginning to seem bleak. Was this chapter of our lives closing before it even got under way? "The End" of my dream for biological children appeared to be nearing.

****

My medical journey began when I was in 8th grade at middle school. Our final exam for physical education was to run the mile, and completing it, regardless of your speed, would earn you an "A" for the class. The grade for the class was the driver that pushed me to continue, even after my body was screaming for me to stop. While I have always been more academic than athletic, it was a task that I felt confident I could accomplish, however pitiful the results. As I was jogging around the track, about three quarters done, I started to feel dizziness, nausea, and significant chest heaviness. I pushed through with the great encouragement of my "closest" friends.

"Come on, you're just out of shape," they chimed. "Toughen up. This shouldn't be that hard."

Twenty minutes later, as I crossed the finish line and accomplished my goal, I fell to my knees and nearly passed out. Instinctively, I knew it was much more than exhaustion and unconditioned lungs. My heart continued to race, long after the run was over and I couldn't catch my breath. My parents were contacted by the school nurse, and they scheduled the soonest available appointment to see Dr. Stone, my pediatric cardiologist, who had been seeing me since birth for an unrelated and resolved heart issue.

By the time I arrived in Dr. Stone's office at age thirteen, my symptoms, which first developed during the mile run, had turned into a prolonged episode and created an electrical "storm" of activity that wasn't relieving on its own. I was in atrial tachycardia (fast heartbeat) quite frequently and had severe chest pains even during rest. After assessing my condition, he referred me to a heart specialist at the neighboring Minneapolis Heart Institute (fortuitously, one of the best heart centers in the United States). They ran some more extensive tests, including an echocardiogram - a cardiac ultrasound, an electrocardiogram (ECG) – external electrodes monitoring electrical pulses, and a heart catheterization – which is a probe placed through an artery in the groin and up into the heart to assess blood flow within the heart. Finally they diagnosed me with Hypertrophic Cardiomyopathy (HCM), an abnormality of the heart muscle involving excessive thickening of the left ventricular wall. During the heart catheterization, they observed that the excessive muscle growth was creating an obstruction, which had triggered my chest pains and arrhythmia.

We were told that this was a genetic disease that should be investigated further to find its origins. The origins were relatively easy to delineate. Reviewing the death certificates of our immediate family, my father's twin brother died in 1977 at age 24 of "acute pulmonary edema and heart failure, as a consequence of congenital asymmetrical hypertrophy of the heart." His mother, my fraternal grandmother, died in 1979 of "probable cardiac arrest" at age 50. Since HCM was not widely understood, especially the genetic component, and imaging with echocardiogram was in early development at the time of both of their deaths, no further exploration was done.

My father went in for testing a few months after my diagnosis and was found to have some increased muscle growth, indicative of HCM, but had not yet experienced any side effects from it. When our genetic mystery had been solved, my grandmother's two sisters mentioned that there were a handful of suspicious deaths (such as a single-vehicle car accident and a drowning by a known proficient swimmer) that had occurred within the extended family. These could possibly have been cardiac events, but there had been no investigations or autopsies to confirm what we now suspected.

The cardiac specialists told my parents that surgery would be required to remove the excess muscle growth along the septum (dividing wall between the left and right chambers) and inside the ventricles (lower two chambers). This surgery, called a myectomy, was at the time, a fairly new procedure, and only a couple of specialized surgeons in the US were performing it. We were referred to one of them for a consultation and to schedule the procedure, but weeks before we were to fly from Minneapolis to San Francisco for the surgery, the surgeon was killed in a boating accident. My parents were left wondering where to turn next while the urgency of my situation intensified.

Days later, while discussing my case in a physician break room, Dr. Stone miraculously ran into Dr. Nicoloff. He was a world-renowned heart surgeon, who had completed the first heart transplant in Minnesota and co-developed the St. Jude mechanical heart valve. However, he had never done a myectomy, but was willing to give it a try. He had expressed concern with my parents that he might be unable to start my heart again after the procedure, but he knew this surgery was virtually my only hope for a normal life.

The surgery took place in December 1990, six months after my initial diagnosis, and was tremendous success. Seven days after my open heart surgery, I went home filled with energy and renewed strength. At fourteen years old, the body has an astonishing ability to recover at breakneck speed, which I have since discovered decreases with age.

While I never returned to gym class or sports during my remaining years of school, there was not much missing from my life. My parents worked very hard to make sure I never felt limited, and they encouraged me to set high goals and believe that, despite my physical limitations, there was nothing I couldn't accomplish. My heart, besides needing yearly monitoring, behaved remarkably well for the next ten years. Though it would never be a normal heart again and always be prone to bouts of abnormal rhythms, the hope was that these anticipated episodes were relatively infrequent and minor in severity.

****

As I was left to ponder the ramifications of the TIA with Ryan in the ER, they were busy searching for a room to admit me into. Finally, after a few hours, I was given a room on the cardiac floor, and taken through the standard admit procedures; ID bracelet, placement of a telemetry monitor, an initial EKG, introduction to my assigned nursing staff, questions about medical and family history, current medications, and a first round of admit stats (blood pressure, pulse, temperature). This was routine to me because although my condition had been stable, I had at least a yearly hospital admission for stubborn atrial fibrillation (a fast and irregular heartbeat).

From all my past emergencies, I have learned that hospitals have two speeds of function; lightning fast when emergency situations occur and slow as molasses when your condition is stable. While it is frustrating to wait for the doctor who never seems to arrive for your scheduled procedure, I know that it is much better to be in the second camp. Although great patience is required (one of my short suits in the dealing of personal strengths) I appreciate why the priority system is essential.

Waiting is excruciating when you only know half the information and anxiously hope to understand the rest before you turn the initial news into a big hairy monster. Ryan and I, sitting in my room, were left to wait for the other pieces of the puzzle. My regular electrophysiologist, it had been inferred, would be relaying the rest of the results, along with the short term and long term plans. On top of the shock of a serious medical event, Ryan and I kept staring at each other in disbelief. The silence was screaming, "What now? What does the rest of our lives look like? Besides starting a family, what else does this new situation impact? What is our new "normal?"

My natural rational inclination is to key in on my known starting point, mentally preparing myself to engage it and then starting to sort through all of the possible scenarios, in an effort to reset my orientation. If I can find a path, albeit circuitous, to my original goal or perceived end point, life is good. If it appears that a new path must be charted with a different outcome, my mind begins churning. While I search for the positive, I am primarily gearing up for the emotional journey of accepting things out of my control and the painful recognition of a new reality. My comfort comes from knowing, from the depth of my soul, that God has an ultimate sovereign plan for my life. This setback and others I've faced, helps to give me renewed perseverance and reliance on God that may have waned during the "easy" times. I have hope that God's gracious hand will guide me through this forest too.

As the morning stretched into early afternoon, the on-call doctor finally stopped in to make his rounds, but he didn't have much more to share with us. The good news was that the CT scan and the rest of the neurological tests confirmed that the TIA had not produced any permanent damage. However, we still needed to figure out if my heart was misbehaving enough to produce another clot. One thing was sure, my heart could not be trusted anymore, and as the earlier ER doctor had told us, I would need anticoagulation monitoring (including medication and frequent blood draws) for the rest of my life.

The other good news, that the doctor in the ER hadn't relayed, was there were other medication options available for blood thinning, which didn't carry the risks of birth defects. These meds were reserved for short-term use due to their exorbitant expense, and required either daily injections or a PICC line (a peripherally inserted central catheter) in my arm to constantly infuse the drugs into my blood stream. So when, and if, we got pregnant, I would be immediately put on this other regiment of medication. Nevertheless, the doctor made it clear that we needed to refrain from thinking about our future family until the current situation unfolded a bit more. Getting my blood thinned in a consistent way and making sure that my heart could be tamed was their first priority. In my impatience, I longed for a timeline, something to give me a sense of forward progress, a target to aim my energy. Deep down, I knew anything they told me would be pure speculation. No one but God knew what the future held. Knowing now all of the challenges that lay ahead at that moment, I probably would have curled into a ball and prayed for the end to come — something I actually did on a few occasions. It is God's mercy that He reveals our journeys one bite at a time, allowing at least partial digestion before the next spoonful arrives.

A few hours later, Ryan went home for the evening to catch some sleep and gather my personal items for the hospital stay. Only hours after his departure, my heart decided to provide further proof of its unpredictability. Around midnight, my heart rate skyrocketed and sent the nurses and doctors scrambling into my room from the telemetry monitoring station. They started some IV medications to lower the rate, but it was ineffective. One of the identifying characteristics of my disease is the inverse relationship of heart rate to blood pressure. As a normal heart speeds up, the pressures rise to accommodate the new flow conditions.

In my case, as my heart rate rose, my blood pressure dropped dangerously, and my heart felt as though it were quivering in my chest. In actuality, it was. Not only was it fast, fluctuating between 140 and the mid 150's, but it no longer had any regular rhythm to it. The blood was not pumping out to my extremities efficiently, and I became lightheaded, on the verge of passing out. Drenched in sweat and cold to the touch, I struggled to stay conscious, an unbearable pressure on my chest. After trying for 20 minutes to stabilize me, they moved me into the intensive care unit. As they wheeled me rapidly through the corridors and down the elevator, each thud of a transition strip or expansion joint in the floor accentuated my uncontrolled pulse, already radiating throughout my body. In the ICU, I had a nurse and doctor monitoring me closely, ready to administer emergency treatment at any moment.

My heart felt like it would explode, and having not yet experienced a shock in my 10-years with the defibrillator, I prayed that it would fire and put me back into a normal rhythm. I was still naive enough to believe it provided the solution to this horrible episode. Only years later would I realize that my device was not foolproof or benign, but actually the source of many of my nightmares.

In the meantime, the cardiology team had determined it was not necessary to perform an emergency cardioversion to restore my natural rhythm. Despite my pleas, the pain was what they determined to be "tolerable." The unorganized manner which it galloped along, while normally just disturbing, was now terrifying. There were a few points during the night that I begged God to release me from this situation in whatever way He saw fit. I was ready to go to heaven, thinking in the moment that death was the preferable resolution. The hospital staff must not have thought I was as close as I felt, and God mercifully agreed. Relief did finally come in the early hours of the morning, and my heart regained its composure. My whole body was completely spent, having done the equivalent of hard core aerobics for the last eight hours, without the added benefit of a thinner waistline.

I slept a good portion of the morning away, and by mid-afternoon, I was back in my regular room. Not only was it my birthday, but Hurricane Katrina had come ashore in New Orleans and neighboring coastline towns the previous day during my own chaotic storm. The pictures and videos of the horrific devastation were flashing incessantly on every channel of the TV. Trapped by my situation, I was equally ensnared in the torrent of sad images of loss and pain transported into my room; a city in the throes of turmoil where over 1,800 people would die before help could arrive. Watching others endure their own life-changing situations helped me realize I wasn't alone or singled out in this broken world. In the immediacy of my crisis, it's easy to lose sight of other people and their needs. I wasn't the only one struggling to find new footing, and this tragedy gave me a group of people to empathize with and pray for, ultimately taking some of the focus off of myself. Self-pity didn't seem appropriate when others were dying without aid in dangerous, deplorable conditions.

Remaining in the hospital for about a week longer, my heart had a few more small joyrides, but nothing like the first night. My heart was undoubtedly in an "electrical storm," which is my term for when it consistently threatens to throw itself into a quivering "tantrum," rivaled only by the most headstrong toddler, lasting minutes, hours, and sometimes even days. Although this was an especially bad episode, at least once a year, it goes through a period of bad behavior, having been irritated in some way. My heart remains cranky for a while afterward, and through new medications or dosages, it eventually finds its happy place again.

Honestly, I'm surprised more people aren't affected by heart rhythm issues, considering what is asked of it. The normal heart beats approximately 100,800 times a day, 36,792,000 times a year, and 2,369,776,000 times in a normal 79-year lifespan. Think about it, that's a lot to ask of an organ the size of a human fist; to keep consistent speed and remain regular, day in and day out, without a moment to stop and rest. It's an unthinkable task for a heart like mine that has become thick and inflexible due to an odd gene mutation. I can go months without giving the work of my heart a second thought. Then, in the blink of an eye, I am not able to focus on anything except each unpredictable and pathetic beat.

Time in the hospital was an arduous slog. It took my blood a significant period to reach acceptable anticoagulation levels, which kept me hospitalized longer than otherwise needed. Several times a day they would do a blood test to see if my INR (international normalized ratio) was between 2-3, considered therapeutic for coagulation. A normal person should be under 2, but they needed my blood much thinner to keep clots from forming. The constant rollercoaster of waiting for lab results led to disappointment every morning when the results indicated that it would be at least one more day before I could go home. I longed to go home, so that I could begin to process the reality of my new situation. Time spent in the hospital leads mostly to stewing, and not productive, emotional healing.

Finally, my lab results came in above 2, and the rounding doctor could begin the discharge process. My discharge instruction was for blood test monitoring to continue weekly until I could prove my INR was stabilized, and my next heart check-up was scheduled in one month. Ryan and I were in an indefinite holding pattern until my electrophysiologist gave us permission to move forward with our family agenda. As it turned out, it would be a full year before they believed my heart activity was under control, and I was given the green light to try for children again. My controlling nature gave way to a very long year, full of frustration, impatience, and anger at the circumstances I found myself in. I regret not trusting God more with my life, and my joy during that period of waiting. He was in control then, as He is now. I was the stubborn teenager, pouting in my room about the unfairness of my situation, unaware of the multitude of blessings and joy He provided each and every day. He missed out on my praise, and I missed out on His peace.

"Be joyful in hope, patient in affliction, faithful in prayer."
Romans 12:12

"Be joyful always; pray continually; give thanks in all circumstances, for this is God's will for you in Christ Jesus."
1 Thessalonians 5:16

But the secret to joy is to keep seeking God where we doubt he is.
Ann Voskamp, *One Thousand Gifts: A Dare To Live Fully Right Where you Are*

2

My childhood was spent in the beautiful, lush valley of the Mississippi River in Minnesota. While always within a 60-mile radius of Minneapolis, we moved rather frequently. The oldest of two children, born to Paul and Jackie Howard, we had a close nuclear family, with only my paternal grandfather and his family living nearby. My family was fun loving, full of laughter, and kindness. Mom had a deviously, playful streak in her that kept everyone on their toes, and my dad thrived on capturing special memories and reliving sappy traditions.

As I was turning five, my father received an undeniable calling from God to go into Christian ministry. His dreams were persistent and clear, and despite my mother's resistance, within a few months, he had left his job in home design to return to school and get his Masters in Theology. She was left to be the main breadwinner until he completed seminary two years later.

The first ministry assignment he was appointed to lead was actually three churches in a small region along the St. Croix River valley, two on the Wisconsin side of the river and one on the Minnesota side. These small towns were incredibly friendly and welcoming to our young family, and they took us under their wing immediately. During my mom's pregnancy with my little sister, Chaya, she was on mandatory bedrest, and they brought meals to our house every night and were happy to steal me away for an afternoon when she needed a rest. These were my first real memories of what Christian community was meant to be; loving each other, supporting one another in times of need, and just being family. While I attended Sunday school and knew my

Bible stories well, seeing the biblical life lessons played out in front of me were much more impactful. I tried to be a model pastor's daughter, not because of some perceived role I needed to play, but because this was the example set for me by other children within the church family and community.

Three years later, I was devastated when the Minnesota Methodist Conference decided to move my father to a church that needed his leadership in designing/constructing a new church building. While the community wasn't significantly larger than his last parish, it functioned entirely different. Many of the families were dysfunctional, the adults unapproachable, and the kids fickle and mean. Fifth grade became a painful slog where I frequently came home crying, being totally isolated from the locals. Even the teacher admitted to my parents that my inability to acclimate was due to the inclusive culture of the school and not for a lack of social skills. Most of the town was owned by one family, which was constantly bickering over power and thought they "owned" the church because they were significant contributors.

In an attempt to fit in and shed my "pastor's kid" label, I started to rebel and take the same indifferent attitude about church that the other kids displayed. I no longer paid attention during service and preferred to be in the nursery helping out. Our household was becoming splintered as my father was working endless hours trying to satisfy the congregation's need to be served, devoid of any reciprocation within the church or community. Even our home was no longer a place of refuge because "The Family" owned that too and felt justified showing up unexpectedly at all times of the day and night. The final straw was when a couple of them showed up drunk and screaming, and could not be convinced to leave. My dog went into an epileptic seizure from stress and my mother made an ultimatum; we would move into our own home or she would take the kids and leave. After much contention with the church leadership, we did finally move, but they couldn't track or control my dad's movements. Reports and documentation were now required to justify his workload, and they made the decision to cut his salary and housing allowance. Again my mom shouldered the burden of the finances, which caused even more friction.

Our family was deeply scarred by the experience they endured as part of this "Christian" community. Within six months, my dad left the church and the ministry feeling failure and disillusionment, something that would plague him the rest of his life. His faith, along with his family's faith, had taken a full body blow. He questioned why God would send him to such an unhealthy church that took such a huge toll on his family. We were all left with a bitter taste of how sinful professing Christians could be. Where was God in all this? Anger welled up in me at how God could let our family be battered by the evil I saw in the people of his Church.

After we escaped from that church, we returned to the open arms of our congregation from pre-ministry days. While it was refreshing to be in such a loving environment, my spiritual growth was not renewed. Our old church lacked a strong, passionate leader, and his sermons were shallow and without biblical substance. I spent most of my remaining high school years fooling around in the balcony with my friends, trying not to get in trouble. I knew all my Bible lessons, but they didn't impact my heart. My personal relationship with God was nonexistent, but since I knew "of" Him and was a "good" person, I figured I was on the right path. Basically, I was just coasting spiritually until graduation, when I could be on my own and not obligated to attend church.

Although lukewarm about church, I had a passion for architecture and was actively pursuing it. With my Fisher Price blocks and figurines strewn about the house, at age five I announced to my parents that I was going to be an architect. As I grew up, I never wavered from my first love and was driven to pursue it wholeheartedly. As a junior, I left my suburban high school and went to the University of Minnesota, where I could begin architectural program coursework for the final two years before graduation. Absorbed in the study of architecture, even my summers were dedicated to my pursuit. Between my junior and senior year, with my parents' blessing, I flew to New York to attend a summer design course for college credit at Syracuse University.

Never afraid of jumping into the unknown and chasing my passions, after my official high school graduation, I decided to finish my Bachelor of Architecture program at Illinois Institute of Technology (IIT), a reputable college in the great, bustling city of Chicago. My parents were not surprised, and although they had some trepidation, they never tried to dissuade me. My mom, in particular, wanted to give her kids all the opportunities she didn't have, sacrificing the last two years of her college degree to support my father's schooling. While I know that my own driven personality and my parents' gift of encouragement played a large part in my fearlessness, I think the awareness of my mortality early in life was the element that propelled my determination.

Trust and reliance on God was never my strong suit. I had to have a plan, loved the challenge of attempting lofty endeavors, and felt my happiness depended on accomplishing the goals I set forth. If my determination appeared to be making progress toward my goals, it must be because God was blessing it, right? Thus far, there was very little that I didn't achieve if I put my mind to it. My heart condition caused little interruption, except for excluding me from sports and gym class, which actually created more time for the classes on my career path.

In the fall of 1994, Chicago became my home for the next five years. Having dropped me off on the South Side of Chicago, my parents went home to ponder the potential error in their ways. To their credit, I never came home again. However, the phone calls home were quite frequent, seeking their guidance and direction.

Ryan and I met during orientation week of our freshman year at IIT, our small architecture and engineering school. While I was relatively used to a big city, Ryan was in the middle of a culture shock, having just driven in from Montana, where the entire population of the state was a third of the size of Chicago. Comfortable within the confines of our small school campus, he had decided to pledge a fraternity house where I knew a few members from a scholarship weekend I attended three months previous. The house was comprised of a bunch of engineering geeks and all-around good guys. Not interested in the party atmosphere of the other social clubs, we both fit in quite well.

As we talked, I realized that Ryan and I had several commonalities, including close-knit families, a dry sense of humor, and a love of the Midwest humor of Garrison Keillor. Ryan fit the profile of my ideal guy; tall, slender build, quiet and reserved, academic, and a strong protestant Christian upbringing. He had green eyes that melted my heart, and eyelashes that any woman would envy. His face was delicately chiseled, with a perfectly tamed nose and strong cheekbones, a chin dimple helping to accentuate his sweet baby face, which is always a weakness of mine. I could tell he was a bit shy, but the crowd of people provided an easy environment to casually mingle on the sunset boat cruise of Lake Michigan.

One week after we met, he attended my 18th birthday party in my dorm room, so I thought he might be interested in me (it wasn't until much later that I discovered that he actually came to the party hoping to see a friend of mine that he had also met on the cruise). I've never been one to hide my true feelings, and my assertiveness can be a rather precarious trait of mine. By trying to appear worldly and spontaneous, I managed to put a good scare into him, but also left a little intrigue. I brashly told him that I was interested in pursuing a relationship, and he kindly told me he would rather remain friends. Although I was disappointed, it was a blessing that this rejection provided the space for a natural, healthy friendship to blossom.

To my surprise, he really did want to be friends. It was during the beginning of the second semester that his love of music lead him to host a radio show that broadcasted from the same building as my studio. The show focused on the 1960's, especially The Doors and The Beatles, and was the reason his fraternity brothers nicknamed him "Hippie." Sitting and talking on the grand staircase of Main Building every week after his evening show, our comfort level grew and conversations became fluid, his shyness dissipating. We began to see each other nearly daily until I started to question whether this was becoming anything more serious.

Neither of us had seriously dated anyone in high school. I had a couple short-term relationships and quite a few infatuations, but nothing more than naïve teenage romance. His exposure to girls was even less, focusing most of his high school years on academics and skiing with the boys in the mountains of Montana. Both of us had a pretty clean slate.

My curiosity got the best of me one afternoon, and I took the opportunity to interrogate David, a fellow fraternity brother while we were walking home from class. His response to whether Ryan was interested in me or not was vague at best. The only thing he said was that Ryan had told him there was a Beatles song called "Her Majesty" that reminded him of me.

About two weeks later, through a rather odd set of circumstances, we each ended up at Borders bookstore downtown at the same time with our respective group of friends. It was a popular place to hang out, having a coffee bar, tons of books to peruse and the opportunity to preview CDs before buying. As soon as I arrived, I raced to the music department to check out the song I had been itching to hear. It turned out to be a hidden track on the end of the Abbey Road album, not even listed on the cover. Very quickly, I got the gist of the song, as it was only 23 seconds. It talked about a shy boy who want to tell his gal that he loved her and wanted make a commitment, but he felt he needed to be a bit drunk to have the courage. Crystal clear! And then Ryan walked in to the store… The moment was painfully awkward as I was still speechless, but I couldn't boldly tell him I knew about the song. So I waited, very patiently, until he got up the nerve a month or so later to finally admit his feelings.

By April 1995 we started officially dating, our first outing together being Easter services, and the second, a military ball for his Air Force ROTC program. Once the cat was out of the bag, our first months were filled with the normal butterflies in the stomach and awkward, emotional jousting, but by the end of the year, a natural calm and ease settled over the relationship. Spending most of our free time together, our feelings grew deeper and more meaningful, our love intensifying beyond merely shared interests. We had fun together and yet had no problem working through tough emotional issues. Over Christmas break our first year, during a road trip from Chicago, we introduced each other to our respective parents and immediate family. Both families seemed content with our selections, although my family's quirkiness and offbeat sense of humor left Ryan guessing what my mom, in particular, would do next (one Christmas, she bought him and my father matching leopard print bikini underwear just to see his reaction). My dad was used to practical jokes like this, but Ryan's reserved demeanor made him a target for my mom, as she loved to see him blush. It was not intended to be cruel, but to welcome and initiate him into our odd family.

Ryan's parents were much more reserved like him and a little easier to predict. His father, Michael, having spent 25 years in the military, had a formal, yet kind temperament. He was frequently quiet, but when he said something, you knew it was well thought through, which matched Ryan to a tee. Kathy, his mother, carried herself with great poise, always perfectly put together. She conversed sinuously, attentively listening and responding with even more questions, making you feel special and valued. Although I knew she liked me, I don't believe, at least early on, that she thought her son should be so serious over the first girl he dated. I'm sure I would feel the same apprehension.

Within the first year, we began to talk about our future, not outright saying the word "marriage," but definitely implying it. There was no on-again and off-again rollercoaster, and all of our fights were resolved quickly without too much drama. Neither of us approached dating in a casual way, believing that there was no point to wasting time with someone we couldn't envision marrying. As a result, I think our relationship transitioned into an assumed permanence in an amazingly natural way.

So when an opportunity to travel for a year in my architectural program arose, I felt remarkably at ease and confident that we could survive the distance and time. In the spring of 1996, when Ryan and I had been dating just under a year, I attended a meeting in my architecture school that introduced our class to a student exchange program at Robert Gordon University in Aberdeen, Scotland. It was specifically for third year students and was a full year in duration. Cautiously, I asked Ryan if he would be supportive of me leaving him for a year. My parents, as always, were on board with the idea, but I assumed Ryan might have more hesitation. To my surprise, he was also excited for my opportunity and encouraged me to apply. We both felt assured that our relationship was strong enough to endure a long spell apart. I didn't have any doubt that he would wait for me and I for him. It would definitely test us, but if we survived, our love would be all the more resolute.

This sounded incredibly exciting to me as I had always wanted an opportunity to travel abroad, but knew I couldn't come up with more money than my loans and grants provided. Fortunately, finances were not an issue because tuition at my current school could be transferred to the other school in an equal exchange. Room and board would be included in the deal, with the only additional costs being travel, books, and miscellaneous expenses. Additionally, it was ideal that Great Britain was an English speaking country, as I knew no other language fluently. While most of the Scots did speak English, I would learn later that it was outlandishly fast and in a rich brogue. The pronunciation of even common words was so drastically different that it forced me to frequently ask people to spell their words.

Fortunately, only two people applied for the two positions, a Polish gal named Dominika and I, so we were both accepted. That summer, prior to leaving for Scotland, I went home to Minneapolis and worked two jobs trying to earn enough spending money to last the whole year. Flying back to Chicago a week before I was to leave for fall semester, Ryan and I spent the week together trying to take in all of our favorite sites and eats; our favorite greasy soup diner, Chinatown, deep dish pizza, coffee houses, Michigan Avenue beach, and an old movie house. We couldn't get enough of each other, desperately attempting to capture enough memories to last the long months ahead. It was so hard to say goodbye that we ended up doing three "official" sendoffs at the airport (during the days when friends and family could escort the passengers all the way to the gate). As much as we wanted every last minute together, it would have been preferable to say our last goodbye at the departure drive, avoiding the long, painful stare as I descended down the flight gate ramp. While I didn't regret taking this trip, the actual leaving part was much more grueling than I had imagined.

Aberdeen is the third largest city in Scotland with a population of approximately 220,000 people and twice that many sheep. It is not small by any means, but it definitely felt tiny in comparison to Chicago. A harbor city located on the northeastern coast of Scotland, it takes the brunt of most of the blustery winds and currents of the North Sea. Fishing and oil platforms are the main industry, thus leaving quite a large number of wives and children on the mainland for extended periods without their husbands. It is known as the "Grey City" because of all the grey, local granite used throughout the city architecture, but I think the nickname is primarily due to the abundance of overcast, rainy days (something I've obviously learned to love, having settled in the Pacific Northwest where the climate is quite similar). Moving from the "Windy City" of Chicago to the "Grey City" of Aberdeen definitely seemed like a lateral move weather-wise, but it got me within throwing distance of the European cities that I craved to explore.

Dominika, my travel companion from school, kept me company for my first overseas journey. It was nice to have a familiar face in the strange land we arrived in. It was cold and rainy when we landed, something I would get quite used to in the next nine months. One of the professors at the school met us at the airport with his tiny car, which was quickly packed to the gunnels with our luggage, primarily Dominika's ginormous bag. I had helped her lug an obscene amount of stuff together all over the two London airports and the Underground, which nearly made us miss our connecting flight. We would soon learn that everything in Europe was much, much smaller, especially the cars, homes, and appliances.

He drove us to our new flat to get settled and sleep off the exhausting jet-lag. The short drive to the school uncovered a beautiful, lush landscape with hills covered in purple heather and stone cottages scattered along the exceptionally narrow roads. The architecture was a strikingly foreign vernacular compared to my modern high-rise and steel vocabulary.

We stayed in one of the two residence halls on campus, the "Square Tower" that was able to locate me on the main floor, accommodating my request to avoid stairs. It was a five-story tower that was of fairly modern design, but used traditional materials. Each floor had five bedrooms, each with their own shower and sink, two separate toilet rooms (the size of a broom closet), a kitchen, and shared living room. The refrigerator was a small, under-counter type that was meant to accommodate five people, which forced us to shop more frequently than I was used to, and on staggered days. The flat was quite homey, yet was pretty tight quarters, especially when the guys from the floor above came over.

My other three roommates were two Norwegians and a Scottish gal. They were very pleasant and I enjoyed spending nights hearing about their different lives and cultures, even getting a Norwegian language lesson or two. My architecture classmates eventually turned into good friends, but were somewhat distant at first to "outsiders," especially Americans who apparently all talked like Texans. President Clinton and the US government were not very popular in Britain at the time, so without joining the "bashing" party, I just steered clear of political talk.

The academics of the school were very demanding, and their education system was challenging to adapt to. Out of 30+ students, A's might have been given to one or two students and B's to another half dozen. The rest were satisfied to receive C's, meaning they were achieving as anticipated. This was quite a departure from the American style of grading where A's and B's were the norm and a C meant you really weren't cutting it. The seminar courses were interesting, but it took a while to pick up everything they were saying and get used to the metric system. Even after nine months, my designs were first envisioned mentally in imperial sizing and then translated into metric as they became more developed.

True to form, I spent a lot of time in the design studio and not much time socializing. My roommates encouraged me to go out on occasion, having a much less rigorous course schedule, but I was never much of a night owl. Though I was now legally able to drink alcohol and Scotland had a loosely enforced over 18 policy, I kept it to a minimum. I was pretty boring and definitely didn't fit into the typical college party scene. Plus, I was pinching pennies for my upcoming winter break tour of Europe.

Over Christmas break, I flew to Minneapolis to be with my family and to spend time with Ryan. He had driven to my parents' house from Chicago to meet me during my three-week long stay in the States. Our reunion was so sweet, and we couldn't stop holding and staring at each other; the physical touch and being face to face was a thousand times better than our crackly, detached phone calls in the echoing basement of the Square Tower public phone. It confirmed for me that our relationship could endure a lengthy separation without damage. Longing to share my new experiences with him, we spent hours telling each other stories about the last four months. Sadly, we knew the "you had to be there" adage still held true, especially in my case, where I was in a brand new environment with people he'd never met.

After Christmas, Ryan and I drove to Montana to be with his family through the New Year. This time with family was priceless, and being with Ryan was just like old times, picking up right where we'd left off. We were both aware of how short our time together would be, which made being surrounded by family the whole time bittersweet. Stealing away moments of alone time was challenging and it was never enough.

As it would come to be, God, in His graciousness, crafted a most ingenious, albeit scary situation that provided us with precious time together. On the drive back to Minneapolis, the weather took a turn for the worst. We had made it to Bismarck, ND on the first day (about an 18-hour drive), and were preparing to leave the hotel the next morning. As we were standing in line to check out, we heard rumblings of a big storm that was prompting many of the guests to request another night. Ryan and I looked at each other and said simultaneously, "Wimps! How bad could it really be?"

Pride, and an urgency to get back to Minneapolis, caused us to be rash in our decision making and our departure. Snow drifts were three feet high in the center of the freeway lanes, and we couldn't see 50 feet in front of us when a truck passed. Cars were stranded everywhere and semis had left the road. Although Ryan is one of the best winter drivers I know, two hours later, he finally admitted he did not want to continue. We had made it only 15 miles down the road when we were forced to plow the car up what appeared to be an exit ramp, in hopes of finding a place of refuge.

Seeing a hotel off to the right, we took a chance that it would have some accommodations. It was a tiny, run-down hotel that was operated by a little old woman who kept questioning why we didn't have the same last name. At this point, I was willing to lie in order to get a place out of the cold, blowing snow. We spent the next two days there, the freeway having been shut down hours after we gave up. Watching football playoff games and playing the Pick-up Sticks game we had received in our Christmas stockings, we were perfectly content to be together in our musty, worn-out accommodations. Thankfully, the motel had a diner attached, which we ventured out to several times a day, but it had a strict "cash only" policy. By lunchtime the second day, we were all out of cash and had to beg them to accept credit for the remainder of our stay. They agreed, as the storm had taken away the rest of their customers, except for a few lone truckers that had made it through.

On the third day, we were forced to attempt the remainder of the trip. I had a flight back to Europe scheduled in two days and I didn't want to attempt rebooking a flight over the holiday season. The roads were open, but they were an ice skating rink, with thick ice coating the areas of the lanes that weren't covered in deep snowdrifts. We could see abandoned semi-trucks that had left the road during the worst of the storm, some of them almost all the way through the median into oncoming traffic. White-knuckling it along with only a handful of courageous (or desperate) drivers, we took it really slow and made it to my parents' house in nine exhausting hours; it should have only taken about six.

Leaving Ryan for Scotland this time was even harder than when I had left in August. In a subconscious move to make saying goodbye "easier," we started bickering about trivial things, picking fights like an old married couple. We knew that the fighting was out of sadness and not anger, but it hurt nonetheless. My heart was so split. While I was excited to get back, especially since I was departing on a solo 10-day trip around Europe prior to heading back to Scotland for spring semester, Ryan would not be with me; another life-changing experience that I would have to share second hand. As my plane pulled out of the Minneapolis airport, tears rolled down my face and my heart ached for him to join me.

My parents had given me a Euro-rail pass for Christmas, which allowed me to travel anywhere in Europe for 10 days. In Scotland, I had lived so frugally on my monthly food stipend that my savings from the last four months became my spending money for the trip. I visited eight cities, including Paris, Rome, Venice, and Prague and was able to eat, sleep, and visit some museums for around $40 a day. Looking back, I have no idea how I had enough stamina, let alone how I was able to stretch my money so well. On an adrenaline high, all I cared about was getting to the next great architectural masterpiece. All of the magazines I read when I was young, and the buildings I learned about in my history courses, were all coming to life. Europe was the candy store of my dreams.

I would walk all day, until my feet gave out beneath me and then I would find the nearest hostel. It was a real blessing that my heart behaved surprisingly well because I had no back-up plan if it hadn't. Ryan and my parents got a call from me in each new city; besides that, no one in the world knew where I was. It was exhilarating to feel so free and impassioned by my experiences, unaware of the limitations that were awaiting me in the near future.

However, the most extraordinary incident that occurred on my trip had nothing to do with architecture. Over Christmas, Ryan had given me a gold bracelet that, in a romantic notion, I was planning to wear every day until I saw him again. On my first night of the trip, while lying down to sleep on the hard floor of the common sleeping room as I crossed to Amsterdam by ferry, I noticed that my bracelet was not on my wrist. After searching all of my bags, I came to the devastating realization that it was lost forever. I had spent the day touring all over London, and it could have been lost anywhere. Crying silently in my sleeping bag, sleep came in broken chunks, punctuated by uselessly replaying the string of events that preceded its disappearance. As unbelievable as the trip was, I found myself thinking about the bracelet frequently.

When I returned back to my flat in Aberdeen after my trip, a package was waiting for me that I had mailed to myself while in London. In the bottom of the box, surrounded by a hodge-podge of personal effects, was my broken bracelet staring back at me. The box was tattered and holey, and I hadn't sealed it well, but somehow the bracelet had remained in the box. I called Ryan right away and shared the fantastic journey of this bracelet.

It was hard to comprehend the events leading up to the box sitting on my bed, but I tried to piece it back together.

Deciding that I had about 10 pounds too much in my backpack for my damaged heart to manage, I had gone to a post office in London, found a discarded, mangled box in the corner, and pulled out some items from my pack that weren't absolutely necessary. Inside the warm building and hot from rummaging around in my backpack, I removed my heavy winter jacket. While pulling the cuffs over my wrists, I must have broken the clasp of the bracelet. The bracelet had fallen right into the ravaged box without my knowledge, not on the floor or any of the many miles I had walked that day. I was meant to hold on to this bracelet and the man who gave it to me. This is how God sometimes imparts His directions for me, through miraculous signs; Ryan would be the one I married. God is so good!

3

It was hard for me not to see God's hand in the bracelet journey, almost like God was telling me that He had not "misplaced" me either, despite my reticent and wavering disposition. My heart was starting to be opened and during the first few weeks of second semester, I accepted an invitation to attend a Pentecostal church service with an architecture classmate of mine. There, I met a woman named Frances. Frances, an early thirties, soft-spoken single mother of three young boys, was desperately trying to keep her family fed. She would soon become one of my closest companions. While my classmates were enjoying all of the partying and ruckus of college life, we began attending church together every Sunday and spent many evenings in prayer and conversation at her house. After meals together, she would counsel me about the character of God and explained scriptures to me that I had never fully understood before.

The Pentecostal religion was an extreme departure from my mild-mannered Protestant roots, and at first I was a little taken back, but slowly I realized how incredible the Spirit of God is. He is the Living God here on earth, and gives supernatural gifts, and while speaking in tongues and prophesying were de-emphasized in the Methodist faith that I was raised in, they were spoken of in the Bible, and could not be ignored. I experienced whole-hearted and full-bodied worship, not the shyly sung, off-tune hymns sang to the floor. My definition of worship and praise changed entirely, as did how I saw my God and Christ Jesus as a kind, loving savior who I could approach confidently with any issue. He was not distant, as I had treated Him, and He cared about me personally.

She brought me back into relationship with God and reminded me how important it was to give my full life over to Him. Somehow, ironically, this journey overseas brought me back "home" again. I had strayed from the spiritual teachings that I had grown up with, and now understand that I had never personalized my faith; it had always been the beliefs of my parents. One evening she even had me phone my parents back in Minnesota to share with them my newly rekindled faith. They initially seemed surprised that I had fallen away from the principles they had instilled, but by the end of the call they realized that this was the first time I had professed my faith openly as an adult.

Forever I will be grateful to Frances for her nurturing and mentorship. Having rededicated and recommitted myself to God prompted me to take action in my life, recognizing that I needed to depend on God in all aspects of my life, including my studies and my relationship with Ryan.

Taking time daily to pray, study the Bible, and ask God for direction, was something quite new to me. I asked Him about not only the big decisions, but also the simple, everyday issues, learning to listen and discern His response. My life no longer revolved around the design studio, and I started taking Sunday off for the Sabbath, which I had never done before. I had never trusted that the necessary work would get accomplished without the full seven days. While I maintained my rigorous work ethic and my passion for architecture, I now handed over my rest to Him, relying on Him to help me work more efficiently, avoid distraction and listen to Him when He told me I was done for the day. My priorities had been totally and uncompromisingly rearranged. I sought out time to be with God and had no doubt He was present and seeking me.

"Ask and it will be given to you; seek and you will find; knock and the door will be opened to you.
Matthew 7:7

In February, my architectural classroom took a trip to Venice for our spring semester project. We rode a double-decker bus across the English Channel on the ferry and all the way to Venice, over two days each way. When we returned back to Aberdeen, life and classwork kicked into overdrive. Everything we had learned about construction and structures in the first semester was now being applied to one building as the final design project. I was simultaneously studying for final exams with much more vigor than fall semester in hopes of pulling better than the "B" I received earlier. Frances and I continued to spend evenings together, but the rest of my available time was spent curled over the drawing table in studio.

Ryan's phone calls were always the highlight of my week, and I waited in my flat with great anticipation when I knew he would be calling, but some of our conversations in the middle of second semester were starting to concern me. Ryan had several classes that he had fallen behind in, and his fraternity responsibilities were occupying most of his time. He was also in danger of losing his ROTC scholarship with the Air Force because he hadn't been keeping up on his physical testing requirements. To my surprise, one evening he informed me that he had made the decision to request dismissal from the military. In the best case scenario, they would grant his request, but he would no longer have funding for his last year of school and would owe the government back for three years of school. In the worst case scenario, they could turn down his request and draft him as an enlisted soldier, he would lose his officer rank, and still have to serve out his eight-year commitment. Either way, it appeared he might not be in Chicago next year for school.

The culmination of all of these stressors, I believe, led to a heart episode that occurred two days before the final exams. Around midnight, I was awoken with a fast and erratic heart rhythm causing shortness of breath, dizziness, and a cold sweat. Stubbornly, I let it continue for about four hours before I decided that my condition was not going to improve on its own. I shuffled to Dominika's door, asked her to call an ambulance, and took a seat at the dining table to wait, head collapsed into my arms, focusing carefully on each erratic beat.

The ambulance took me to Aberdeen Royal Hospital, where they admitted me immediately even though the symptoms were starting to wane a bit. I was assigned to the "Florence Nightingale" ward where I was hooked up to all of the usual monitoring equipment. The floor definitely lived up to its name, and I felt like I was back at the turn of the century. There were long rows of beds lining the window walls of the tall, narrow wing.

They parked me right next to a patient who moaned all night, and my own monitors were so sensitive that they kept going off whenever I rolled over. Although I was admitted for a heart condition, I was never seen by a cardiologist. My main attending doctor during the three-day stay was a gastroenterologist. Coming from the US, this was odd and a bit upsetting. Socialized medicine was a complete departure from the specialized care and relatively comfortable conditions that I was used to in America. Even the nurses on the ward mentioned to me that it was a good thing I didn't come in with an open wound because they were out of bandages until their monthly shipment came in 10 days!

The upside of being in a Scotland hospital was that I never had to show an insurance card and I never received a bill. The tea cart offered me tea and biscuits seven times a day - before breakfast, at breakfast, before lunch, at lunch, before dinner, at dinner, and before bed. Ironically, they had no decaf tea, so I always declined for fear my heart would act up. The thought of all these patients lying in their beds wide awake all day, wired by the tea, with nothing, not even a TV to occupy their time still makes me laugh.

On the day before I was to be discharged, I phoned my parents to let them know what had happened and that I was alright. Knowing that it wasn't a life threatening episode, I didn't want to call when I was admitted because it would just worry them and there was nothing they could do besides needlessly get on an airplane. They were not happy with me, but seemed to understand my reasoning a bit, although my mom still not-so-jokingly mentions how she baked bread non-stop to relieve the stress was until I was discharged (my point taken). Being so used to hospitals and viewing them as a fairly routine part of my life, however unpleasant, I hadn't seen this event as something to panic over. At this point, my heart seemed to go into a little storm about once a year and would last a few days, and then life would resume where it left off.

Frances volunteered to pick me up on the day of my discharge and took me back to my flat. The teachers decided that since I missed the exams, and they didn't have multiple versions, I would not be able to take them. They agreed that the only fair solution was to assume that the grades I received first semester would be what I would have done second semester. I thought that was more than fair, though I'm not sure my friends, who struggled through eight hours of testing, would agree. I was rather relieved that I didn't have to put any more thought into those subjects. Now I had only my semester project to finish, which was nearly complete, and I would be on my way home to the States in one more uneventful week.

When I arrived back in Chicago in mid-May, Ryan was still in the midst of his finals. I felt guilty for being such a distraction, albeit a pleasant one, especially since I knew he had a lot of catching up to do. Once he was done, I pushed my way back into top priority. We spent the next few weeks getting reacquainted and revisited some of the great Chicago eats together (yes, the food in Britain is bland and boring as rumored). Boy, did I miss good Chinese, Mexican, and real deep dish pizza. Not wanting to leave Ryan after just returning to the States, I had decided to stay in Chicago for the summer and take some classes in order to complete both my construction management and business minors.

Initially, there was some awkwardness trying to get familiarized with each other's nuances again, and realizing that we had both noticeably changed during our time apart. The time away from one another was very healthy and it showed us how important it was to have our individualities, but also how much we needed and complemented each other. With the response from the military still pending, Ryan was unsettled about where his future was headed and, therefore, in his distraction, had let some of his studies slide. On the flip side, he noted that my intensity had increased (if that was possible) and my overall seriousness amplified; I was less fun-loving and spontaneous. We balanced out each other; Ryan kept me fun and tried to keep my intensity in check, and I helped encourage and motivate him.

However, seeing different parts of the world, living entirely on my own, and most of all, reconnecting with God and my faith had set me on a new path. I was still as passionate about architecture as I had been previously, but I had a new sense of my identity and my priorities. I was hopeful that Ryan and I could realign our faith lives, putting God first in our day to day lives, and find a church where we could continue to mature and put our faith into action. My desire was that Ryan and I could engage each other the way Francis and I had; learning from each other, praying together, and sharing how God was leading us.

This faith journey, which for me began in Scotland, is one that has shown God's hand in our lives the strongest. Our relationship grew stronger as we inched closer to God, but it has taken patience and perseverance, which have also been gifts from God. Upon my return from abroad, Ryan and I both began looking for a church to attend together. Although we never found one in Chicago that met both our needs, Ryan showed me his longing to seek God's direction in his life. I felt confident that though the search could be long, at least we would be on the same road.

By the end of May, he asked me to marry him, and by mid-June I had accepted. I knew in my heart that he was the man God had chosen for me, but I had been concerned that he was asking me too quickly after my return to the States and was acting out of nostalgic emotion. After more deliberation, I understood that we were both mentally and emotionally ready to make the commitment. Sadly, we had no choice but wait two years to be married, after we were both graduated. This was a decision that was entirely predicated on being able to retain financial aid for school and medical insurance, which I would lose if not under my parents' charge.

Having left Air Force ROTC and given up his scholarship, Ryan worked feverishly to secure monies to complete his last senior year so he wouldn't have to leave school (and Chicago) three quarters of the way through a degree. After spending a summer on pins and needles about whether he would be enlisted, the Air Force informed him in August that he would be discharged without obligation to enlist and he could pay them back for the first three years after completion of his degree. Again, God showed us His great mercy and grace. Fortunately for us, that summer happened to be the only time when the Air Force had an excess of officers and felt able to relieve some of duty. The following year, a fellow student we knew in a similar situation, was denied the same request and was enlisted immediately.

Through the help of a teacher and mentor, Ryan got a half-tuition scholarship, but it still meant that he would need to work every other semester. Thankfully, one of his fraternity brothers offered him a great job in construction in Washington, D.C., which was flexible enough for him to work one semester and go to school the next semester for his remaining coursework.

We now spent the next two years alternating between being together and being apart. By graduation, Ryan was gone the equivalent amount of time that I had been gone. But the silver lining was that he would finish his degree, and we would graduate at the same time. My Bachelor of Architecture program had always been five years, and now his 4-year Structural Engineering degree was elongated to match mine; again, God's provision at work. Despite some painful times apart and awkward times reuniting, our relationship flourished, and at the end of the two-year wait, we were more than ready to spend the rest of our lives together. We hoped for a little less chaos than the last three years, but comfort and consistency can lead to complacency, and God knew that would not be beneficial for us.

4

Life in the months following my TIA was precarious at best. The "electrical" storm my heart was in continued to intensify, and showed no signs of letting up. In an attempt to continue everyday life as normal, I went back to work soon after being released from the hospital. Unfortunately, "normalcy" didn't appear to be in the plans. It was clear that as long as my projects were continuing to demand long hours and fast deadlines, my heart rose to meet the challenge. The quandary of my heart condition is that if adrenaline was pumping, I could keep blazing through late nights, stressful clients, and a barrage of seemingly impossible deadlines. The moment I stopped to relax and take a breath (which was inevitable), my heart would jump out of rhythm and land me in the hospital, where I had all the time in the world to stew in self-pity, fear, and apprehension.

However, staying busy with work was a frustrating, but somewhat effective way of "forgetting" about my previous aspirations for parenthood, which had been indefinitely put on hold. Although my life was preoccupied with my current health situation, sadness lingered, and answers about my future remained out of my grasp. God appeared absent and only willing to give me enough light for my next step. I knew this was an opportunity for me to learn, yet again, that I had to put my faith first and walk with open hands down this dark path. Despite his endless blessing and provision, I still questioned His goodness for me personally. I never doubted that I was a part of His perfect plan and sovereignty, but I assumed that the "greater good and salvation of the world" didn't necessarily include my happiness.

Deep down, I didn't believe He wanted to heal my heart and end my current chaos, let alone bring joy and the hope of children back into my life. Struggling with depression and anger at why my situation continued unabated left little time or interest to seek a more meaningful discourse with God.

The following eight months saw an unprecedented number of ER visits and hospitalizations. As soon as my heart saw a Friday or Saturday approaching, it would start racing like a horse in the final lap of the Kentucky Derby. Nearly every two weeks we were right back at the ER or floor 5NE (cardiology) of University of Washington Medical Center. My boss even started making jokes that they weren't going to let me go home for weekends or take a day off because it was almost predictable what would happen.

When my heart rhythm would go askew, assuming my heart rate stayed a manageable 100-110 beats a minute, Ryan and I would give it an hour or so to see if the bad rhythm could resolve itself. When it didn't, Ryan would pack an overnight bag (if it wasn't already packed), and we'd head to the hospital, nearly on autopilot. About half the time we made the thirty-minute drive to the hospital, my heart would regain its composure, and we would turn the car around before reaching the ER doors. I began to theorize that the ER and impending hospital stay would scare my heart right back into sinus rhythm. The other half of my heart episodes, at least a half dozen times, led to admittance to the hospital and a subsequent cardioversion.

It was happening so frequently, that sadly, the whole scene became routine. I'd get to the ER where they would evaluate my condition, taking the same family and medical history, which by this point I could say in my sleep. If I was unable to talk due to my breathlessness, Ryan could spout it off verbatim. Based on my frequent flier status, I had the same group of doctors and nurses, which I had come to know quite well, and we'd begin a familiar, friendly banter.

The medical team would then administer the same regiment of medications in an attempt to slow the speed down and let my heart (and pacemaker) try to restart its own rhythm. It appeared to be part of their protocol to start with beta blockers, gradually increasing the dosage until they finally acknowledged that my heart rate wasn't going to budge. Then they moved on to the calcium channel blockers, which essentially did the same thing, but much more effectively. Most of the time, they were eventually able to slow the speed, but more often than not, the atrial fibrillation or flutter would persist. However, once my rate was stabilized, they could find a bed on the cardiac floor, get me settled, and schedule a cardioversion for the next day.

The cardioversion, which is a procedure where they shock you back into cardiac "submission", is not as dramatic as you see in the ER television shows — when it's done under emergency situations. They have a kinder, gentler approach where they put you to sleep with anesthesia for a short period of time and do the "dramatic" shock while you doze, only to wake up back in rhythm minutes later (hopefully). Due to a curtain malfunction, I had the misfortune of watching the patient across from me in the pre/post-surgery ward having it done. It certainly looked quite barbaric and painful. Knowing I was next on the docket made me less than enthusiastic when the cardiac team wandered in my direction.

"Does everyone cough and convulse like that?" I asked.

"No, his reaction was a bit unusual," the doctor reassured me. Who knows if he was blowing smoke up my smock? I'd be asleep when they converted me, and no one ever tells a patient how horrible they look during a procedure. I think it's written in the bylaws somewhere, and even visitors seem to understand that it's impolite. Regardless how good or bad you react to a cardioversion, it's still no wonder you wake up sore, with every muscle seizing up at every shock. To add insult to injury, the shock pads they place on your chest and back create the equivalent of sunburns and leave red, itchy blotching for several days.

After a poor night's sleep due to the irregular rhythm of my heart, I couldn't wait for the procedure to be done and over. For me, being out of rhythm meant not having a good, deep breath since the beginning of the episode, and the lack of oxygen made me anxious and light-headed. I was required to fast, from midnight before the procedure, to ensure that I didn't throw up during the shock and aspirate on it. My stomach would growl, having food withheld up to 24 hours, frequently having to wait long into the afternoon for my turn to be cardioverted.

So needless to say, when the hospital volunteer was finally wheeling me down to the procedure room, I was so happy to be closer to feeling better. In a way I was almost cavalier about the whole thing, waving to the nurses on the floor and whoever was visiting me at the time and shouting, "See you on the flip side," as I went around the corner. While the doctors were obligated to review the risks of the procedure each time, I never fully paid attention to the fact that, although rare, it had the possibility of actually creating a life threatening rhythm that they wouldn't be able to stop and could lead to death.

All I could focus on was how wonderful that first breath would feel after I woke up from the anesthesia. The first breath I could take all the way into my lungs was glorious, without the feeling of an elephant sitting on my chest and the fluttering that created my shallow, pathetic breaths. It was worth all the discomfort and anxiety. But the cardioversion, while it always worked on the first or second shock, never lasted long. I would be back, sometimes within days.

Each hospitalization, they would send me home with a new medication or different dosage to try, in hopes that they could get the "electrical storm" to dissipate. Finally, they had had enough of me. It was quite apparent to everyone involved that a different course of action was required. In April 2006, I was referred to another electrophysiologist (EP) in the cardiac group, Dr. Robert Rho, who specialized in a procedure called an atrial ablation. In his early forties, but incredibly wise and skilled beyond his years, he exuded a gentle confidence, honestly interested in how you were doing as a person, not just a patient. He took the time to thoroughly explain his proposed course of action, always seeking input and answering questions. He treated his patients as fellow comrades in battle, never belittling or assuming they were ignorant lab monkeys to try out his innovative new techniques. Little did I know at the time that this mild-mannered, kind-hearted doctor would play such an integral role in my life. He would be someone I entrusted my life to, but also my friend, my surgeon, and my cheerleader, caring not just about my health, but also my happiness and future.

The procedure in which he specialized, involved inserting an ablation catheter into an artery in my groin (under general anesthesia), and burning the sections of my heart around the blood vessels that were creating the electrical misfirings. This was a fairly new procedure at the time and had proven quite successful in patients like me. It was hoped that the burns would create scar tissue inside my already damaged heart that would neutralize the bad activity. The key to its success was "mapping" where the source of the misfiring was occurring and targeting it.

The procedure was anticipated to last 6-8 hours because they had to do an initial mapping and strategizing before they could execute the plan. Ryan waited for nearly 10 hours in the small, sterile cardiac procedures waiting room, staring at the crazy art installation of different shaped and colored buttons; a TV-less room he would get to know well in the coming years. I was wheeled into the operating room around 7:30 a.m. in the morning and it was nearly 6 p.m. by time Dr. Rho came in to discuss the results of the operation. He drew a sketch for Ryan, circling the perimeter of the arteries that he had burned around in the upper chambers. He explained that while it had been incredibly complicated to search for the misplaced activity around my heart, he felt the surgery had been successful. Many of the electrical misfirings had been eliminated, but a few "stubborn" locations remained, that may or may not continue to cause trouble.

For me, the procedure itself was a breeze. A few good whiffs of the gas mask, counting to 10, and I was out for the day. The recovery, on the other hand, sucked. I awoke groggy, but relatively comfortable. Within minutes however, I was struck by the fact that I had a horrible backache from being on a metal gurney for over 12 hours. They had immobilized me by putting a sand bag on each side of my groin which was preventing the newly opened arteries from bleeding me dry in minutes; merely the thought of this occurring sends Ryan into a cold sweat to this day. He has always had an aversion to graphic medical images, and despite my relative detachment of gory procedures, the TV channel can't even linger on a medical show if he's in the room.

Although I was incredibly thirsty, they couldn't give me anything to drink in fear that I would become nauseated from the anesthesia and throw up, thereby opening my healing arteries. In my hazy state, I asked Ryan how the surgery had gone and whatever questions I could think up.

"I'm so glad the procedure went well," I said in a fog, looking around at the smiling faces of my family, "but do I look as bad as I feel?"

There was an awkward silence as Ryan's mom reached over to my bed and applied some Blistex. "Let's get you some chapstick sweetheart, your lips look a bit parched."

No one had the heart to tell me I looked bloated like a marshmallow. I would find out only later that my face had swollen significantly, as well as all my extremities due to the fluids they were pumping into my system during surgery. It was startling when someone from the hospital administration came in to have me sign a document hours after surgery, and I couldn't wrap my sausage fingers around the pen!

After about 12 hours, my pleas for water were finally mildly satiated, only allowing me to have ice chips to rub on my lips. Hours later they teased me by putting an ice chip in my mouth, but I had to immediately spit it back out into a cup. Finally after almost 18 hours, following my transfer to a patient room, they let me suck on one glorious cube. The nurse was parsing them out so sparingly that I wanted to rip them out of her hands and toss the whole cup in my mouth. Never have ice chips tasted so divine.

The first three days after surgery were miserable. My blood pressure kept dropping too low, so they started holding back my pain and heart meds. This caused me to panic because I knew what my heart is capable of when deprived of the anti-arrhythmia medication. It seemed counter-intuitive to me to fight one issue by causing another potentially serious one. Eventually I was able to talk to Dr. Rho, instead of the attending physician, and he got my heart medications reinstated, agreeing that the alternative consequences were not worth the risk.

My heart continued to show some irritation with the procedure in the form of fast, irregular bursts of beats, but nothing that sustained itself. Daily blood draws were unpleasant since I was now so dehydrated that my blood vessels had shriveled into nothing. It was quite usual for the phlebotomists to take 3-4 pokes each time just to get a vial of blood. I dreaded the morning rounds from the lab (affectionately referred to as the vampires), starting to recognize the really successful phlebotomists and asking for them by name. For the "newbies", I wasn't very forgiving and sent them packing after two unsuccessful attempts.

By the third day, I was back on regular food and allowed to get up and walk a bit. It took me a while to have enough strength to walk around the halls, but I definitely had the urge to keep trying. I knew that my release was based partially on my ability to regain my strength. The entire hospital stay lasted about a week, but would have been shorter if they hadn't eliminated my blood thinners prior to the procedure (to reduce the bleeding risk). When my blood was back to acceptable anticoagulation levels, I was finally free to go home.

My heart made a phenomenal recovery, and I started to feel better each day that would go by without having atrial fibrillation. The days turned into weeks, and the weeks into months, and I started to regain my confidence that life could be normal again. By August, four months later, I ventured to ask Dr. Rho if we could try for kids again. Unbelievably, he said yes.

Reactivate: Operation Build Our Family. Full speed ahead. As far as I could deduce, God must have meant for our plans to only be delayed, not changed. Right? My faith still didn't give over the plans of my life to God, I had only given over the speed He would fulfill them. Giving lip service to His sovereignty, I still wanted my way, and believed if I worked hard enough and persevered long enough, He'd give it to me. My joy came in a new pursuit, not in knowing the path was already written, and I could rest with Him in control. Only later, when more storms of life arose again, did I meditate and rest in the scripture verses that could have brought me peace much earlier.

"Many are the plans in a man's heart, but it is the Lord's purpose that prevails."
Proverbs 19:21

"However, as it is written: 'No eye has seen, no ear has heard, no mind has conceived what God has prepared for those who love him', but God has revealed it to us by His spirit."
1 Corinthians 2:9

5

My last two years of college, after returning from Scotland, flew by in a whirlwind of activity and preparation for the future. The majority of my time was focused on school, packing my schedule tightly between architectural studio courses and two minors. In an effort to earn some money for the wedding and a potential move after college, I took an internship position at a small interior design firm in downtown Chicago. Working over twenty hours a week, on top of a full-time course load was trying, and caused some friction with my architecture professors, who thought working during school took away from academic pursuit. My time management skills produced a rather anti-social student. I spent my studio time working intensely, not straying from the time I had allotted to each task or project, and certainly not taking any time to hang out in the lounge with my classmates discussing deep architectural theories (or often – the latest movie release).

It was incredibly rewarding working in the field, not only for real on-the-job skills/portfolio building, but also in the professional relationships that I formed. My boss, Jeff, was a kind, hard-working single guy in his late thirties that made an excellent mentor. He was incredibly patient and worked with me closely to provide thorough training in space planning and in the Autocad software he utilized. Thankfully, he gave me a solid foundation for my future work experience, and a fair wage with flexible work hours — both of which were especially rare for an internship.

By July 1997, just two months after my return to the States, Ryan and I announced our engagement to our families, with the wedding to occur upon graduation in May 1999 (nearly two years away). During our engagement, my health remained relatively stable despite a few hospital stays. However, in February 1998, after a series of holter monitors (24-hour monitoring devices) revealed that I was having frequent, and potentially dangerous ventricular rhythms. My cardiologist in Chicago decided it was an appropriate time to install an AICD (Automatic Implantable Cardiac Defibrillator) in my chest. Based on my family history of sudden cardiac death, he felt that the risk was too great to continue unprotected.

They also wanted to do an electrophysiology study that involved a catheter being inserted into the femoral vein in the groin. The catheter is then threaded into the heart, allowing them to artificially reproduce the problematic rhythms in a controlled environment and then stop them through different medications and/or electrical shocks; "poking the lion" as I like to call it. The procedure gives the doctors a good idea of what my heart is capable of and what medication solutions work best, but it is not a repair surgery.

So in late February, my father, Paul, flew in to snowy Chicago from sunny San Diego to be there for my surgery. Ryan had also arrived just hours before from Washington D.C., where he was working to raise money for school next semester. During his visit, my dad stayed with Ryan at the fraternity house, which was sitting cold, empty, and untidy, having been hastily vacated during spring break; the heat set just above where pipes freeze.

Nearly strangers, this was the first significant amount of time they had spent together without me, and a unique opportunity for a soon-to-be father and son-in-law. Just recently engaged, Ryan felt a pressure to show my dad that he could care for me, but he also knew my dad's need to be the father figure for his struggling daughter, so he walked the line very cautiously. Ryan was as accommodating as possible in an unkempt, frigid home, setting him up in a spare room with as many extra blankets as he could gather. My dad, as always, was courteous and kind amidst this stressful situation. This was Ryan's first foray into hospital adventures with his soon-to-be-wife with a serious heart condition, and my dad could provide insight and encouragement, although I know, deep down, he was just as scared as Ryan.

Having a surgical procedure for the first time in six years, I definitely had some apprehension about not only the procedure, but also the device. It would be a foreign object placed uncomfortably in my body, that I may or may not ever need, but I understood the rationale and found no reason to fight it. The procedure itself went off without a hitch, and I was home that evening, and relatively pain free within a week. The electrophysiology study did reveal what the doctors had suspected. I had serious ventricular rhythms, but at least for the time being, they were controllable. I was grateful to feel a sense of protection from these potentially fatal occurrences.

However looking back, I could have never fully grasped how much I would be impacted by this tiny little device, about the size of a small wallet, placed in the muscular pocket below my left collar bone. It seemed so benign, and I would have never imagined my future distain and paralyzing fear of it. While I recognized that there was a possibility of needing it to save my life, I never thought I'd actually utilize it. Years later it would be excruciatingly clear that while the AICDs can save lives, they are not infallible, as the doctors seem to suggest. At the time of the implantation, I was naively under the impression that when the need arose, the shocks it administered would always right the rhythm, even if it took multiple tries. The truth is, when your time comes, no amount of medical intervention will supersede God's will. He has numbered all of our days, and this device will not change His plan.

By Christmas of 1998, Ryan and I were in full job-hunting and wedding-planning mode. We had set the date of our wedding as the Saturday following college graduation. Since Ryan and I had not established a home church in Chicago, we decided to hold the wedding in a place sentimental to me — Taylors Falls, Minnesota. About an hour's drive away from Minneapolis, stood the most majestic white-washed Civil War-era church, where my father had the privilege of serving as pastor in during my early elementary years. The Methodist church was perched high on a hill, with only the top of the steeple visible from the lush St. Croix River Valley below. It had always held a special place in my heart, and I was so fortunate that the congregation welcomed me back with such open arms. Nostalgia overwhelmed me at the notion of being married in the same place where I sat at my father's feet, listening to his special children's sermons.

It was still yet to be determined where our first jobs would be, but we knew it would not be in Chicago. As much as we loved the city, it didn't fit our image of the best place to raise a family. We wanted a smaller town that accommodated short commute times for homes outside the city core. We did not want suburban, but also preferred not to be in the inner city. Both of us being involved in the construction industry, we needed a population center capable of supporting infrastructure growth. Our choice came down to Denver or Seattle. Ryan desired to be back in the mountains, which he missed immensely during his time in Chicago. I agreed to move out west because I didn't have any need to stay in the Midwest, especially since my immediate family had moved from Minnesota to California during my fourth year of college.

The week before Christmas, after sending out a hundred resumes to firms in both cities, we headed to Seattle to conduct interviews and explore the area. The steep hills were definitely a negative for me since my heart protested on even slight inclines. However, the lush greenery of the environment and a brief glimpse of Mount Rainier sold me. At spring break, we headed to Denver and repeated the same fast-paced agenda of interviews and sightseeing. It was a great city, but deep down we both wanted the job offers to come from Seattle. Leaving both cities, we were told by potential employees that they would make a decision closer to May and let us know. So we jumped back into our studies and waited three more months, which flew by rapidly.

Meanwhile, in March we took a week and flew to Minneapolis to conduct our own set of interviews with potential wedding services. My grandfather let us stay at his house during the visit, and we used it as home base to travel back and forth to the wedding site an hour away. We met with cake makers, caterers, DJ's, florists, our minister, the church coordinator (who happened to be my old Sunday school teacher), reception/rehearsal dinner sites, and hotels. A million decisions to make, but we completed the whole wedding day planning in those few short days. It was craziness, but exciting and fun. It was wonderful spending rare and precious time with my paternal grandfather, his second and younger wife, Wendy, and his children (my aunt and uncle, who were about my age). They were so welcoming and made every night relaxing after each busy day.

A mere two weeks before graduation, we received the employment calls we were anticipating. Although we were blessed to get offers in both cities (the construction market was still strong at the time), we made the easy decision to move to Seattle. Researching the area a bit, we rented an apartment over the phone, sight-unseen and proceeded to reserve a U-Haul trailer that we would drive behind our car from Chicago to the wedding in Minneapolis. The grand plan was to drive to Billings, Montana for a brief stop in order to drop off the trailer at Ryan's parents' house, and then to continue on to our honeymoon in Banff, Canada. After the honeymoon, we would then head back to Montana to pick up the trailer and complete the 15-hour drive to Seattle. All of this would be accomplished in a matter of two weeks, as our first professional jobs were to start the Tuesday following Memorial Day. We were always looking for an adventure and this definitely fit the bill.

The week before graduation both of us had our wisdom teeth taken out, hoping to take advantage of our parents' insurance while we still had it! Somehow, through the discomfort, we studied for and completed our finals. In the spirit of cramming everything in, the bachelorette party was the Friday before finals. Not surprisingly, this was a bad idea (who's going to miss the last party of the school year?). Only Chaya, my sister and maid of honor, and Cindy, my bridesmaid and closest friend, committed to going.

Cindy, a well-grounded Iowa farm gal who taught elementary special education, had just married Brian, Ryan's fraternity brother, a year previous. Cindy nannied for a family north of Chicago and would spend the weekends with Brian at the fraternity house. Being one of the few other girlfriends in the fraternity, and this being a fairly nerdy engineering school, Cindy and I developed a fast friendship. Once Brian had graduated, and they married and moved out to the suburbs, my already limited social life at school was dulled. Even when the house was filled with people, I felt her absence profoundly. She loved people more intensely than anyone I'd ever met, and her hugs could literally take the breath from your lungs. Her smile was contagious, and her whole body shook when she laughed, yet she also had a serious side. Stubborn and determined, she faced life head on, a quality I understood quite well. Neither of us took "no" for an answer. Brian, a computer engineer, was easygoing, able to laugh at his own nerdiness, and smitten by her strong, yet kind nature. They were a great pair and one of the few couples where conversation flowed interchangeably. I could just as easily talk to Brian, and Ryan with Cindy. We shared the same values about faith and family, and had many serious discussions randomly intermixed with stupid college antics.

Ryan felt sorry that everyone had bailed on the bachelorette party and asked if I wanted him to join us; rather unconventional to have the groom attend, but I was happy to have him and there was not much chance of things getting out of control. We went to our favorite Mexican restaurant, as Chaya wasn't old enough to drink, let alone drive. With the help of a few margaritas and some awesome burritos, we ended up having quite a good time, but certainly nothing we would regret the next morning (well, maybe the burritos). The same could not be said about Ryan's bachelor party.

With equally bad timing, the bachelor party was the night before graduation. The entire fraternity house, along with Ryan's dad (who could proudly hold his own against a bunch of college guys), went bar hopping and stumbled home early the next morning. Ryan, slumped forward, with his face buried in his hands during the graduation ceremony, and his dad a bit green around the collar, were both feeling the full effects.

The And

Packing up and leaving Chicago was filled with the sadness of leaving our past lives behind and the anxiety of the unrevealed future that lay ahead. Heading out west, we were saying goodbye to our friends, most of which were also graduating, but planned to stay near Chicago. This included our best friends, Brian and Cindy, who had already made a life in Chicago. Our wedding was the last time we saw many of them. As we were driving out of the city, we vowed to return to visit often.

Despite all of the difficult goodbyes, May 22, 1999, the day of our wedding, was more wonderful than all my childhood fantasies. All of our family and friends were there from all over the country. It was a weekend and party many still regard fondly. Three days in a tiny town with a population of just under a thousand people, where everything was within walking distance, it was a great opportunity to meet with all our guests, and thank them for all their support and love. There were plenty of happy tears, but surprisingly, neither Ryan nor I stumbled through our wedding vows. My father gave the sermon, but insisted upon letting someone else do the official vows and send off.

The reception was held inside an old railroad depot with dark wood benches wrapping the exterior walls. With about 100 guests, everyone had come together for us: my family, Ryan's family, his sometimes rowdy fraternity brothers, my architecture classmates, my high school friends, and my dad's old congregation.

And then, as soon as the party had started, it was all over. The next day, we literally packed the presents into the back of the U-Haul, cleaned up the reception hall and church, said our final goodbyes, and set forth for our new life. Running on adrenaline and desperately requiring some rest before our new jobs, we were hoping the week in Banff would be just what we needed, breathtaking scenery, sleep and recuperation, and relaxing from the craziness of the last six months. The last four weeks had been especially intense, and were much more of a sprint than my body would have preferred. But my heart held up exceptionally well with no hiccups.

Sightseeing every day, eating vast amounts of exquisite food, and sleeping whenever we wanted, the honeymoon was everything we'd hoped for. Enjoying our luxurious vacation, we were acutely aware that this time was just a brief pause before life had to begin for real. After returning to Montana to retrieve our belongings, the remaining drive to Seattle was exciting, but a bit somber with the realization that we were at the end of our college days and its inherent freedoms. We were now officially "grown-ups."

The excitement of settling into a new home and city was immensely enjoyable. Despite feeling a bit hesitant in our responsibilities, our job placements appeared to be good fits, and we began making some new friends at work. Our home, a rather spartan two-bedroom apartment, was like playing house, and we immediately started a new family with a sweet kitty named Java from the local animal shelter. Weekends were spent exploring in the city and the mountains; camping, road trips, and finding new eateries. Our future was so promising and filled with possibilities, and we were excited to take full advantage of it.

Right away, our careers jumped on the fast track, and we were both working significant hours and being given increased responsibility. Extraordinarily blessed, I had been promoted to Associate by December the following year and was the project manager for tens of millions in construction dollars.

Simultaneously, Ryan and I had decided to make our student loan repayment a fast track priority, which we put on a highly aggressive five-year pay-off schedule. After our first big hit in end-of-year taxes, we realized quickly that since our student loan payments couldn't be deducted from our taxes, the only sensible solution was to have some tax shelter. Our solution was to buy an inexpensive home with the seed money we saved from college.

Even with a busy work schedule we found the time to buy a cheap fixer home in late 2000, during the start of the housing boom. The house we selected had been vacant for five years, and had been a condemned home by the Port of Seattle for a Sea-Tac Airport runway expansion. Consequently, in the early '70s, it had been physically relocated several miles and placed on a new foundation, with new plumbing and electrical. Essentially, we were buying a 1920's home, with 1970's bones. The realtor we had chosen for our search was very concerned that we were making a big mistake choosing this home and tried to talk us out of it.

"I've shown you several homes, but this one appears to need the most work. Projects this big take a real toll on marriages, and you are just newlyweds. The divorce rates are very high. I think you should reconsider one of the other properties," she said. "It might be easier to start with a small remodel to see how your marriage handles it."

Ryan and I looked at each with a smirk on our faces. "We'll be just fine. I think we can handle it," confidently we replied together. "Please draw up the papers. We'll get this done in 18 months, max." Although the marriage stayed intact, it took seven full years to gut and remodel every room of the house.

During the first three years in the house, I was traveling weekly to Los Angeles and Las Vegas for retail projects, and

Ryan filled his evenings with house projects. We had a lot of fun spending our weekends working side by side, designing and reconstructing our "new" home. I loved sketching up "napkin" drawings and handing them to Ryan to make them work. He was quite the problem solver, and nothing seemed beyond his ability to accomplish; just two hours staring at all the electrical components on the shelves at Home Depot and he figured out how to rewire half the house. Laughter was abundant during many of the projects, especially the time we forgot to open the windows while priming with an oil-based paint and the fumes made us dizzy and slap-happy. We were giggling so hard that it took us a while to realize there was a problem and a few hours more to come down from our paint intoxication.

In 2000, we attended to two special weddings. The first one in May, a close fraternity brother, Bryan, gave us an excuse to fly to Long Island, New York, and spend the weekend with many of Ryan's AEPi friends and their girlfriends/wives. During our time at school we enjoyed countless weekends with the other couples within the fraternity house, a good number of which went on to marry. Bryan and Angelikis' wedding was great fun, including being treated to a reception on a boat in the New York Harbor, circling the Statue of Liberty.

The wedding also gave us a great opportunity to soak up time with Brian and Cindy, who we had only seen once since our wedding. Talking late into the night, they revealed to us that they were expecting their first child in a couple of months, which was wonderful, especially knowing how much they wanted to be parents. They were the first of our friends to start a family, and although we knew we weren't ready for this dramatic step yet; we saw their life progression as a reflection of what our marriage journey would look like. When sweet Maggie was born that November, we made a special trip out to Chicago and loved on her as if she was our own firstborn; with a little apprehension, but armed with the knowledge that someday soon, we would be caring for our own little one.

The second wedding for the year was Travis and Rachels' in August in beautiful Kalispell, Montana. Ryan's younger cousin, Travis, a towering 6 foot and 4 inches, wide-shouldered college basketball player, had made a surprise appearance at our wedding, reigniting their strong childhood friendship. Ryan had not seen him since his grandfather's funeral several years previous. Travis was attending the University of Montana and had shared that he was dating a gal named Rachel, which he inferred might be getting serious; only 6 months later he asked her to be his wife. Both of them had been part of the same church and their families knew each other since they were young kids, but neither had any romantic interest until they met again by chance at college.

Meeting Rachel for the first time, we knew right away why he liked her. Besides her stunningly natural beauty, she was incredibly kind and smart as a whip. Unfortunately, they moved to Texas shortly after the wedding, so our hopes of seeing them more faded. Lucky for us, Dallas did not suit them well, and within the year they moved to Portland, Oregon. Since it was only three hours away, we were able to see them often, starting an incredible journey of friendship. By 2002, their Montana roots brought them back permanently to their hometown of Kalispell.

As far as cousins go, you wouldn't have known they were related. Ryan has thinning (significant understatement) brown hair, is average height and build, while Travis has difficulty with door headers, and a full head of blond hair. Rachel is relatively tall, with dark, almost black hair and olive complexion with a slender build. She exudes gracefulness having danced ballet since childhood. Although opposite from me in physical appearance, her personality matched well with my own, both being independent, highly focused and organized, decisive and with a few control issues thrown in for good measure. Travis, on the other hand, is much more like Ryan in his rational and calm demeanor, and steadying patience. He is intensely loyal to his family and cares for them well, working hard and entrepreneurial. Yet when you get the four of us in a room, conversations last until all hours of the night, and there is no shortage of laughter or tears.

****

In 2003, my work life became a bit more manageable, being moved into a slower and more reasonably-paced education studio. My new workload consisted of small school renovations and additions which had much longer deadlines than the fast-track retail projects I had grown accustom to. These new projects gave me a better understanding of normal construction schedules, taught me patience, and the value of slower, more deliberate decision-making. This new speed of life gave me an opportunity to pursue my architectural licensure, which would take months of studying and involve over 40 hours of testing. For the next six months I spent most of my down time sequestered away studying, while Ryan worked tirelessly on our new master bathroom.

By August 2004, I completed my licensure; and by September, we had finished paying our student loans. To celebrate, we took a three-week trip to Ireland, England, and Scotland, which we had been saving for in addition to making loan payments. We visited countless castles, villages, and amazing countryside, as well as seeing some of my friends, including Francis back in Aberdeen, Scotland. After scrimping and budgeting for five years, this felt so luxurious.

The year following our trip was filled with even more house projects, but also a good share of painful events. In January 2005, we had demolished our kitchen down to the wood studs and began rebuilding it from scratch, which left our lives quite discombobulated and without a kitchen for an extended amount of time.

During what should have been a three-month remodel (we finished in five), two funerals took us out of state. In February, Ryan's grandmother passed away in Montana of a heart attack, although she had been ill and already bound to a care facility since we were married. We flew out to attend the funeral with the rest of the family. Her service was held at the local "Cementery" in the middle of nowhere Montana, close to the family's original homestead. We were fortunate to have good weather so they could actually bury her in unfrozen ground. Any other winter, explosives would have been required, likely disrupting Grandpa's restful sleep by her side.

In April, just two months later, as we were nearing the end of the kitchen project, we received devastating news from Brian and Cindy, in Chicago, that their daughter Maggie — the new life we had celebrated in New York just three years prior — had passed away. While her death wasn't unexpected, as she had been suffering from an unknown degenerative muscular disease that was discovered when she was six months old, this was especially painful to accept. Although we had been walking this journey with them, until the last few months when the outcome became clear, we continued to hope for a miracle.

Going to her funeral in Chicago was beyond comprehension, seeing a tiny little casket and devastated parents. Taken at such a young age, never having reached even the simple milestone of a smile, her parents were left childless and searching for answers — answers that did not exist, at least not within earthly comprehension. Even her official autopsy was inconclusive. The bigger question is why do things like this happen. God must have a purpose to allow such sadness. But the sadness we felt as observers of this event only touched the surface of the agony experienced by her parents. We would never be able to understand what it means to lose a child until we ourselves were parents. We expect our children to be our legacy and that they will outlive us. Maggie's death flew in the face of this rationale.

In September 2005, just as we were facing the fallout of the TIA, I was promoted to Senior Associate and about 10 months later my first big school project was entrusted to me to project manage. Our firm had been awarded a brand new $30 million middle school in Dupont, Washington. The project schedule from design to final post-occupancy inspection was over four years, and I was given the responsibility of leading its design, documentation, and construction.

These four years would prove to be the most trying time of my life, balancing a new school project, battling health problems, and struggling to create a family. During that time, God had many lessons He wanted to teach me — many that I'm continuing to relearn. The beauty of God's mercy, in retrospect, is that many of the lessons began months or years before, in gentle preparation for upcoming hardship. As Brian and Cindy's loss showed Ryan and me, the preparation came through walking with other people through their hardship first.

6

The wheels of change were in great force for Ryan and I in the summer of 2006, almost a full year after my stroke. I'm not sure the logic behind it, but it seems that whenever I am stirred up emotionally (good or bad), the urge to start in a fresh location emerges. It's not an escape I'm looking for, more like a new mountain to climb that corresponds with my desire for forward momentum. A new locale is the physical representation of forward momentum to me. Maybe this desire comes from moving every three years as a child of the pastor, not putting roots down deep enough to really hurt when pulled out. New is exhilarating for me, and I relish the opportunity to experience a new environment, even at the loss of the familiar, including close friends. We had been living in our home in Sea-Tac for six years at this point, far longer than any other residence in my entire life. In this time, we had both realized that the neighborhood we were in was not conducive to long term family settlement.

We still only knew a few neighbors because the area was very transitional and contained large enclaves of non-English speaking people. As the hope of starting a family became more palpable, we felt that it was probably a good time in the housing market to put out our "feelers." Sadly, we knew our home, which we had grown to love, had been only a place to sleep at night. Both of us had 30-minute commutes in opposite directions, and with our heavy workloads, we had invested little time in our community. Ryan, a principal in his structural engineering firm, had now been running the Tacoma office of Swenson Say Faget for two years, and we agreed that it made more sense to look in the Tacoma area due to lower housing costs and the proximity to Ryan's office. I would be the one with the hour-long commute, but I thought it would be manageable since I eagerly expected to go part time when we had children.

It was hard to believe how fast six years flew by. After initially thinking that our remodeling flip would take two years maximum, we were in for a rude awakening. We had completed our kitchen remodel less than a year previous and hadn't touched the house since. The last chunk of the remodel to tackle was the back entry foyer and laundry room, which was in a pretty sad state since it had been the materials staging area for every project that had been done. My laundry room was strewn with lumber, paint, and construction debris, so it was a wonder that anything clean came from that room.

Ryan and I endeavored to finish a few small tasks in order to get the maximum buying potential from this home that had caused blood, sweat, and some well-earned tears. It was our goal to have the house on the market by July, in time for beautiful weather and to capture anyone with school-aged children looking for a home before the school year started.

Since we moved to Seattle in 1999, we had been attending a Lutheran church near our first apartment, but our Sea-Tac house was now five miles away. We were the only people in the twenties to thirties age range, and a majority of the folks were well into retirement. Choosing this church had been a compromise between Ryan and me. I had wanted a very contemporary, young, upbeat church, much like the Pentecostal church I attended in Scotland. Ryan, raised in the Lutheran Church, was more interested in the traditional Protestant service format. We decided that we would attend the "contemporary" service they offered. But in the end, we both realized that is was really only the tempo of the music that varied between the "traditional" and the "contemporary" styles.

The first time I entered this Lutheran church building I knew God had placed us here. Architecturally speaking, it was nearly the exact same floor plan as the church I designed for a missionary complex in Lagos, Nigeria while I was in college. While home in Minnesota for Christmas during my fourth year of college, and after my recommitment to God, some Nigerian friends of my parents approached me about a school and church complex they were helping to fund and build. They asked if I would be willing to design the church, which would be the first structure built on the site. Excitedly, I agreed, and during the second semester I completed the design and mailed it to them. Although I never saw the final product, these friends attended our wedding and shared with us the successes of this new missionary community.

It was not surprising how comfortable this Lutheran church felt, as I had walked through it in my mind so many times before. Attending and serving in our first church together was a crucial first step in finding our common faith walk, but after seven years, we had both come to realize that our spiritual growth had stagnated, and we needed to honor God and continue maturing. We had found many areas to serve, on committees and work groups, but not much learning or growing was occurring spiritually; busy work, not a deeper passion, knowledge or relationship with God.

It was apparent that the aging parishioners were unwilling to try new ways to reach people, began bickering about even miniscule decisions, and were drowning in the overwhelming maintenance of the large facility they had painfully been dwarfed by. Most importantly, the leadership in the church was nearly non-existent. The pastor had left about a year into our attendance and had never been replaced with someone permanent. Trying to be helpful, I sat on the committee to find a new pastor, only to realize that the Synod seemed unable to supply fresh, motivated voices, and most of the candidates had no desire for missional work outside of regular worship duties. The church was passionless and the fire that had blazed just one generation previous during their prime, had been extinguished.

Moving homes gave us a reasonable and gracious excuse to move on from the Lutheran church. It was important to us that our home and church were in the same community, not 40 minutes to an hour away. We felt a strong motivation to actively engage in the community around us, sharing our faith and our lives with other families.

While at this church, we had "moon-lighted" at a large non-denominational church in Seattle a few times, which gave us a better sense for the type of church we were yearning for. The heady messages that the young, dynamic minister gave spoke to our hearts and didn't try to sugarcoat the truth of the Bible. The packed warehouse space had multiple services each Sunday that lasted two hours, but flew by with powerful, engaging music and truly God-inspired teaching. I had a strong urging from God that we needed to find a similar home church in Tacoma before we picked up and moved house. So one afternoon on my lunch break, I called the Seattle church we had been attending, asking for a reference to a possible sister church in Tacoma. They referred us to SOMA (meaning "body" in Greek), which was a newly-formed church, part of the Acts 29 church-planting group. Acts 29 is a reference to the non-existent chapter of the Bible that would follow the call of Paul in the Book of Acts to make disciples amongst the gentiles throughout the world.

We started attending a few weeks in a row and immediately we both felt a conviction that this was the place that we need to be connected with. Their main thrust was that as Christians, we were to be on mission together in the community, living it out practically every day with neighbors and friends. We joined a small home group and spent as much time as possible getting to know them well and immersing ourselves in the idea that we could no longer live isolated and attend church in a bubble. This was a real turning point in our lives, both in our marriage and how we interacted with the people around us. When we moved to Tacoma, our choice in homes would be made focused on hospitality and sharing resources, not just for the hope of a growing family.

As July approached, our goal of completing the house remodel looked attainable. Besides a nasty episode with yellow jackets pouring into our kitchen and finding a broken waste line pouring into the crawl space just two days before our home inspection for a potential sale, we were ready to move on to the next great adventure. By God's grace, we were able to get an offer on the house in just seven days and close on the property 30 days later.

We had never figured on our house selling so fast so we had to kick it into overdrive to find a new one that fit all of our criteria. From all of our trips to Tacoma looking at the different neighborhoods on Sundays after church, we knew we wanted to be in North Tacoma. The north end was only 10 minutes from work for Ryan and reminded me so much of my neighborhood growing up in NE Minneapolis, with elegant Tudor and craftsman houses. However, the most important criteria for the neighborhood was a large expanse of flat ground and sidewalks so I could go for a long walk and not have to maneuver hills, my nemesis. The house had to have character and not need any major renovations, as we were pretty worn out of house projects. More importantly, the idea was to start a family, and working kitchens and baths were essential!

We found a home on the second round of serious looking, and I fell in love with it immediately. Ryan took a bit of persuading because he had his heart set on a craftsman style home, and I had to show him the merits of a Tudor. There was a ton of natural light and a great fenced backyard. It had already been beautifully remodeled and there were enough bedrooms for kids and visitors. It seemed like a bigger house than we might need, but it seemed to fit the bill hospitality-wise, with a large kitchen and open dining and living spaces.

In the middle of August, moving day had arrived and went smoothly with the help of Ryan's sister, Lisa, and her husband, Cody, and two strong guys from a moving company. Somehow from the move into the first home, our furniture had increased in size and weight, and we no longer had living room furniture we could bench press. It's amazing how the hodge-podge furniture from college that you think is totally adequate becomes unacceptable when you become "adults."

The move went off without a hitch except for one little incident. As we were driving away toward our new adventure, having traveled only four blocks from our old house, I glanced behind me into the bed of the pickup truck in just enough time to see my nicely packed wardrobe box, holding my wedding dress, catch some good wind. As if in slow motion, it lifted silently straight up and floated gently into the turning lane of the two lane road. In a few more blocks we would have been on the freeway, the dress never to be seen again. Screaming at Ryan to pull over, we were able to retrieve it fairly easily, dodging a few oncoming cars and re-securing it tightly for the remainder of the trip. The box was unscathed, and the dress still snugly inside, which is the reason I can still laugh about it.

Having waited four months following my atrial ablation surgery in April, we were itching to move ahead with again trying to have a child. Within a week of moving to Tacoma, Dr. Rho gave us the authorization to proceed in the family creating business and we started in earnest. The excitement and anticipation was reignited in my heart, simultaneously pulling out the old fears associated with our decision for children the first time. Was I strong enough physically to carry and deliver a child, and once they were born, could I handle the demands of a young child? Was it selfish to knowingly predispose my child to the same struggles that I endure daily?

Both of us were hopeful that this time was going to go more successfully than the first. Nothing could have prepared us for what lay ahead. Although at the time, we thought we'd already endured the worst of it. We didn't realize that the measure of success for getting pregnant was not in weeks, but in months.

The next six months flew by so quickly that I am hard pressed to remember most of it. Work was incredibly busy for both of us, and I was getting used to my horrid commute, trying to make the most efficient use of my train/bus time. I got used to leaving for work early and arriving home late, utterly exhausted every night. There was still a lot of design work needed for Pioneer Middle School, which required me to be in the office every day, the commute adding almost three hours to my work day. My glimmer of hope was that construction started in January, and I would then be able spend a few days on the job site each week, only 15 miles from our home.

The And

We spent Thanksgiving 2006 in Montana with Ryan's side of the family. Every year they do a big potluck feast at Ryan's uncle and aunts' farm. His cousin, Travis, and wife, Rachel, invited us to stay with them for the weekend. On Saturday, the night before we were driving home to Washington, they invited us out to a nice dinner. They had gotten Rachel's parents to watch their son, Jasper, who was two at the time, and so we thought it was to be a double date just like old times. However, at dinner right after the waiter had taken our orders, they exchanged glances and launched into their true agenda for the evening.

"We know how the last few years have been very rough on you emotionally and physically," Rachel began as if her speech had been rehearsed, "I've been doing a lot of reading lately about gestational surrogacy and after much thought, Travis and I want to offer to carry a child for you." Jaws dropped and crickets chirped.

Still speechless, she continued, "We know that being parents has been the most wonderful thing in own lives. We think you would be missing out on an incredible experience if you couldn't or didn't have children, plus we know you'd be great parents. My pregnancy with Jasper went really well and actually, I kinda enjoy being pregnant, minus the delivery. Travis even says I'm a bit nicer when I'm pregnant. However, the raising of babies and toddlers is a different matter completely. As you know our son was very colicky, which was painful, so there are no 'backs' in this offer," Rachel said with a smile.

"What we're trying to say is that we hope you'd consider our offer if you aren't sure Erin's heart can take it," Travis concluded.

Ryan and I looked at each other dumbfounded. What a generous offer, so selfless and kind. "Wow! We can't thank you enough," I said, "It takes our breath away that you could love us so. However, we have, in fact, decided to try for kids on our own. We feel really good about our chances, and think that my heart has stabilized. We are hopeful that we can experience the joys of parenthood as you have. You are such great examples for us."

Travis smirked playfully, "Anything we can do to help, let us know," as the boys snickered. "We just wanted you to know that we are excited for you to have children too."

The amount of love they showed us was tremendous. I never would have thought someone would be willing to give that much of themselves for our happiness. The ironic part of the story is the Rachel called us a month later to tell us that she was pregnant with their second child quite by accident and was actually pregnant at the time of her offer. Good thing we didn't take her up on it!

In January 2007, after attending my sister, Chaya's college graduation in Marquette, a city in the Upper Peninsula of Michigan, she and a friend of hers, decided to road trip across the country and move to Tacoma. She stayed with us a few months until she got a job in Seattle. It was wonderful reconnecting with her after 12 years apart (I graduated high school and moved out when she was nine, and we lived across the country from each other; her in California, me in Illinois, and then me in Washington, and her in Michigan). I was so grateful that she wanted to be in close proximity to me, and 30 miles separation was so much better than 2000. She is such a special woman, and I really enjoyed the evenings together just catching up and realizing how much we now had in common.

Growing up with nine years apart, she was always in a different stage of life, and we had a hard time relating. From about 11 years old, I spent most Friday evenings babysitting her while our parents had date night. She was an adorable little blond girl with a crazy tangle of hair that always stuck out in back, no matter how often it was brushed. Although she was generally reserved, she frequently wore a mischievous grin, and had a stubborn streak that wasn't easily pacified. I was the "second" mother that she never wanted, but she put up with me. Incredibly bright and sweet, she managed to tolerate my bossiness with an impish smile and a "we'll see who ultimately wins this one" kind of mentality. While she was the typical little sister pest who got into my stuff, I loved her even then and was happy to let her tag along with my friends, and they were equally OK to have her around.

About the same time my sister moved in, I went to a fertility specialist to see what was wrong with me or Ryan or both. After an exam, they told me that everything looked normal and they don't usually start any testing or intervention until you've been trying for a year. In my mind, I counted both periods of time together. So though it felt like it was never going to happen, I got pregnant in February, just a month after seeing the doctor. After so many single-lined pregnancy tests, it was hard to believe I was now looking at two strong lines. Immediately, I ran into our bedroom, nearly hitting the doorframe with my shoulder. Holding my pee strip and shaking my head in disbelief, "I think it has finally happened," I said to Ryan under my breath; almost afraid that saying it out loud could reverse it.

He looked up from the book he was reading, and his eyes became saucers. "Really? You're not joking, are you?" a mischievous smile forming on his face, a look of both triumph and relief. Fooling around would no longer be compulsory and stressful, ruled by the calendar and not by the heart. The mission was accomplished.

We looked at each other in total disbelief and simultaneously said, "Oh my God, what do we do now??" The planning and practicing for a child never prepares you for the fear you experience the moment you realize the deed is done, no turning back now. Sheer terror and pure joy are a potent combination!

"The Lord is my light and my salvation –
Whom shall I fear?
The Lord is the stronghold of my life –
Of whom shall I be afraid?"
Psalm 27:1

" 'For I know the plans I have for you,' declares the Lord,
'plans to prosper you and not to harm you,
plans to give you hope and a future.' "
Jeremiah 29:11

"Trust in the Lord with all your heart and lean not on your own understanding;
in all your ways acknowledge him, and he will make your paths straight."
Proverbs 3:5

7

The waiting was now over. We had conceived our baby (much too close to Valentine's Day for our comfort). Ryan and I both detest Valentine's Day – nothing worse than corporate profits veiled in cheap love trinkets. After all of the negative pregnancy tests, this time I knew I was pregnant right away. It was like my body was transformed overnight by extreme fatigue, nausea, and heartburn. My senses were heightened; so like most women, my reaction to different foods was either love or hate, no neutral ground. I couldn't stand many of my favorite items anymore, and odd cravings for lemonade and hard boiled eggs emerged. One night early on, Ryan and I were watching some children from our church small group, and we had decided to have popcorn and movie night. Unfortunately, I didn't realize that the smell of popcorn was now intolerable and sent me running to each little child, doing the squish check for soaked diapers. Nope, just the popcorn, which had a pungent urine smell to me. Much to Ryan's chagrin, his favorite snack would have to be shelved for the remainder of the pregnancy.

The first three months were immensely stressful, as I had a tendency to worry about every conceivable problem we might encounter. Jumpy with the slightest odd twinge or symptom, I never felt at ease and I was afraid to get my hopes up too high for fear that we would lose the baby. I now understood why so many soon-to-be mothers wrap their arms protectively over their bellies even to cross the road. It's not just to have a place to rest your hands. It is the start of years of instinctually vigilant and preemptive protection like a mama lion with her cubs.

While most of my concerns were normal to every mother, the fears Ryan and I carried were not entirely unfounded. This was not going to be an uncomplicated pregnancy. We knew it would be a challenge, given my health, but I was not prepared for all that was yet to come. My prayer life began to focus on asking God for release from my fears about the pregnancy and impending birth and seeking peace in the outcome God was going provide. It was excruciatingly hard to give over my worries and rest, but I knew I had no control over the situation. My Bible was constantly flipped to the following verse, especially the part about each day having its own troubles:

Therefore I tell you, do not worry about your life, what you will eat or drink; or about your body, what you will wear. Is not life more important than food, and the body more important than clothes? Look at the birds of the air; they do not sow or reap or store away in barns, and yet your heavenly Father feeds them. Are you not much more valuable than they? Who of you by worrying can add a single hour to his life?
Therefore do not worry about tomorrow, for tomorrow will worry about itself. Each day has enough trouble of its own.
Matthew 6:25-27, 33

Immediately (within days) after the pregnancy was confirmed, I had an intravenous heparin line installed in my arm. The doctors needed to move quickly to something safer for the baby than the dangerous blood thinners I had been on previously. The result was a five pound bag that was constantly attached to me. It went everywhere I went; by my side in bed, to the bathroom in the middle of the night, outside the shower, to the grocery store. I had about a two-foot leash which brought me back to reality with a startling tug every time I allowed myself to forget about it. Getting a shower was now a two-person job where Ryan would wrap my arm in a towel and then in plastic wrap and medical tape, and then hang the bag on a hook just outside the stall. We had to protect the insertion point from getting wet and possible contamination.

Weekly in-home nursing visits were needed to change the heparin bag and dressing, sometimes quite a painful venture. My arm, about 12 weeks into the treatment, began to itch and burn under the adhesive dressing and grew quite red and bloody. We found out the hard way that my skin was sensitive to the chloroprep used to sanitize the wound and it was getting trapped under the bandage, not allowing it to breathe and dissipate. The switch needed to be made to alcohol swabs, but it involved scrubbing the enflamed area with more alcohol than should be legal and then slapping a new adhesive bandage on the angry skin. The intense burning was enough for me to cry out in pain like a baby.

The heparin bag was a great way to remind me daily and hourly what was yet to come, and I mentally counted down the weeks until the bag would be gone. It was a true physical burden I had to carry. Not only was I already fatigued by the stress put on my weak heart by carrying a child, but now I had another weight that sometimes was too much to handle. I found myself sitting continually so I didn't have to carry the additional weight, and when I did have to walk more than a block, I would have someone at my side carrying the bag for me. I looked forward to the last two days of each week when the bag would be significantly drained and gloriously lighter.

Maybe it was a blessing that I struggled to put on weight during my pregnancy. My nausea and heartburn made most food very unappetizing. I developed an intense jealousy of the women who seemed to have no problem conceiving and carrying a child full term. Their lives only minimally impacted, with a few cute food cravings and manageable fatigue thrown in for good measure.

In addition to the heparin bag, however, I had many more hurdles to overcome. The burden of pregnancy quickly became overwhelming for my heart, much more than I had imagined. Only four weeks into the pregnancy, while standing at the kitchen counter at work, my defibrillator fired inside my chest for the first time ever. While I was aware that my heart was having a difficult time staying in rhythm, and I was extremely fatigued, I assumed this was just my lot for the next nine months. However, I knew I was especially tired that day, and the walk from the train station had been a laborious trek. After arriving in the office, I put my bags and coat away and went to the kitchen to make my morning toast. The flutterings of my heart grew stronger and faster, but thankfully gave me enough warning to grab the counter before the shock. I was knocked to the floor and must have uttered a yelp because the front desk attendant peaked in from around the corner (ironically, the same gal who had driven me to the hospital during my TIA). Landing on my knees, fully conscious, I quickly moved to my bottom and braced myself, gripped by fear for whatever else was to come. Getting a shock, while perfectly awake, is equivalent to getting kicked by a horse (I'm assuming) with a sharp, jolting thud to the back and chest simultaneously. To this day, I shudder when someone claps me on the back because the startle brings me viscerally right back to getting a shock.

It took a bit of convincing for me to get up off the floor and move to a chair. My heart was no longer my friend and could not be trusted. The ambulance arrived within minutes and the techs began taking my history and vitals. Diana, a close friend, sat with me during the evaluation and held my hand while they found an adequate vein for an IV, which isn't always an easy task given my small veins. Within a half hour, I found myself on the way to the hospital. I was shaking with fear, not just for my condition, but what might have happened to the baby. In the immediate, I was anxious that the shocks could continue to occur with no improvement to my heart. My heart had settled a bit, but I knew that it could be racing again in no time.

My coworkers were unaware that I was pregnant (having decided not to tell anyone until the second trimester), so I couldn't ask the ambulance technicians in the office lobby how my baby would be affected by this shock. Once inside the privacy of the elevator and free to speak candidly, I was assured that the baby would probably be just fine, as they are perfectly protected inside the womb. I dreaded the thought of the baby experiencing the same horror I just went through. The main concern the techs had was whether my blood pressure had dropped significantly, which is frequently associated with my arrhythmias.

When I arrived at the hospital, the doctors were able to quickly assess what was happening to my heart. The anti-arrhythmia and beta blocker medication levels that I had been on prior to getting pregnant were no longer adequate due to metabolism and blood volume changes associated with the pregnancy. They hoped that by raising my prescription levels up slightly, they could stabilize me now and throughout the rest of the pregnancy. Ryan took about an hour and a half to get to the hospital due to traffic between Seattle and Tacoma. He was just in time to meet with the doctor from my OB's office, who checked the baby on ultrasound and were able to confirm that there appeared to be no negative impact from the defibrillator shock. This was first time that we saw our little one's mesmerizing heartbeat on the screen, a marvelous moment brought about by a terrifying situation. I was discharged from the ER by 4:30 p.m., just in time for the evening rush hour commute home.

Obviously, we now needed to tell our immediate family what had really happened, so their fears could be relieved. When I was stabilized in the ER, Ryan had called my parents and his parents, as well as both our siblings. We hadn't updated anyone during the course of the day because there was a constant flow of doctors and tests, and we wanted to disseminate the complete news to everyone all at once. So Ryan and I called everyone on the cell phone while we were stuck in traffic. They were overjoyed with our news about the baby and amazed that the solution to the problem was so quickly identified and resolved. I know they were equally worried about the remaining 36 weeks of the pregnancy. Everyone suspected that we had a long road ahead of us, but our decision for children was already made and well under way. Before the calls concluded, they each promised not to share the news with people outside the family because we had not yet passed the 12 week "safe" point. I had convinced myself that if I just made it to 12 weeks I could breathe deeply knowing I wouldn't miscarry.

The weeks seemed to drag on, with every little symptom or twitch appearing to be an indication that something could be wrong. I continued to have debilitating fatigue, and commuting 80 minutes each way to work only exasperated it. Pregnancy was miserable; my body was not cooperating in any regards, from my stomach to my heart. Fear stood at the door most nights during my quiet moments and threatened to jump out from behind every corner. Ryan and the high risk OB doctor got really frustrated that I couldn't relax and just "enjoy" being pregnant. The doctor, in a lousy attempt to comfort me, frequently gave me talks about how other people had it much worse and I should just cherish this time. Ryan felt comforted by the doctor's reassuring words. What I heard was "buck up and get over yourself. If you just relax, you'll enjoy it." He obviously was not speaking from personal experience.

At 11 weeks, when my parents were visiting from San Diego, we experienced another dramatic episode. After a day-long family outing (including the desperate search for my go-to craving- cupcakes) I was climbing the painfully steep stairs to go to bed when I recognized that I had gone out of rhythm, my heart racing and erratic, and extreme shortness of breath that was cause my head to go fuzzy. Slowly, I made my way down the long narrow hallway to my bedroom and carefully lie down in bed, desperately hoping and praying my heart would regain its normal speed and rhythm. No such luck.

Bam! My device fired. This was now the second time. In a panic, I shouted for my mother who was downstairs to come be with me. As she rushed up the stairs, I realized that I now needed to pee like a racehorse. As if this wasn't bad enough, whenever I go out of rhythm, the panic of the situation makes me urgently need to use the bathroom. Tragically bad timing!

As I knew we needed to head to the hospital, I asked my mother to assist me to the bathroom. With her nurturing, soothing care, she could keep me composed even when I knew the fear was overwhelming her. My heart in the meantime had not slowed, and as I sat fully clothed on the toilet trying to muster enough energy to pull my pants down, my device fired for the third time. By this point, I didn't want to attempt to make it down the stairs and to the car, so we called 911.

A fire truck and ambulance arrived at our house in minutes, clipping several low hanging trees along our narrow residential street. This commotion brought out many of our neighbors, some of whom we'd never met formally. Once inside our house, the firemen assessed the situation and recognized that making me move might cause another shock so they began the precarious process of carrying me down our narrow staircase. Not only would a stretcher not fit, but it wasn't wide enough for both men to go down on either side of me, so one had to go backward and one forward with me scrunched in a makeshift seat in between. The craziness of the situation brought out my nervous humor, and I joked a bit with the handsome, muscular firemen, even trying to get my sister a few names and numbers for later.

Inside the ambulance, we asked them to take me to the University of Washington Medical Center, where my physicians knew my medical history and the best course of treatment specifically for me. Unfortunately, they told me they could only take me to a Pierce County hospital, so we decided on the closest major hospital, thankful to have the option of two major facilities within a five-mile radius.

Once in the emergency room, I requested that they call my doctors at UW so they could give them the full medical background and decide on treatment options together.

"I don't think that'll be necessary. We can handle your condition just fine here," said the ER doctor in charge of my treatment, pompously refusing to call. "Anyway, the medication levels you are on are not advisable and we can't recommend any further medication increase to slow your heart rate."

"But I know that my doctors at UW would not agree. When I was there just a couple weeks ago for the same problem, they told me that my pregnancy had affected my metabolism, and my heart was no longer getting the correct dosages. They had to raise my beta blocker levels to bring me back into rhythm. Please, please call them to confer. This will not get better on its own," I pleaded. Draped in sweat and shaking, I felt trapped and scared. My heart continued to race unabated, and I feared another shock at any moment, my worry only intensifying the situation.

"Actually," the doctor continued, "pregnant women often have elevated heart rates, and I would feel comfortable sending you home if it went down to 120 beats a minute." What garbage! Had he talked to my regular cardiologists, he would have been more informed that my damaged heart doesn't handle high speeds well and for long periods of time. My head was spinning, overwhelmed that I might have to live in this state of distress for another 30 weeks. But nonetheless, after four hours, he sent me home, still out of rhythm and racing, and desperately afraid I would be shocked again.

Sleep was hard to come by that night, and I spent the whole next day on the couch sleeping on and off, having no energy to go upstairs to bed. I still didn't feel any better; just walking to the bathroom would almost make me pass out. That night, less than 24 since my last ER visit, my defibrillator went off for the fourth and fifth time while I was once again trying to muster enough energy to pull my pants down in the bathroom. This time, there was no question where we needed to go. The question was how many more times would it go off before we made the 30-mile trip between Tacoma and Seattle. Ryan had packed my overnight bag (he had become a pro at this over the last eight years) and he was putting it in the car when my heart slowed to the point where I could "make a run for it." Actually, it was a snail's pace, but I made it to the car without it going off.

We left immediately with my mom riding in the backseat with me. We got only five blocks before it went off for the sixth time. I held my pillow to my chest and just prayed that God would give me the strength to endure the pain. Fortunately, it was 10:30 p.m., and the roads were pretty empty. Ryan raced along fully anticipating getting pulled over by a cop, but just hoping that it would be past the Pierce County line so they wouldn't force us to go back to the local hospital. Who knew, maybe they'd even escort us the rest of the way to UW. Somehow, accrediting it to a miracle and a lot of prayer, we made it there without it firing again. The doctors had all my medical history and moved right into action, giving me some medications to slow my heart to where I didn't worry about getting shocked. It took quite a while to stabilize the atrial fibrillation, but it finally happened about four hours later, and I didn't need to be cardioverted.

During my time in the ER, I was equally worried about my father, alone and scared, back at the house. He suffered from the same condition as I do, and his health had deteriorated significantly over the past five years. Once strong and driven, he was now a shell of his former self, fragile and broken and at the end of his medical options. He was constantly having to be cardioverted and was in end-stage heart failure. He understood the pain of the defibrillator firing and had been deeply distressed the past two days watching his daughter go through the same struggles. Both of us lived with our worst enemy and closest companion in the same small box nestled inside our chests. I was deeply grieved just watching him in the hallway with tears in his eyes, his body trembling, staring helplessly as his daughter limped along searching for something to relieve her agony. His profound empathy for me caused him physical pain and brought on his own rhythm issues. He was tortured by seeing his child in pain, but also aware that he had inadvertently caused it. The guilt was palpable. We were intricately and tragically woven together in this family curse.

While I knew leaving him at our house was difficult for him, I think if he had accompanied us to the hospital, the urgency of the situation would overwhelm him and inevitably cause two hospitalizations. Consequently, we decided he should wait at home. Ryan promised to check in often to make sure he was doing OK and give him updates on me. As inconvenient as timing always seems to be, my parents had a flight home scheduled for early the next morning, and we needed him feeling better and somewhat rested in order to make it.

Luckily, I was stable enough the next morning for Ryan to be able to leave me at the hospital for a few hours to take my parents to the airport. They obviously didn't want to leave, but we insisted that we'd get this sorted out and I'd be fine. We put on a good face and tried to act like adults.

It took two weeks for the doctors to stabilize my rhythm problems. I was in a constant state of atrial fibrillation and flutter, and my heart rate would spike during the smallest movements, such as sitting up in bed. They made adjustments to my device programming, which lessened the chance of it firing, including raising the heart rate speed that triggered a shock. Sadly, my anxiety level didn't decrease proportionately. We were fortunate that all of the shocks thus far had been atrial related and not the deadly ventricular rhythms. They would not have been able to decrease the device settings if the ventricles were causing the disturbances. In the following months, I was plagued by dreams that I had been shocked, only to wake up and find that it wasn't real. The doctors explained that the phenomenon occurred because the heart, being a muscle, has a memory of the shock and so it would involuntarily spasm, appearing just as real and as frightening as the real thing.

The doctors also played around with myriad of drugs and dosages hoping to find the perfect combination that was both safe for the baby and that would alleviate my symptoms. My original pre-pregnancy dosages all were multiplied by eight (one of them went from 40mg to 600mg). Normally these dosages would be enough to kill a horse, and none of the doctors had ever prescribed this much to any of their patients, but it seemed to be working for me, without the serious side effects, such as dangerously low blood pressure. I became known among the cardiac doctors as a "super-metabolizer." Although my body could tolerate high drug dosages, there were significant impacts to my daily existence, the top two being extreme exhaustion and breathlessness, dramatically more than normal pregnancy fatigue. We were also told that there was a good probability we'd have a low birth weight baby.

The doctors were so intrigued by my drug metabolism that they asked me to be a part of a drug study involving pregnant women who were taking beta blockers, and how their metabolism changed during the course of their pregnancies and after birth. At the end of each trimester, they asked me to check into the hospital for the day, get an IV placed and they would take blood at prescribed time intervals to test the levels of medication throughout the day. I was happy to contribute to science, and if it helped women's treatment plans in the future, it was well worth it. Plus, it was fairly relaxing, and hospitals, sadly, had become quite comfortable and homey to me. I loved interacting with the nurses, and this was one way I could be useful, since most of my time was spent on my butt at home.

Due to my lack of energy and cautiousness about having more arrhythmias, and out of necessity, I decided to work part time for the rest of the pregnancy. My company was really supportive and set up my home computer so that I could work from home entirely, answering construction and design questions, and reviewing pay applications and construction schedules. I rarely left the house except to go to a doctor's appointment or to visit my project's construction site for a project meeting and to monitor the progress of the work. Even then, I was normally driven by someone else who made sure I got home if my heart started acting up, which it did, especially when I climbed the construction scaffolding. No amount of logic or reason kept me from doing my job. Only my body could tell me "no" and it did often; but by then the damage was done, and I needed to be dragged home.

My ability to be independent was a thing of the past. Not only did someone have to escort me around, but I couldn't even contribute around the house with my normal tasks. Ryan was forced to handle all of the household duties such as cooking, cleaning, grocery shopping, and laundry, all on top of his full-time work schedule that frequently required overtime. He never complained, even though I knew it was really hard on him. His family was his upmost concern and responsibility; self-sacrifice and loyalty were part of his nature.

Ryan worked really hard to involve me in tasks that he knew were important for the baby nesting process. One weekend, his parents came over and painted the nursery the colors that Ryan and I had picked out together. My job was to sit in a chair and paint the homemade dresser that Ryan and I had designed and created for our last house. We loved this dresser and were excited to see it be used in the baby's room. I had chosen a creamy chocolate brown that went well with the buttery yellow and sage green we wanted on the walls. I got part of the way through the front face and lost all my energy. I felt like a failure, unable to accomplish the simplest of tasks. As I found my way to bed for a short nap, my mother-in-law, Kathy, kept reassuring me that I was doing the most important part of all by caring for the baby inside. My one job was to stay rested, eat well, and try not to exert myself too much. It seemed so simple, yet so hard. I wanted to do, but I could only be.

Eating well was a challenge since my nausea endured throughout the pregnancy. Peanut butter and jelly sandwiches were the only reliably appetizing meal, and I couldn't leave the bed in the morning without a couple of saltine crackers. Taking my huge handful of pills daily proved difficult because my gag reflex was so sensitive. I had to find something besides water to keep them down. My doctor told me to eat anything that appealed to me, including as much ice cream as I wanted. I would buy the food that looked the most attractive, but by time I got home from the store, it had lost its appeal. Ryan benefitted the most from my snacky purchases and gained measurably more weight than I did.

Staying rested was difficult because of all the arrhythmia that I had fairly consistently, especially at night. I would lay awake trying to slow my heart down by myriad of relaxation techniques, slowed and deliberate breathing, mediation/prayer, different positions, etc., many of which I think I repeated out of pure superstition, since it may have appeared to work one time before. Truth be told, there is no way to convince a stubborn heart to find a smooth easy rhythm, but I can say that anxiety does not help.

At our 18-week ultrasound, we were again assured that the baby was doing well and developing on a normal track. We also found out that we were having a little boy, without too much ambiguity. While we both would have been delighted with either sex, having a boy was an extra special gift. He would be the first grandson born in Ryan's family and knowing that he would probably be our only child, we were excited to be able to pass down our family name to the next generation. Ryan and I were quick to choose a name and share it with everyone. We wanted

Aiden Michael to be known, well before his birth. Aiden means "little fire" in Irish, which we felt was very appropriate based on the all that he had been through during this pregnancy and the spunk he displayed despite of it. Michael is Ryan's father's name, and we were proud to have him share the name with such a fine man.

Using my relaxation techniques in the middle of the night, I was now able to speak to Aiden, using his given name, telling him about his family and all the fun we would have when he arrived. Most of the time my erratic heart rhythm and shallow, labored breathing would wake him up anyway, and he would toss and turn with me during the countless sleepless nights. His movement was such a salve to my emotional and physical discomfort. I would go as far as to poke at him every morning to wake him up, just for the reassurance that we were in this together.

Trying not to exert myself was really an oxymoron. Depending on the crankiness of my heart, standing too long or bending down to get a dish from the oven could prove too strenuous. I had to gauge my energy level hour by hour, the mornings normally being the most refreshed and likely to be in rhythm. Once in a while, I would have a good day with a little extra energy and I would try to help out with a quick grocery trip or emptying the dishwasher. Unfortunately, I would frequently overdo it and end up out of rhythm and sleeping most of the next day. It was one of those "good days" that forever changed my life. Rarely can people actually point to the exact moment and location that carried them into a new reality. Sadly, I can.

It was August 8th, 2007, when I was 27 weeks pregnant, and it was one of those days where I had a little extra energy so I decided to run a few errands. I had been in rhythm for a few days in a row so I felt a renewed sense of confidence and was comfortable taking a quick drive by myself. It was actually invigorating to have a bit of independence back. Our truck needed emissions testing, and I had to go to the DMV to renew my driver's license that was expiring at the end of the month on my birthday. I had just left the DMV to go home and get some lunch when I made the decision to try a new route home. I enjoyed taking unexplored streets and seeing new neighborhoods and homes from the different eras of development. I did this whenever I got the chance.

Today I would take 12th Street home instead of 19th or 6th. As I was passing a Catholic Church and school, I approached a slow moving vehicle in the left lane of a four-lane arterial street. The speed limit was 35 miles an hour and there were no kids around, as it was summer. I decided to move into the right lane to go around them and noticed a car creeping toward the street from a driveway entrance of an apartment complex, a few hundred feet away.

As I would later learn, inside the car was a young teenage driver that was out practicing with her mother. As I passed the driveway, she got confused and hit the gas instead of the brake. She accelerated forward and caught the back wheel well of my narrow-bodied pick-up truck. The truck began to spin and as it did, it rolled onto its top. I remember each detail so perfectly because it seemed to be going in slow motion. For a brief moment, I was suspended upside down by my seatbelt. The windshield was shattered and the top had been crushed slightly. If I had been any taller I probably would have sustained head injuries. Fortunately, I was fully conscious and pretty sure I wasn't injured. I found my seatbelt clasp and after jiggling it a bit, it finally released, dropping me into a pile of windshield glass below. Carefully, I maneuvered myself into a kneeling position on the roof. Although I tried desperately to opening the driver's side, I knew I wasn't going to have any luck because the frame was obviously dented and jammed shut, so I leaned over and started pushing my weight against the passenger side door.

People had started to gather around the vehicle and weren't having much luck on the door from the outside either. The door was unlatched, but only able to open an inch or so, painfully scraping the asphalt. All the while, fluids were leaking from the hood, and the radio was playing surreally in the background. Fumbling with the knobs, I finally got the music shut off, but I couldn't get the keys out of the ignition. The police and fire department had arrived about the same time, secured the street from further accidents and gotten the door open to a width that I could shimmy out. I had been concerned the whole time I was stuck that someone would hit my overturned truck from behind while I was still sitting in the mangled cab. I slid out of the truck on my hands and knees crawling through the broken tempered glass chunks. When I got to my feet, I noticed the only injury I had was a small cut on my elbow, not even big enough to warrant a band-aid. In a trance, I found my way to the curb and sat down in the grass.

A priest from the church I had passed came and sat down quietly next to me. He asked if I was alright and if he could pray with me. Sheepishly I said yes, but inwardly I hesitated. Aiden had already starting to move around, and I felt a wave of relief. Confident that my baby was alright, my prayer had already been answered. After all that we had been through, God wouldn't possibly take him away. I did a quick "thank you" prayer silently as he prayed, but nothing more. I am embarrassed to admit that my first response was not to cry out to God with more than just a "popcorn" prayer in a terrifying moment such as this. I hope that it was the pure shock of the situation that made me numb and word-bound. At first glance everything appeared to be fine, except for the crumpled truck in front of me, right side up now but awkwardly askew.

As I continued to sit on the curb after the priest had left, I frantically tried to get a hold of Ryan on my cell phone. In the end, I accepted that the only way to reach him was to leave a message for him with a coworker in the office. I wanted Ryan to be assured that I was okay before he arrived panicked at the hospital. A policeman walked over to inform me that I was going to need to be evaluated at the hospital, standard procedure for a rollover accident. I agreed that it would be good to have Aiden checked out, so I took the ambulance to the same local hospital that failed to help me 16 weeks prior. So strapped to a hard backboard (again, standard procedure, but really difficult for a pregnant women in her seventh month), and hopeful that this experience would be better because my heart wasn't involved, the ambulance shot down the road. Aiden kept moving around in my belly, obviously unhappy with my position as well.

When I arrived at the hospital, I was told that after accidents they typically monitor the baby for a minimum of four to six hours. The nursing team put me in a bed on the Labor and Delivery floor and strapped a baby monitor around my belly. They were able to find the heart beat right away, strong and even, but it kept moving out of the monitor's range. The nurse joked that he must be a hyperactive little baby because we ended up chasing him around my belly all night. He was 27 weeks at this point, and still had plenty of room to maneuver. All the signs looked positive. No bleeding, contractions, or fetal distress were observed. After about an hour, Ryan found me in the hospital. He had been absolutely panicked. The message had not been passed on that I was okay, only that I was in the hospital after a car accident. I was so happy to share with him the miracle that had taken place today. Very few people make it out of a rollover unscathed, and it appeared that Aiden and I had both received the same gift. We felt so grateful and blessed.

After a few more hours and a pork chop dinner (which ironically looked rather appetizing), they let me go home with a clean bill of health. That night, we called all of our family and friends to share the wonderful news of God's protection on this very upsetting day. However, as the next few days went by, I noticed less and less activity from Aiden and began rethinking my original assessment. Ryan assumed I was worrying needlessly again and tried to downplay my concerns, instead focusing on the euphoria of the 'miracle' that had just occurred. "God took care of everything," he reminded me. "But if it would help to ease your mind, you could to stop by the OB doctor after your heart appointment on Friday."

Husbands and doctors: take a lesson here, never ignore/downplay the intuition of a women, let alone a fiercely protective mother-to-be.

8

The following Thursday after the accident I spent the night with my sister, Chaya, at her apartment in Seattle. I had a previously scheduled cardiology appointment at UW the next morning, and we had decided it would be easier physically for me to make the appointment by driving up the night before, so my morning nausea wouldn't be kicking in during morning rush hour traffic. It had been one week since the accident, and I continued to have uneasiness about Aiden's lack of movement. I shared my concerns with Chaya over a Thai dinner that night telling her that I no longer felt the normal flutterings and only felt him move when I moved. She listened intently and tried to be as reassuring as Ryan, but my unease would not be relieved. In the morning, as I lay awake trying to motivate myself to get up from my sister's much-too-comfortable bed, I poked and prodded at him until I felt meagerly satisfied that I felt him move.

I drove to the hospital in my rental car, as my truck had already been deemed "totaled," and we were now waiting for an insurance settlement to replace it. As Ryan suggested, immediately after my cardiology check-up, I stopped by my doctor in the OB/GYN department. They also expressed concern when they heard I had been in a car accident and took me back to an empty exam room right away. Staring up at the cold, white ceiling tiles, my stomach was in my throat with dreadful anticipation. Trying to muster up the same optimism of Ryan and Chaya, I longed to hear Aiden's heartbeat, but as the nurse struggled to find one, frantically moving the doppler wand over my belly; all my suspicion came rushing back.

"I'm sorry, I need to go get the doctor. I'll be right back," was all she said as she rushed out of the exam room. He came in pushing the ultrasound equipment cart and began probing my belly once again. Aiden appeared on the screen immediately, flawlessly beautiful, but eerily still. I knew instantly something was very wrong. There was no reassuring smile from the doctor, only a somber look of recognition and resignation.

He slowly reached over and lightly grasped my arm, looked me in the eyes and said, "I'm sorry, your baby is gone." I stared back in disbelief, and then the tears started flowing uncontrollably. As I was weeping, he continued talking, "I will need to start the induction process, but it may be up to 24 hours before you deliver."

Shock and denial set in at the same time, right along with frustration and confusion. I couldn't believe what was happening. How could I go through such a tortuous pregnancy, only to walk away empty handed? This could not be part of God's plan. I have no doubt that Aiden had been part of His plan for our lives. How then could He end it so abruptly after we had pronounced His miracle of the accident only a week earlier?

The doctor excused himself from the melancholy of the exam room and went about retrieving the supplies he needed to start the induction. The nurse remained, and I listened through the tears as she shared more specifics about the procedure and what the next few days looked like. I'm not sure how much I heard because I kept telling myself that it couldn't be true. I interrupted her train of thought, "Please bring the doctor back in to 'double check' the ultrasound because I certainly wouldn't want to start the induction if he was mistaken." She looked at me thoughtfully and left the room quietly. As I had requested, the doctor returned to verify the results of the last ultrasound just five minutes before. Seeing Aiden on the screen again was so painful. He was this perfectly-formed child who looked like a real, little baby, not the large headed, disproportionate fetus that was in our second trimester ultrasound pictures. He had grown so much since our last ultrasound at 20 weeks and was right on track to be a small, but healthy baby.

We had just celebrated his 27-week milestone, when his lungs were supposed to be developed enough for him to make it on the "outside." Despite my aching desire, the doctor was right; the tiny little heart that we had seen blinking on the screen a few weeks earlier had disappeared and would not inexplicably reappear. He was totally still and looked to be merely sleeping. Questions filled my head. How long had he been gone? Had he suffered? If we had known something was wrong a week ago, would delivering earlier have saved his life? How could the hospital have missed seeing that something was wrong?

As the doctor and nurse prepared for the induction, they brought me to the office next door to make some phone calls. A social worker came in within a couple minutes.

"Hello, I'm Patty, a social worker here at UW. I want to extend my deepest apologies for your loss and offer any assistance possible in this difficult time. I'm sorry we had to meet under such circumstances, but I want you to know I'm available if you need anything, even if you can't think of anything at this moment." I sat there silently, blinking back a few tears and trying to give her a polite smile. She was offering resources, not counsel, and certainly couldn't do the only thing I longed for — bring Aiden back.

Only one request came to mind, "Could you show me how to dial an outside telephone line from the exam room? I have a few calls to make."

"Absolutely," she gave me the instructions and walked to the door to leave, "I'll be down the hall if you think of any other questions." A quick smile and she was gone.

Laboriously I choked back the tears and dialed Ryan's cell. When he answered, I simply said without preface, "Ryan, its Erin. You need to get up here. Aiden didn't make it. They are going to start the induction right away and they think he'll come within twenty four hours." The silence on the other end was deafening. But really, what more was there to say?

Finally after a long pause he answered, "I'll be right there." He later described to me how vacant and dazed he felt as he jumped into the car to drive up from Tacoma; anger welling up in him as he listened on the radio to the drone of an afternoon Seattle Mariners game. They were having another lousy season and were an easy target of displaced emotion.

The second call I made was to my mom. Her tears were as uncontrollable as mine were minutes before and they just seemed to amplify my own. Knowing the importance of this pregnancy to her and my father made the disappointment unbearable. In retrospect, Aiden had been lifted up, higher than any person should be, as the redemption of all the trials and hurts our family had endured during the last ten years, punctuated by the rapid decline of my dad's health. I was trying so hard to stay calm and keep myself together, that I began speaking in a monotone manner, hoping that I could regulate the tears and not betray my prideful sense of self-control. Tears are rare for me and maybe that is why the flood seemed bottled, ready to explode, and yet awkwardly held back.

It took all of my mental strength and focus to survive the essential phone calls in a somewhat even tone. My friends were gracious enough to not ask many questions, and through Diana at work and Lissa from church, I was able to disseminate the news to everyone else. I hoped that if the news spread quickly, I wouldn't have to talk about it anymore or go through awkward encounters of "how's your new baby?" at the grocery store.

Ryan arrived within an hour and we fell into each other's arms, sobbing and shaking. The flood gates had opened and continued unabated until the nurse stepped soundlessly through the exam room door. I stood up straight, wiped my tears and tried to direct my thoughts to a faraway place. Numbly, I climbed onto the table as instructed and closed my eyes. It was now time to begin the induction process.

The whole ordeal was a terrible nightmare. They informed me it could take a while for the medication they had implanted to take effect. Once the procedure was complete, all I wanted was to hole away in the privacy of a patient room. Unfortunately, they needed a little more time to get a room ready for me on the Labor/Delivery floor. Ryan and I had no choice but to find refuge elsewhere. Knowing the hospital as intimately as we did, we thought the most anonymous (and useful) place to waste some time was the cafeteria, as all of the waiting rooms seemed too exposed or isolated. We both knew we didn't want to wait in the doctor's office anymore, and our stomachs were starting to show signs of the waning day.

We found no solace sitting in the sea of people. There were no words left to say so we sat in silence, avoiding eye contact and the chance of more tears. We knew that we were not the only people here choking down sandwiches while their lives crumbled, and people they loved died. It's eerie to be in such a public place during such an intensely private pain. We picked at the tasteless food on our plates until our hunger was meagerly satisfied and decided to leave. Overcome by the chaotic ebb and flow of the cafeteria, we found ourselves walking around aimlessly in a trance.

After languishing a painfully long time, we made a beeline for Labor and Delivery praying the room would be ready. Taking an elevator to our room, we were greeted by the nursing staff who took great care and discretion with our situation, speaking in hushed tones and smiling tenderly, but still avoiding direct eye contact. They led us to a room at the end of the hall, one where we wouldn't have the agony of seeing all of the other families and their new bundles of joy. My sister was already there waiting and threw her arms around me. Some close friends from church, Ryan's parents, and his sister, Lisa, and her husband, Cody, arrived shortly after. A room full of people awkwardly making small talk; some of them meeting each other for the first time. It's so peculiar to be surrounded by everyone you love and have nothing to say, sharing a moment that doesn't require words.

When the nurses began prepping the room for the approaching event, my family and friends politely made their departure, deciding to walk to the local shopping complex for some palatable food outside of the hospital. While it was wonderful being so well cared for, it was a relief having alone time with Ryan to sort through the crushing emotions of the day and the impending birth. The conversation flowed into a prayer in which we pleaded with God to keep me healthy during the labor and to be present in our pain. We told God how confused and wounded we were, and how only He could help us accept this tragedy, find peace and restore our joy; it seemed unfathomable in our puny brains. Tears continued to ebb and flow in our communion together, along with expressions of frustration, fear, and palpable sadness. I know He was with us at that moment, but the salve of His healing could not yet penetrate our despondency.

My parents, upon hearing the news, had scheduled a flight from San Diego, but they couldn't get there until noon the next morning. It was initially my hope that the delivery wouldn't happen until my mom was there, but God, in His graciousness, granted Ryan and I this private time together. My water broke around 5 p.m., and I knew that labor was going to go quicker than the doctor originally thought. Throughout my pregnancy, my high-risk OB doctor had assured me repeatedly that he would keep me comfortable during the labor with great medication (which I was in favor of given my intimate knowledge of its powerful effects), going as far as telling stories about his patients playing cards right up until they were told to push. I thought he was full of crap, but I was willing to believe it if I could gain some peace from it. I knew that pain increased my heart speed, labor would do likewise, and I was deathly afraid of not being able to complete labor on my own due to arrhythmia and shortness of breath. As a back-up plan, he also assured me that if I couldn't finish, they had the "tools" to do the job on their own. Again, not a reassuring thought.

As the night drew on, Ryan hurried home to gather some items for spending the night. His family went home as well so they could get some sleep before they picked my parents up at the airport early the next morning. This left my sister and me to sit and talk about everything, except the big elephant in the room. We weren't deliberately avoiding hard discussions, but most everything had been said and it was much more fun to laugh, watching mindless movies on bad hospital cable. We sat together just content with each other's comforting presence.

When Ryan returned, Chaya took her leave. We settled in for the night, but sleep didn't come easy or last long. The Labor and Delivery bed mattress was much too thin for my comfort, and I asked the nurse had anything to help my aching back (only partially due to the bed). She pondered it for a brief moment and then ran out of the room, only to return pushing one of the standard hospital beds. I realized, without further explanation, that since this wasn't a normal delivery situation, their concern about normal birthing procedures didn't actually apply. They only needed to worry about me and not about the quick care of a newborn.

Not long after the bed was changed out, I started to have a lot of cramping. However, my physical discomfort was dwarfed by my emotions, feeling Aiden's little body moving around when I rolled over; knowing he was no longer with me. It was so deceptive and gut-wrenching. I'm so thankful that God didn't make me endure the physical pain long.

Around 3 a.m. the cramping was more than I could bear. The nurses gave me some morphine to dull the pain, but after a few hours it was no longer effective. I knew I was in labor, but the nurses didn't help to quell the pain as I was requesting. It was frustrating that the great pain meds that the OB doctor had promised me earlier were not going to materialize. No epidural for me because my heart was becoming unstable and my blood pressure had dropped too low. They wouldn't even give me more morphine, so I just had to tolerate the pain.

Finally, about 6 a.m., they said I could start pushing. I've always thought I was a pretty strong woman, but I know that I could not have endured without Ryan at my side holding my hand and speaking calming words into my ear. My emotional and physical pain were nearing my threshold. I just kept repeating the prayer, "God, please give me the strength to get through this," — a prayer that became my mantra for months to come. He did on that day and many others. He kept my heart in rhythm and gave me enough physical energy to finish the delivery relatively quickly. These had both been my main concern during the pregnancy. Now it was done. As much as I had earlier wanted my mother to be at the labor, I now realized that this was something Ryan and I needed to do alone.

Aiden was born at 7:30 a.m., August 17th, 2007, weighing in at 1 lb. 5 oz., small but potentially viable. Yet he made no sound, no nurses running to and fro, no happy tears shed, no pictures with Mom and Dad, no people sitting expectantly in the waiting room— a great crescendo with no sound.

The nurses let us hold him, a tiny package wrapped in a hospital receiving blanket. How I wished it was just some big mistake, and they would hand me a squirming little bundle. Reality was really a slap in the face. He was perfectly formed. I could see little bits of Ryan and me in him in his delicate face, long fingers and toes, and even his eyelashes; features that would never develop further. So he was the one who would move around inside me while I lay awake in the middle of the night, out of rhythm. It was him whom enjoyed the bumpy rides in the car, kicking with every corresponding pothole. It was him that I harassed every morning by poking at my belly until he would kick me back (Ryan thought I was so cruel). It was him that caused me to use the bathroom five to six times a night because he used my bladder as a punching bag. This would be our last memory of him, our Aiden. There would be no more.

Several hours later the entire family arrived. They consoled us as best they could, but there's not much more one can say besides, "I'm sorry for your loss." No one knew Aiden, not even I really, except for a few hints of personality in utero. They couldn't celebrate his short life. They couldn't even provide hope for the next child because they knew how difficult and precarious this pregnancy had been. The last thing I wanted to hear was about God's plan, purpose, and provision. What kind of plan was this? My months of struggle had been in vain. My joy and future hope were simultaneously obliterated. The miracle had been a sham.

Although some might think it odd, I felt comforted by having Aiden still bundled in the delivery crib through the later part of the morning. Somehow, it was not final until he was gone. When my parents arrived, my mother was the only one who wanted, or felt able, to see him, and we spent a few minutes together alone holding him, crying, and praying. It was a very special moment, one that I will always cherish. We said our goodbyes as the nurse came to take him. She said Ryan and I could call for him whenever we wanted today, but they needed to care for his little body in a specially-warmed room. I didn't want any of the details, I just wanted to know that I didn't have to say goodbye just yet.

The day slipped away quickly between my naps and nausea from the pain medication. That evening, after everyone had gone home, Ryan and I asked to hold him one last time to say our goodbyes and pray over him. This was really the first and only time since he was born that tears seemed uncontrollable. It was so hard calling the nurse back to take him away, knowing that it was truly the end of our time with him. Leaving the hospital the next day without him just as arduous, especially passing all the giddy new parents and their families in the hallway. They were beaming with the pride and optimism of new life, blissfully unaware of the pain around them.

On the day we arrived home after Aiden's birth, the nursery door was quietly closed. Everything was left in its pre-August 17th state, with an assembled crib, a partially-stocked changing table and dresser, and lovingly painted walls. All of the emotions surrounding the preparation, decoration, and nesting were too raw for Ryan and me to tackle. Although a majority of the natural light that reached the long, narrow upstairs hall came from the nursery, the trade-off of a closed door was worth not walking passed the "what-could-have-been" countless times a day. A week or so later, when I was parked on the leather couch downstairs because my heart was still misbehaving, my parents-in-law snuck upstairs and quietly dismantled the furniture and carried them out to their truck.

Our excursion for the day, and one of my first times out of the house, was a trip to Fort Lewis Army base to return the baby furniture to the store. While I sat numbly in the car, Ryan's mom, Kathy, went in to discuss the situation with the manager. I didn't ask any questions when she returned to the vehicle, but from what I gathered, she was initially met with opposition. They had explained to her their policy of not taking back assembled furniture, but she was extraordinarily persuasive in her sweet, but firm "I will not to take a 'no' for an answer" technique.

In the end, we all had the comfort of being rid of those physical reminders. Kathy's graciousness was more than she could know. Also in hindsight, I am thankful that my struggles during pregnancy had spared us the opportunity for a baby shower. It would have been much more painful coming home to precious gifts needing to be returned.

One afternoon while I was sitting in my bedroom, I found myself staring angrily at a small, wood-carved figurine, a gift my mother had bought for me when I was about four months pregnant. It depicted a heavily pregnant woman, but now it represented a cruel reminder of what we had lost, a reminder that needed to disappear quickly. As I picked it up, I took time to examine it and I noticed a sticker on the bottom of it. The collector's tag stated this piece in the series was named "Cherish." Cherish what? The child, or the hope of a child during pregnancy? Either way, I was not ready to do what it suggested. It was put immediately into the closet. Fortunately, I am not one to throw away even the most heinous of gifts, so it was spared the finality of the garbage, or worse being smashed into bits against the wall.

Over the first few weeks we had a blur of family, sympathy cards, flowers, and well- wishers. If it weren't for people coming by to bring food, we probably wouldn't have remembered to eat, and definitely wouldn't have bothered to see anyone. While I love flowers and cards; the flowers quickly became a burden, a reminder of life and death, and the shortness of it all. While they were beautiful at first, they eventually and slowly died, covering the entire dining room table. Each day I went through a process of identifying the ones that were dropping petals and cherry-picking the ones that would make it another day. Painfully slow, the table became empty.

Ryan was given a leave from work, and together, we got through two seasons of CSI, sitting in a dark family room, blinds pulled, watching gruesome scenes and trying to guess who-done-it. It was strangely therapeutic to watch someone else's horror and anguish. Maybe therapeutic isn't the right word, but it was definitely a transference of pain and a thorough absorption into depression and isolation. The CSI series had come to represent mourning to us, as this is what we watched when we were grieving two years ago with Brian and Cindy when they lost their first daughter, Maggie. Spending a week in Chicago during the summer following her death and with beautiful sunshine outside, we watched episode after episode in their dark family room.

Unfortunately, in both situations, there weren't a lot of conversations with God during this stage of grief. While I believe that God was present the entire time, He was waiting to be invited back, to be given the chance to help us heal. But once anger and confusion started to set in, it was hard to invite back in the friend that I knew had the power to stop this tragedy from happening in the first place. What was His plan? I didn't feel like I could trust Him. I was numb.

While we were in the throes of accepting our loss, there was great joy that surrounded us in the birth of two babies in our family. My sister-in-law, Lisa had given birth to a little girl, Erika, in June, just two months previous. Only a month later, Rachel and Travis had their baby girl, Grace. Seeing these beautiful girls and their beaming parents, it was so hard to feign happiness. Despite my half-hearted attempts to celebrate these new lives, my thoughts always led back to Aiden, and inevitably, self-pity.

My faith was not gone, but it was undeniably strained. It's not that I ever questioned God's existence, but in this situation I struggled to see His love and goodness, let alone His desire for a personal relationship. Was He good or were we all puppets in a play that ultimately had no redemption or satisfaction? I'll never forget something a close friend shared with me during the first month after Aiden died. Having confided with her in my struggle to understand why this happened and how God was going to "fix" it, she answered in the kindest, most sincere voice, "I am going to share my faith and hope with you until you are strong enough to have your own again." I admit, I didn't fully understand how that could work, but I trusted her love for me enough to believe that faith might be a transferable gift. Looking back, she helped me see that there remained in me a little mustard seed of faith that desperately needed God's nurturing and healing. Through God's unwavering grace, and admittedly more prayer from others than myself, my faith began to grow stronger and more deeply-rooted than ever before. While Scotland had been a time of passionate zeal for the Lord, this time of testing was meant to establish an unyielding assurance of His love and promises.

"Consider it pure joy, my brothers, whenever you face trials of many kinds, because you know that the testing of your faith develops perseverance. Perseverance must finish its work so that you may be mature and complete, not lacking anything."
James 1:2-4

9

After nearly two weeks trapped at home, the desire for escape was too much to ignore. As I had started to feel marginally better physically, we decided to take a long road trip for a few weeks to lower Alaska and British Columbia (where we had honeymooned eight years earlier). In order to go, we first needed the doctor's blessing, and I planned to ask at a follow-up cardiology appointment on my birthday, August 30th, two weeks after the birth of Aiden. Although I wasn't feeling great cardiology-wise, I thought my heart would benefit physically if it healed emotionally too.

At the end of my appointment while talking to Christine, my physician assistant and close confidant during my tumultuous pregnancy, I broke down sobbing when she asked how I was doing with the loss.

"I'm not sure how to handle all my emotions. There seems to be no end to the tears. My mind feels like it has detached itself, and I'm an empty shell in a trance," I said as tears streamed down and I struggled to catch my breath, on the verge of hyperventilating.

"All of these feeling are very normal," she said looking into my face with eyes that exuded empathy, her hand gently resting on my knee. "Don't feel like there is a timeframe when you should 'feel better.' Let yourself feel the sadness, don't suppress it. But also know that there will be a day when you will know joy again, even if you can't imagine it right now."

I didn't realize how emotionally fragile and hormonally unbalanced I was. Once I had composed myself, with an arm resting on my shoulders, she walked me back toward the waiting room to meet Ryan. On the short walk to the lobby, I sneezed and the flood gates were released. I began to hemorrhage. With my pants soaked in blood, I ran to the restroom just 20 feet down the corridor. Safely inside, but now all alone, I continued to bleed, eventually slipping on the blood-soaked floor. I started screaming hysterically, and Ryan and Christine ran into the restroom. I was sitting in a pool of blood. It looked like a scene of great carnage and the smell of iron was enough to send Ryan reeling. CSI was playing out right here in the office restroom. I'm not sure how Ryan stayed upright knowing his extreme fear of blood and medical gore. Thankfully within minutes the hemorrhage slowed considerably and they were able to help me clean up, change into scrubs, and Ryan pushed me in a wheelchair down the hall to my OB doctor's office.

Although we described the horrific scene to the OB doctor, he didn't believe that I had lost that much blood, saying it probably looked worse than it was. After removing several more large blood clots in a very unpleasant procedure, he told me to go home to recoup for a few days. He said that the blood loss and clots were due to my blood thinner levels during delivery, and the issue should resolve itself shortly. Additionally my blood volume and iron levels would quickly regenerate itself, and my heart would go back to normal. Whatever normal looked like.

By the next day I was feeling faint and my heart was acting so erratically that we headed to the UW emergency room. The ER quickly assessed that I was in need of a blood transfusion, and they ordered several units of my blood type. Halfway into the first unit of blood, I started noticing an itch along the top of my legs, which then started down my arms, and then to my back, until there wasn't a place on my body that wasn't affected. When the nurse pulled the covers down, she saw that I had angry hives over my entire body. The itching was uncontrollable, and I felt myself starting to go crazy. Quickly they administered some Benadryl through my IV, and the welts began to disappear. They explained to me that although the blood type on the donor blood matched mine, I was having a bad reaction to it. I guess this happens sometimes and could be as simple as the donor had eaten food recently that I was allergic to. Still, I was very disturbed at the parody my life had become. My second unpleasantly memorable birthday! What more could happen?

After the Benadryl, I began to get drowsy and fell asleep while they continued to administer the blood. Unit after unit was slowly pumped into my IV, revealing the severity of my anemia. The doctors were finally satisfied that my blood volume was stabilized when I had three units (the body has about 10 units normally). Having continuous rounds of Benadryl gave me the opportunity to sleep the rest of the day away. I took it happily.

Two days after the transfusion my cardiologist gave us permission to leave on our trip. We would travel through the Canadian Rockies, and then out west to the coast, where we would take a ferry to Alaska; about a three-week journey. The hospital had finally released Aiden's ashes to us, and we were hoping that we would find a special place on our journey that would be appropriate to spread his ashes, some place meaningful that we could forever hold in our memories.

Truthfully, this was the most unplanned trip I'd ever been on, spending more time buying new music for the car ride than making reservations or organizing the route. The only reservation I made was for Chateau Lake Louise, an immensely beautiful castle-like resort nestled at the bottom of the most breathtakingly, blue glacial lake. We were very excited to splurge and spend a night away in absolutely lavish accommodations. I think the spontaneity of the trip was healthy for our state of mind. Thinking too much about anything still hurt our brains. So, by the seat of our pants, we packed up and headed out the next morning. Lazily waiting until all of the commuter traffic had finished for the morning, we had clear sailing for the 120 miles north to the Canadian border. The sun was shining so brightly, and we were filled with the exhilaration of a new adventure, so hopeful that we could clear our thoughts and lighten our hearts. Truly, we were escaping.

The first two days were great, and the drive was beautiful. We listened to a bunch of fantastic music, and the scenery was spectacular. After spending one night in Kamloops, we arrived in Banff, enjoying a wonderful night of dinner and romance, upgrading the hotel room so we could have a hot tub for a night. There had been signs along our trip that my heart was a bit out of sorts, extreme fatigue, small runs of tachycardia and dizziness, but I tried to believe that any episodes would pass on their own and were just part of my recovery from the past eight months. However, by the third day, my symptoms began increasing in intensity and the heart arrhythmia episodes lengthened, my energy sapped. It got to the point where we were pretty well confined to the hotel room for fear that I'd get stuck some place with no ability to leave without passing out. Simultaneously, panic started to set in that my defibrillator would go off again.

One night, after a few hours of relative peace from my heart, Ryan talked me into going to a restaurant for dinner. After being cooped up in a hotel room putting jigsaw puzzles together for hours on end while marvelous scenery and spectacular fall weather awaited, this outing was too tempting to pass up.

Despite my initial hesitancy, I relented and agreed to go. The evening started off with jovial chit-chat during appetizers, but slowly throughout the meal, my heartbeat became more and more irregular, so much so that by the end of meal I couldn't talk because my heart was racing too fast. Seeing the urgency in my eyes to depart quickly, Ryan paid the bill and went to get the car, which was a few blocks away.

The time it took for him to double park in front of the restaurant seemed like an eternity. My panic was in full force, only complicating the symptoms. My blood pressure had dropped dramatically, I had become lightheaded, and all of my limbs were cold, clammy, and tingling. I was convinced that I was going to have a medical emergency right there in the restaurant (or maybe I already was). The only prayers I could muster were pleas to God for relief and strength to endure.

Despite the rational solution to head to the local hospital in Banff, we decided that it that might not be the answer to our problem. The small Banff hospital mainly treated ski injuries and other common ailments, and did not specialize in heart rhythm problems. It wouldn't cut it for us, and we'd probably end up getting transferred to Calgary, and from my experience in Scotland, I was not enamored with socialized medicine. I know this wasn't a time to get picky about my health care, but my faith in hospitals unfamiliar with complex cardiac cases such as mine, gave me great pause. There is nothing more frustrating than spending hours in an ER while the doctors run around with blank faces, having implemented all of their known solutions with no success. Worse yet, is when they won't listen to requests to consult with my primary cardiologist, assuming if they can't solve it, no one will be able to. Sometimes they act as though I'm a hapless patient without intimate knowledge of my condition. On the contrary, I have a highly tuned ear to my body, especially my heart. If I've learned one thing from living with a chronic, life-threatening disease, it's this: you must be a strong, educated advocate and know your body signals well, even being willing to be labeled pushy and difficult.

Ryan hurried inside the restaurant to get me and slowly helped me to the car, stopping to catch my breath every few feet. I can only imagine what the wait staff must have been thinking; then again maybe they were completely unaware of the situation occurring at table 9. A gentleman abruptly asking for the check while food remained on their plates and rushing out the door; leaving a women sitting alone, slowly taking deep, forced breaths, frequently checking the pulse in her wrist and neck, sweat building on her forehead, her face as white as ash.

Finally inside the car, we drove to the hotel and into the entry and passenger loading area. Ryan assisted me into a chair in the lobby, knowing that I couldn't make it any further. He rushed back to the car in the loading zone and parked it in the underground parking ramp of the hotel. When he returned, I was still sitting in the chair, my heart not yet slow enough to make the trek to our room, only 100 feet from the lobby. I sat there another 30 minutes with Ryan in the adjacent arm chair, still cold and clammy from a dangerously low blood pressure and teetering on passing out. I took a fast acting beta blocker pill meant to help to slow my rhythm and eventually it worked. Immediately after regular rhythm was restored I took a long, heavenly deep breath in, the first in hours. Carefully, I stood and gingerly made a beeline for our room, wanting to get there before it started again, but also not moving fast enough to create another episode. I climbed into bed when I made it back to room, now totally drained of energy and feeling like I had just completed a marathon.

At this point, most level-headed people would throw in the towel and recognize the vacation was over. Mentally, we were not about to surrender and admit defeat, but I also don't think we were at full rational capacity. In a state of foolish optimism, fueled by emotional overload, we decided to continue on. We truly believed that we were merely waiting for the electrical "storm" to pass and then we'd be in clear skies again. We stayed another day at this hotel trying to assess my condition before heading on to Lake Louise. We relaxed, put puzzles together, got delivery food, and slept the remaining part of the day. Despite being tired, my heart stayed in rhythm. The clouds must have parted a bit.

The next morning I was feeling quite a bit better and we decided to push on to Lake Louise. A beautiful room awaited us at the Chateau and we were not going to miss our opportunity. This was our one splurge of the trip, the rooms averaging over $400 a night. It was only 30 miles down the road, and we took our time enjoying the magnificent mountains along the way. At the Lake Louise ski resort, we took a gondola ride to a scenic overlook. Being summer, we had the place nearly to ourselves and didn't have to fight crowds in the nature exhibit housed at the top of the hill. Standing on the deck of the upper lodge, bathed in the bright sunshine, surrounded by glorious mountains on all sides, with Ryan tight to my side, I believed, for a brief instant, that a ray of light was shining into my broken heart. The moment was so breathtaking that, literally, on the way back down the mountain I went out of rhythm again.

I was in full atrial fibrillation (A-fib) by time we reached the bottom. The resort staff had to escort me by golf cart to the car in the parking lot because I didn't have the strength to walk. As we drove to the hotel, which was five miles away, I was in excruciating pain. This was significantly worse than the previous episode, and I thought my heart might explode. We pulled into the entry roundabout and when my heart had slowed for a brief period, Ryan ran in to get the keys to our room. Beyond frustrated and in full panic mode, I still wasn't in any position to get out of the car. It took 30 more minutes before I had the strength to transfer to a wheelchair that was waiting for me.

The bellboy pushed me to my room and I transferred to the bed; not exactly the regal entrance I imagined when making the reservations. The room was plush and well appointed, but all I cared about was how soft the bed was and how many steps it was from the door. Although I took my "fast-acting" medication to slow my heart rate, after four more hours, I had gotten minimal relief. I realized I had no choice but to call my doctors in the States. They told me I should drive home, and they would see me tomorrow as soon as I arrived.

Hoping to give Ryan a few hours of sleep before the long drive, we decided to leave in the morning. We ordered room service for dinner, and during short bursts of energy I choked down a tuna sandwich. Since we didn't spend the extra $50 a night for a room on the lake side of the building, I never actually got to see the crystal blue glacial water, surrounded by beautiful snow-capped mountains. My picture of strolling arm in arm with Ryan along its banks was not to be. The entire hotel stay was spent lying down trying to calm my quivering heart. While the bed was comfortable, it was a fretful night of broken sleep.

So at 4 a.m. the next morning, we headed back home, hoping we could make it in 14 hours to the 2 p.m. doctor's appointment. As we rounded the mountain passes in moonlit darkness, the vividness of seeing Ryan's clenched jaw and his white knuckles on the steering wheel was seared into my brain. Initially numb from Aiden's death, Ryan, had now reached an anger that I have never seen before in our 12 years together. He was raised in a faith that told him to be stoic and not think much of himself, and therefore to not burden God or others with outward displays of suffering. God was not someone to run to during pain, but someone you were not worthy to approach, a faraway being that was impartial to our feelings.

"What's the point of praying to God when He's not listening? He couldn't even let us heal," was the only thing he said the entire trip. That drive home was the crisis point in our faith. We both felt entitled to rest and grieve, and believed that God was callously withholding it. What kind of good God would do that? While I hadn't stopped talking to Him, I definitely was not praising, or even pleading with Him; I was downright yelling and demanding answers. "Why, Why, Why? When is my pain enough? How much more before I have learned what you are trying to teach me?" During the next few months, I spent a lot of time in the book of Job, crying out for him to sooth the bitterness within me. I was not yet at the place where I was ready to repent as Job did 30 chapters later.

"I loathe my very life;
therefore I will give reign to my complaint
and speak out in the bitterness of my soul.
I will say to God: Do not condemn me,
But tell me what charges you have against me."
Job 10:1-2

"Then Job replied to the Lord:
'I know that you can do all things; no plan of yours can be thwarted.
You asked, 'Who is this that obscures my counsel without knowledge?'

The And

Surely I spoke of things I did not understand; things to wonderful for me to know."
Job 42: 1-3

I spent the entire 14-hour car ride reclined in the passenger seat, which allowed my heart to be relatively slow (I was still about 110 beats per minute). Bathroom breaks at McDonald's were a long, painful ordeal, racked with fear that I would move too quickly and send it racing at uncontrollable speeds again. Panic consumed me in the restroom stall, my thoughts focused on my fear of dying alone, with no one to hear my final cries. Anything left of redeeming memories from our trip was washed away during the laborious drive home. Even the music that we had enjoyed on the drive out now became background sound that filled the deathly silence, but didn't quiet the soul. Aiden's container of ashes remained in the back seat of the car, a stark reminder that our plans had once again been thwarted.

We arrived in amazing time, and Dr. Rho saw us right away. Having been through so much together during this pregnancy, I could see the tears in his eyes as he reached out with a gentle hug. I've never had a doctor so personally engaged in my life, my family, and my overall well-being.

"I'm so sorry this nightmare won't end," he said. "Let's do whatever we can to settle your heart down again so you can move forward." Instantly, I was transported to the image of him standing over me in the operating suite during my first cardioversion when I was pregnant, laying a hand on my shoulder and reassuring me, "I will do everything in my power to protect you. I can't wait to meet your little one in a few months." Now he would be caring for me alone.

After running some tests, he concluded that the dynamics of my heart had changed with the pregnancy and was unable to adjust back; my ablation surgery that he had slaved over just 16 months earlier had been nullified. The underlying truth revealed in their assessment was that another pregnancy was not in my best interest, if not outright dangerous. Deep down, I knew early on that this would be my only pregnancy; I had just hoped that it resulted in a child. All of it, for nothing. What a waste of pain and discomfort, with no reward at the end.

After they cardioverted me from this episode of a-fib, they expressed that it would not likely hold me in rhythm for long and they recommended we repeat the same ablation surgery, but they were unable to fit me in the schedule for another six weeks. We scheduled it, hoping that maybe my heart would start acting normal again before then and we could cancel it. I spent the next month and a half nearly strapped to the couch, some nights sleeping there to avoid the long climb to my bedroom. Fearful that I'd have another serious episode, I kept my activity to a minimum and rarely left the house. Slowly the weeks passed by, but I was still having enough symptoms that Dr. Rho didn't want to cancel the procedure, and looking back, I'm glad I didn't. I was desperately in need of physical healing, which I hoped would start me on the path to emotional and spiritual healing.

"Come to me, all you who are weary and burdened and I will give you rest."
Matthew 11:28

10

My second ablation surgery in October went relatively well. Once again, Dr. Rho struggled for endless hours to eliminate every source of electrical disturbance, appearing after the procedure looking drained. He shared the results with Ryan. "I've been chasing ghosts around for hours, only to have them to reappear in new places, we quit when it became a fruitless exercise with diminishing returns. Her heart was stretched out from the pregnancy, and scarred from the previous surgery, which required us to re-ablate areas done earlier. I'm generally pleased, but not whole-heartedly convinced it will be effective."

Having been on the hard, metal operating table for over 12 hours, and on my back for a dozen more, the healing was slow and difficult. Again, I was overloaded with fluid administered during the procedure which caused some discomfort, but the pain itself wasn't as bad as last time because they could give me more medication, my heart having been better behaved. My back ached and my heels had gone numb with my legs pinned straight, but I wasn't allowed to move or shift my weight. My sore, parched throat stood in stark, mocking contrast to my bloated face and body.

After a week of stable heart rhythms and having shed the water weight, I was fully mobile and itching to be discharged from the hospital. Being chained to an IV and heart monitor, getting poked and prodded at all hours, and requiring assistance to shower or use the toilet, had gotten old. Dr. Rho's concern about rhythm problems due to scar tissue never manifested, and he proclaimed the surgery a success.

Remarkably, I was ready, at least physically, to go back to work part-time two weeks later. It was difficult facing everyone on my first day back, but I knew that this moment was unavoidable. It meant finally accepting that my life had to go on and it would look much differently than I had imagined a year ago. Slowly, I gained my strength back and recommenced full time work. This gradual immersion back into work life allowed me time to update myself on the status of the middle school construction, reconnect with the owner and contractor, and reassume control of the project. The familiarity and routine of work was comforting and healthy, but I took care not to let it become my escape. It would have been too easy to be consumed by busyness and not take the time desperately needed to work through my emotional healing.

However, I was not done with all of the medical procedures and my physical healing. My defibrillator still needed to be replaced because the batteries were running low. So at the end of December, just when I had gotten in the swing of life again, I went in for day surgery to replace it. It was a bit more painful than I remembered from four years previous, but I recovered quickly enough to return to work after a few days. Finally, I felt a shimmer of hope that all of the medical problems were over, for now.

Thankfully, the pacemaker replacement in December of 2007 was the beginning of a full year of calm, and Ryan and I took the opportunity to process all that had transpired. These past two years were not just a delay, but it was a full change in direction from our plans to get pregnant. During this reflection, God was actively revealing to me His sovereignty and His compassion. He required open-handed living that effectively extinguished my will and put Him in charge. I was in full surrender, right where I think He wanted me. I could either choose Him or let myself fall into the depths of depression and self-pity. I needed hope. I needed Him.

My work commute on the train was spent journaling, praying, reading my Bible; and processing the garble of thoughts that sped through my head. By writing down my thoughts, I could process through whether it made sense, or whether it was garbage that didn't deserve mental space. It was a time of great exploration and discovery about what the human spirit and body is capable of enduring with God's help. I recognized God's desire and ability to make me whole again, physically and spiritually. The depth of His desire for me to have rest and peace led me often to a highly quoted, but no less impactful scripture that reminded me of my significance to Him in times of struggle.

"The Lord is my shepherd; I shall not be in want.
He makes me lie down in green pastures,
He leads me beside still waters,
He restores my soul.
He guides me in paths of righteousness for his name's sake
Even though I walk through the valley of the shadow of death,
I will fear no evil for you are with me
Your rod and your staff, they comfort me.
You prepare a table before me in the presence of my enemies.
You anoint my head with oil; my cup overflows.
Surely goodness and love will follow me all the days of my life,
And I will dwell in the house of the Lord forever."
Psalm 23

During my prayer time with God, I began to trust that He wanted to speak to me, and this time, I actually sought His voice, instead of doing all the talking. I had frequent revelations about why all of this pain and trial had happened. He spoke very clearly to me about the blessings amidst Aiden's death; one of the greatest revelations was that my life had been spared by the accident. Had he gone full term, we would have both gained weight that my heart couldn't bear, and delivery would have been even more dangerous. I also received supernatural assurance that Aiden was now in the mighty, gentle hands of his true Father. This was the poem He gave me during one bus ride to Seattle:

"The Gardener"
The Gardener has scattered his seeds
In places that will never know weeds
...but also in hearts that are filled with sorrow
For the seeds contain hope and faith to borrow
Until the day your strength is restored
And you are harvested for the Lord.

Aiden had been spared the heartaches of this world. He will only know the love of His Father, and my prayer has always been that one day we will have the opportunity to tell him how much Ryan and I love him. Yet, God's still got work to do in me before He brings me home. The challenges we've faced continue to test our spiritual hearts and speak volumes about what we truly believe. Is Christ, with everything stripped away, the hope I seek? If not, what do I put my hope in? A perfect family, perfect health, a comfortable life with bountiful resources? The biggest revelation He gave me was that even my agony should be considered blessing by bringing me back to a closer walk with Him. I need to give over my life to Him daily. Below is a scripture I meditated on repeatedly when I was struggling to experience blessing in pain, or peace with God:

"Therefore, since we have been justified through faith, we have peace with God through our Lord Jesus Christ, through whom we have gained access by faith into this grace in which we now stand. And we rejoice in the hope of the glory of God. Not only so, but we also rejoice in our sufferings, because we know that suffering produces perseverance; perseverance, character; and character, hope. And hope does not disappoint us, because God has poured out his love into our hearts by the Holy Spirit, whom he has given us."
Romans 5:1-5

Especially during this time of contemplation, my desire was to walk with God daily and resist jumping ahead of Him. This forced Ryan and I to put off all discussions about future family plans to a later time, which for a naturally meticulous planner, was exceedingly hard, but well worth the challenge. For the time being, we were going to live in the present only. Our lives in the past had been so focused on the hope of future blessings, that many times we missed the everyday ones.

Now almost seven months free of significant symptoms, in May 2008, for our nine-year anniversary, we took a three-week vacation around Europe. We decided to visit France, Italy, and Spain, with a luxurious week aboard a cruise in the Mediterranean. After spending the days touring every nook and cranny of quaint seaside villages and sprawling historic cities, we gorged ourselves on scrumptious food until we passed out in bed each night. We were surrounded by fantastic architecture that reignited my passion for design and construction. We walked everywhere, and went to all of the cathedrals and museums that one could possibly absorb. The adventure of traveling did wonders for our state of mind, and we were able to focus on having fun, something we had almost forgotten how to do. Even with the exhausting walks we undertook, my heart did phenomenal and didn't even threaten to fall out of rhythm! To my astonishment, my fear of having an episode while overseas, although always in the back of my head, did not overshadow my ability to relax and enjoy this special trip.

In November we threw an enormous party we named, "Celebration of the Mundane," to recognize a whole year of drama-free living; no hospitalizations, no surgeries, and no loss. All of our friends and family came to be a part of our grand day. I had officially been weaned off all of my heart meds (except blood thinners), which I never believed was possible. I had taken heart meds ever since my first open heart surgery at 14. As the ablation appeared to be so successful, Dr. Rho said it might be worth the try see if I could do well without the "crutches" of my medications. It was hard to imagine, but it seemed to be working. I had an unprecedented amount of energy that, as far back as I can remember, had been greatly suppressed by my artificially reduced heart rate and lowered blood pressure. It felt like a new lease on life. The future (although we were not talking about it) seemed so bright and filled with possibilities.

Unfortunately, two days after our momentous party, I went into atrial fibrillation and needed to be hospitalized and cardioverted. Dr. Rho finally conceded that my heart obviously wouldn't behave without some form of medication to control its speed and how much it had to work. The less stressed it was, the less erratic electrical activity took place. I guess we knew that all along, but it was still fun while it lasted.

Even this setback didn't take much wind out of our sails. We were pushing full speed ahead. We were working hard at our careers and taking time to have some fun along the way. But all the work and play were not able to fill the void that remained in my heart. While I loved watching Pioneer Middle School reach completion and filling with children in the fall, it reminded me that this chapter was now complete, and I needed a new project to undertake. My parents, having flown into Seattle to spend the weekend with us, were fortunate enough to be able to attend the school's official dedication ceremony on September 20, 2008 where I handed my "baby" back to the citizens of Dupont and Steilacoom.

Although architecture had been my first passion, I was looking for another purpose in life. I had experienced a tiny, little life living inside my body and longed to attempt parenthood again. Even as a new, exciting high school project emerged, and I was given the reigns to make the design sing, I knew it couldn't satisfy my desire to be a mother. My mind would daily ponder the possibility and I still held out hope for a family. Ryan hadn't wanted to talk about it, and I had agreed to stay silent on the subject for a year. But ironically, although I had impatiently peeped up a few times prematurely, the subject of kids was actually officially reintroduced by an unsuspecting party— Ryan's cousin, Travis, and his wife, Rachel.

Travis had started a letter-writing campaign, touting the merits of having children. He reminded Ryan that the offer made previously, before Aiden was even conceived, not only stood, but was strenuously encouraged. He was practically begging Ryan to let them help us have a family. Simultaneously, Rachel had begun an intensive research on the subject of surrogacy, emailing me websites' links, and mailing me books to read. Without question, my interest was piqued at the chance to be a mom, especially to children that would ultimately be our genetic offspring. On the whole, I just kept praying that my desire to nurture and teach be fulfilled in whatever capacity God chose—

whether surrogacy, adoption, or something altogether different, I would be satisfied, or learn to accept it and be content.

Ryan was still really struggling with the thought of children. Although he sincerely desired to be a dad, he was keenly aware of what all of the risks were and that he would carry the burden if or when my health issues arose again. His deepest fears had already been tested in my pregnancy. He recognized real possibility of having to raise a child without me, or worse, having to care for both of us. As soon as our conversations about the future of our family began, it immediately became clear we were at an impasse.

Through our prayers for guidance, we were both directed to seek outside, unbiased counsel. We invited an older and wiser couple from our church over for dinner early in November. Enjoying coffee in the living room, we shared with them our story, much of which they already knew, and asked them how we could decipher God's will for us in this situation. They counseled that we should continue praying, separately and together for God's revelation to be given to BOTH of us. We had decided that during this time of deliberation, we should keep our decision-making very tight to our chests. Although we had many family and friends that carried great weight in our lives, we knew ultimately, the resolution had to be ours to make and live with.

We were also acutely aware that God would have the final say. Our hearts had been softened to His mercy and grace in the past several months. God had revealed Himself plainly to us during our mourning time, His gentle presence was clearer than either of us had ever experienced before. Ryan had spent a considerable amount of time praying that God would show him that his prayers really did matter. And He did. An inexplicable peace had settled over him that allowed him to see that God wasn't some distant deity doling out chaos and pain to His undeserving followers. Nothing that happened was a surprise to Him and He had an intricate plan that could not be thwarted; a plan that desired good for those who loved and believed in Him. He desired a relationship with us and relished acknowledgement and to be called upon in both the good and the bad times.

On the one-year anniversary of Aiden's original due date, we took a trip to the top of Hurricane Ridge, our favorite local mountain overlook. Exactly a year before, we had scattered Aiden's ashes on a cold, windy November day and said our final goodbyes. Beautifully, the ashes appeared to evaporate into thin air, being effortlessly carried off in the wind as if God lifted him upward. Just as Aiden's feet never touched this earth, his ashes didn't either.

Again this year, we felt God was urging us to make the pilgrimage, not just to remember Aiden, but also to reflect on all of God's blessings and promises. Mustering enough courage to step out of the car into the frightful gale, we welcomed the wind and the rain on our faces, God's power fresh and alive. Life needed to start again for us, and we felt God was giving us permission to stop mourning. The Holy Spirit was actively renewing our hearts in the midst of the storm.

After a thorough soaking, we jumped back into the car and sat looking out through the driving rain on the windshield, the longing to hold another child in my arms caused a great ache in my soul. The conversation gradually shifted from the past to the future. We discussed the attributes of a good parent and how greatly we could grow in our understanding of sacrifice and selflessness; learning to be a true parent in the way God modeled. As parents, we were there to point children in the right direction by correction, wisdom, and love; love that put their needs over ours and brought glory to God. While much of what we knew about parenting had been by watching others, we knew the most critical aspects of parenting well was raising them to love God and be thankful for His gift of salvation through Jesus. All else was a product of this understanding; that God loves them and created them (and everyone else) in His image, exactly as He intended. Therefore, they could be "God-assured" enough to share His love and grace to others with kindness, gratitude, respect, and forgiveness.

We attempted, with the help of the Holy Spirit, to tackle the most significant questions concerning God's guidance in our possible parenthood. If we didn't have children, how could we keep from living a self-centered, career-focused existence? Did He have greater purposes for our childlessness? If we did have children, how do we handle times of my possible absence or inability to care for them? Was it selfish to even want children, knowing that our lives are unpredictable and potentially unstable? Knowing also that my heart disease is genetic and the transmission rate is 50%, is it fair to knowingly risk passing down a painful condition? Is it better to go the adoption route to avoid the genetic ramifications? Is adoption even a possibility, since we might not be eligible due to my health history? Besides, even if we were accepted into a program, we knew adoption wasn't a sure thing. We have seen the agony in families when their prospective children were taken away, sometimes after a year with the adoptive parents. I knew I was not prepared for that kind of loss again. While I knew that adoption has given millions of children new hope and a better life, my maternal yearning for hereditary children made me eager to at least attempt the surrogacy route, even if it was meant another painful failure.

Revelation came on the mountain. Ryan and I both had reached a place where our hearts and prayers were fully in-step together. God showed us that we needed to trust Him with our future and let Him take care of the bumps along the road. My heart condition, while it has brought tremendous pain, has also made me into the person I am. I believe that I appreciate the life I have much more than someone who has never experienced their own mortality. I remember my father once saying that if he had known before my birth of his genetic heart condition, he would not have chosen to have children. It pained him to see his struggles repeated in me.

My immediate reaction was to remind him how wonderful my life is, and how much joy I experience daily. I am part of God's plan, heart problem and all. We all have some burden to bear, and God does not make mistakes. If my child is given this burden, then it was part of God's will and He will see us through the trials it brings. While it would be painful to see them go through what I have, I know that they can live a rich and contented life, filled with happiness and love, solid in their faith and blessedly aware of their need for Him. We are all dependent on Him, but many either don't understand this or choose not to acknowledge it. Awareness of your own frailty and mortality is one of the greatest gifts that you can receive from our sovereign God. It widens our view of God and humbles our haughty nature.

After a long period of reflection, punctuated by countless cries for clarity, the decision was made. We would give the surrogacy process a chance, only trying an egg retrieval once, and if it didn't work, then that was part of God's sovereignty as well. We knew first hand that hearing God and obeying the direction we received didn't always translate into the expected outcome or presumed path. Aiden was part of God's purpose for our life, just not in the way we had hoped. His pregnancy was not something we undertook without prayer and guidance, and the surrogacy journey would be no difference.

We had assurance that God would be there to guide us each step, but we would be given only enough light for the next step, not the whole path. Walking with open hands, on faith we would proceed, constantly watching and waiting for Him to speak. It was disobedience to ignore his initial call, even if He did not intend children to be the final outcome. He would make each decision clear along the journey.

On Thanksgiving, a few weeks later, we took the train to Montana, where the annual family Thanksgiving celebration was held. While we were staying with Travis and Rachel, they arranged for Rachel's parents to take their kids for a night. This afforded us the opportunity to talk openly about the subject we were all itching to discuss. As we excitedly shared our decision with them, the room exploded in giddy anticipation; champagne was poured and glasses were raised. Ryan and I were still dumbfounded by the notion that someone could be so sacrificial and giving. They had all of the normal craziness of parents of a one and three year old, all of the daily demands and stresses. Yet they were willing to put their lives on hold, endure pregnancy, and the excruciating pain of delivery for our happiness. They were prepared to forever entangle their lives with ours, accepting the good with the bad. While we were immensely hopefully that surrogacy could be successful, we all were cognizant of what could go wrong in any pregnancy; anything from sickness, hospitalization, bedrest, or even permanent health issues. Not only was Rachel taking a risk with her own body and lifestyle, but also potentially offering up the discomfort and heartache of her own family. I am hard-pressed to think of a more tangible comparison to Jesus' selfless sacrifice for me on the cross.

We discussed some details, but mainly we were walking into the unknown. We were in agreement on all of the major issues, including that the pregnancy would never be terminated, and we would not have a selective abortion (in the case of multiples). All efforts would be made to keep Rachel close to her family during the pregnancy, and the child would be born in a hospital in Montana, if at all possible. Everyone was excited to get going on our new adventure as soon possible. When we returned to Washington, we made an appointment for all of us to see an infertility specialist at their soonest available appointment, which happened to be early January.

Prior to that, we made plans to tell the family at Christmas about the decision we had reached. We thought it would be fun to surprise everyone with the announcement, since no one even knew that we were considering this wild idea. My family had a vacation planned a week before Christmas, a three-day cruise departing out of Long Beach, California. A spur of the moment idea that my dad and I hatched up mid-summer, this was to be the first family vacation we had since I was in high school. The cruise terminal was just a short drive from San Diego, where they were living at the time, so it made before-and-after cruise planning a breeze. Days before Christmas, we would fly home to Washington and tell Ryan's family the news. It seemed so efficiently timed and easy to execute.

The cruise turned out to be wonderful time cooped up on a big, luxurious boat because the weather was, for the most part, torrential rain. It was such a different experience than our cruise around the Mediterranean, where the purpose of the boat was essentially to feed us well and take us quickly from port to port. That boat had been sized for 150 passengers and 100 crew members. This one could easily fit 3,000 people and entertain them in every way conceivable, even if they never got off the boat. We spent most of our time hanging out on the deck interior playing a dice game, and sharing side-splitting stories and jokes. Our surrogacy announcement was met by sheer delight, and we toasted with some smuggled booze in our stateroom. My parents were overjoyed at the thought that we might still provide them with grandkids. My dad's health was continuing to diminish, and this news brought him great hope of becoming a grandfather.

Our flight out was scheduled for two days after we returned to port. Again, nature had ulterior plans. The weather from California had taken a turn up the Pacific Coast while we were at sea. Flights, including ours, had been cancelled all along the Pacific Northwest for the next two days. However, when we tried to rebook, along with the thousands of other people affected, the earliest we could get home was two days after Christmas. It was disappointing to miss the official holiday celebration, but we were promised by Ryan's family that Christmas could wait until we got home.

As for us, there were much worse places to get stranded than beautiful San Diego (now that we had sent all the bad weather north). We spent a lot of time at the beach and even managed a trip to Sea World. The most significant benefit of the delay (and I'm sure divinely orchestrated by God) was the special, unexpected time I got with my parents, especially my dad. One spectacular sunny day I found myself sitting on a park bench at the beach with him, breathing in the salty air, mesmerized by the tide rolling in and out, and the seagulls gliding in the gentle breeze above. There was no question that this was the place he ultimately loved, and where he wanted to retire. Despite this great affection for San Diego, my parents were willing, if not eager, to relocate to rainy Washington to be with my sister and my family.

This trip to his favorite park had an agenda though. I knew it before we even left the house, as he specifically asked that we go alone. My father talked openly with me about the status of his condition. Because we shared many of the same experiences, he knew I would understand his anxieties about the newest developments in his health. Unlike only a year before, his heart failure was steadily increasing, and his energy level remained low most of the time. He confided that he knew his time left was very short and he asked that I take care of Mom when he was gone. She was having a difficult time hearing him speak about his impending death and would no longer listen to him, chalking up his "death talk" to depression and futility. I know he felt an urgency to have someone who would acknowledge the reality of the situation. It was hard to hear, but I knew he was speaking the truth.

Travis and Rachel drove out for the first office visit to the fertility specialist, which was primarily an information-gathering meeting to learn the steps of the process. All four of us packed into the tiny consultation room giddy with enthusiasm. The nursing staff pulled each of us out separately, performing the required physical exam and collecting the necessary medical history. The doctor then came in to our packed office and interviewed each of the couples, told us the success rates, and potential issues that might arise. Since Rachel had already had two children, and I had gotten pregnant successfully without any intervention, she was very optimistic of our chances of success. She told us that our coordinator would start to prepare a personalized fertility plan for both Rachel and

I, and we could get going as soon as the required legal paperwork was in place.

We were required to complete an FDA evaluation to confirm no diseases would be transmitted, and Rachel had to have a psychiatric evaluation to make sure she was of sound mind to offer this crazy gift. Finally, Ryan and I needed the appropriate legal documents to solidify the contractual agreements that were made verbally. Once that was all complete, they would see us again and start the actual process of preparing Rachel's and my body for our profound undertaking.

By early March everything was ready to proceed with syncing our menstruation cycles together. Through medication, they would stop her cycle and not allow any more eggs to fall. Conversely, they had to speed up my egg production so they could gather a number of eggs together for fertilization. It was a finely tuned dance of days, each with a choreographed medication schedule to follow. The early weeks of this dance would prove a true test of faith, endurance and determination.

II

Ready. Set. Action. The decision had been now made to move forward with the surrogacy. Initial appointments regarding timing and process were done and now the hard work had to begin. The fun "what if" discussions with Travis and Rachel over wine and cheese had grown teeth and become reality. Unfortunately, it did not take very long before all of my hopes and dreams for having children would be put to the ultimate test of emotional and physical endurance, including an encounter with one of my closest friends.

After we announced to our friends and church community that we were going to proceed with the surrogacy process, the out-pouring of support was phenomenal. Many didn't fully understand the process, but they were willing to support us because they knew how much we longed for a family. I knew that our church held strong opinions about the protection of the unborn, and some even went as far as rejecting anything that interfered with natural conception; but most of them were okay with some assistance in the reproductive process. However, the conflict that arose with my dear friend Lissa, who was there for me through so many painful moments, was a reminder to me that God wanted to use this journey to reveal my heart to Him and His heart to me. There were questions about my beliefs that I hadn't yet answered for myself, which presented themselves in issues that most people never have to face.

One night, a few gals were gathered at my house for a time of prayer, reflection, and discussion. Within our church, these groups are called DNA, where it is the goal of each member to provide Discipleship, Nurturing, and Accountability for the other members of the group. The group was some of my closest friends, united by our faith and a safe place where we could ask tough questions, share hard situations, and lead each other in the truth of the gospel. That night I shared with them my excitement, yet nervousness, about moving forward with the surrogacy process. A gal named Heidi chimed in immediately with delight, but Lissa remained awkwardly silent. This was not the first mention I had made to what we were endeavoring to do, but it was now a confirmed direction. Slowly, and very deliberately she begin to speak of her concern that we might in fact end up with more embryos than we would use. I knew it was hard for her to speak up, but she felt a strong need to share her apprehensions and make sure we had taken them to God.

"What are you planning on doing with the remaining embryos?" she asked gently.

"Ryan and I discussed it, and we are fine with donating them to science research if there are any extra. We know that we won't be able to donate them anonymously because of the chance of a genetic heart condition. Likewise, if we donated them to hopeful parents, we aren't ready to accept having other biological children in the world, which we wouldn't parent," I answered without hesitation.

Lissa took a deep breath and looked me in the eyes with a loving but resolute expression. "I grieve with you in your loss and am excited with you about the possibility of children, but giving the embryos over to research is destroying life and I can't knowingly give my endorsement of something to which I don't agree."

"So you are telling me that you can't support our desire for children and the happiness they bring?" I was beginning to go red in the face, my temper starting to flare. I felt judged and was furious that my decision could be seen as murder. Yet inside, I began to question if I misunderstood what God wanted for me. Maybe the means didn't justify the ends. Maybe I was meant to be childless.

"No," she replied, "I will love any of the children you have, but I feel I must share my sadness that you could be simultaneously taking life that God created."

"You are basically saying that I will be committing murder," was my retort. Pridefulness, and the fear that she could be right quickly built a desperate defensiveness in my heart. The distress that I felt about the potential of an incredibly close friendship ending only added to the snowballing anger.

The conversation only degraded from there. I was no longer able to rationally (or quietly) communicate and was pacing like a caged lion in and out of the room. I began throwing a verbal barrage of the meanest things that I could formulate in my growing fury; even citing her strained relationship with her father as an example of how her judgement of people pushed them out of her life. These were tender areas in her life, shared in confidence and I was twisting them in hideous ways. My venom seemed to have no end. Taking all that she could withstand, she finally walked out of the house, quietly shutting the door behind her.

After Lissa left, Heidi, who had been sitting quietly on the couch while her friends were quarreling, laid her hand on my shoulder and spoke gently, "I am confident you will resolve this, I know it," she said with a loving assurance, "You are too good of friends to hold this bitterness toward each other. God will bring you back together." She gave me a hug and left as well.

Sleep did not come that night, and tears were hard to contain. Ryan was much more level-headed, and when he returned home, he quietly listened to me spill my venom again. I was livid; after what we had endured the past few years, she couldn't just be happy for us. Yet, as I prayed that night and a good portion of the next day, God settled my heart, removed my bitterness, and helped me recognize that I needed to understand what I believed about the life He creates. Almost immediately God brought me to a scripture, Leviticus 7:14— "Life is in the blood."

My journal entry on God's revelation of this passage shows my further exploration of the tree and branches metaphor, used frequently throughout the Bible, as it related to the passages about Jesus supplying the vital connection to God. This is what I heard and wrote down:

Life is in the blood for all creatures. Where there is no supply, there is no life. An embryo in a petri dish is simply a seed or building block that has not been planted. Just as a seed plant can only live so long without a source, it needs nourishment to have life. If there are embryos remaining after our family has been created, my sin will be in not planting every seed that has been given to me, not in "killing" life. Just as everyone has some seed (gift, talent, blessing, etc.) that God has given them, not all of them will come to fruition. Apart from God there is no life. He is the tree and we are the branches. God has allowed women the special opportunity to understand this model in a physical form. Through our wombs, a seed is planted and God enables it to grow through the nourishment of our blood. When the nourishment is taken away, the life dies. Aiden's life ended this way, and ours will too. When our hearts stop, our blood will cease to flow.

Jesus provided us the ultimate gift of eternal life through His death and has grafted us back to the Tree of Life with God, but it came at a heavy price in the shedding of His blood. God is the ultimate Gardener and has planted many seeds in the lives of His people. Some of them will be given life and grow roots; some will not. We must remember that God chose us, we did not choose Him, and it is our job, with His help, to grow strong and help nurture the seeds He has planted in ourselves and others.

Three days after my blow up (yes, I will take full blame), I called to talk to Lissa. I told her that I loved her and apologized for all my harsh words. She replied with an apology, not for her beliefs, but for the way the argument spiraled out of control. After reading her my journal entry, she thanked me for taking the time to meditate on the issue she brought to light. It had been such a blessing to have God's intervention in our hearts, and for Him to force my spiritual examination with the fight. While I don't think I changed her belief, that wasn't the point. God showed me how Christian conflict should be resolved and that it is acceptable to have differing opinions, while still holding fast to the truth of the gospel. It is a lesson that will impact my relationships for the rest of my life. Lissa remains to this day, one of my dearest friends. The ability to be painfully honest and yet, inexplicably humble with each other, has served to fortify our bond.

****

Part of the initial phase of the surrogacy process is the egg retrieval, and it involves a finely tuned synchronization of my menstrual cycle with the surrogate's. Rachel was put on Lupron to stop her eggs from maturing and dropping, while simultaneously allowing her uterus to prepare for transplantation by thickening its lining. My cycle had to be pushed into overdrive by stimulating the follicles to grow quickly, and in larger numbers than a natural ovulation cycle through additional estrogen supplements. The doctors initially started me on a birth control level of estrogen (about 50 mg) with the intent to increase it slowly to an astronomical level (about 3,000 mg) at the time of retrieval. After two weeks on the estrogen, I was feeling energetic and much more confident that I could make it through this process. All I had to do was produce the eggs; Rachel would be doing all of the heavy lifting.

At the same time as the start of our cycle synchronization, my parents, after months of deliberation, had finally made the decision to move to the Seattle Area from San Diego to be with my sister and me. They had found a place to rent on Anderson Island, which is a small island, populated mainly with retirees and vacation homes. It lies about 20 miles south of Tacoma, and a ferry ride away from my house. They decided not to sell their home in San Diego during a significant slump in home prices and to keep most of their belongings there so they could return for visits. It was my responsibility to procure the main furnishings, and so Craigslist and I became good friends during the month of March. It was during the purchase of a stupidly heavy microwave that I realized all was not well in the egg retrieval process.

I had spent the day at work in Seattle, climbing on rooftops and inspecting flashing installations of a local community college, and was feeling pretty good, with more energy than I could ask for. When I returned to Tacoma early from work, I stopped by a home advertising a microwave. Although I have been told not to lift heavy weights, I figured it wouldn't hurt to carry it down to my car. As I was I setting it into the back seat of my car, I felt my heart speed up. In the short time it took to get seated in the driver's seat, my heart was racing right along. I was only about six blocks from home in a quiet residential area so I thought getting home was the best solution. Pulling away from the curb, I felt my heart start to quiver oddly from the pit of my stomach. Only 100 feet down the road and before the intersection, I received a massive shock from my defibrillator. I was conscious and alert, but horribly frightened, and still in a dangerous heart rhythm. Since I had only been going about 10 miles an hour, I was able to stop the car immediately.

However, I needed to find an appropriate place to pull over, so I inched through the intersection at a slug's pace, and just as I pulled to the curb, I was hit with another terrifying jolt of electricity. I had never been shocked by my device with this little of warning. All of the times before, I had been out of rhythm at least a small period of time before the shock occurred; enough time to prepare myself mentally (as much as possible for something that is so startling). This time, however, the total time between initial symptoms and both shocks was less than one minute.

I fumbled in my purse looking for my cell phone, careful not to move too quickly and increase my heart rate any further. When I located the phone, I realized that it was out of battery charge. I had spent the day making phone calls back to the office, relaying information about the roofing status, and the phone was now totally dead. Having no way to contact anyone for help, (FYI, I now always have a charger in the glove box) I noticed a student walking past my car on his way to class at the University of Puget Sound, only a couple blocks away. I waved to get his attention, and he walked to my car window. Carefully and unsuccessfully trying to act nonchalant and calm, I explained what had just happened and asked if I might use his phone to call my husband.

He was more than happy to assist me, and after I got a hold of Ryan at work, he then waited with me the 10 minutes until Ryan arrived to drive me to the hospital. Although I was in no shape to carry on a conversation, I tried to be polite and slowly, and breathlessly eked out questions about his major and whether he worked. His name was Forest and he worked at the college's facilities office, and we actually knew some of the same people because I had done some architectural work for the school. I knew that I might never see him again so I wanted to know as much as possible about the kind person who had been there for me in a moment of unbelievable need. When Ryan arrived (I thank God he hadn't been in Seattle for the day), Forest asked if he could assist further. We told him that he had done more than enough and he continued on his path to class, with a good story about why he was late.

I got into Ryan's truck, and we headed straight to the UW. By the time I arrived in the ER department, an hour later, I was still having significant rhythm issues, feeling lightheaded and short of breath, but fortunately I hadn't had another shock. The staff flew into action and got me a room immediately. While the electrophysiologist (EP) was taking my medical history, my heart sped up, and monitors indicated that a shock could be imminent. He talked me very calmly through some breathing exercises, and while it didn't change my arrhythmia, it did allow me to decrease some of the panic-induced beats that would have put me over the defibrillator's monitoring threshold for a shock.

My arrhythmia continued for a few hours, but after several IV doses of beta blockers it finally slowed to the point where my heart could find its own rhythm again. The cardiologist and EP specialists looked carefully over the data collected in the ER and on my defibrillator and determined that I had experienced ventricular tachycardia (VT), which I had never had before. This type of rhythm is in a whole different category, one that is truly life threatening. While I had experienced many, VERY uncomfortable atrial fibrillation or flutter episodes, they would most likely not become fatal. The realization that my heart was now capable of this degree of seriousness put me in a state of anxiety and panic that defied my own ability to reason through.

I spent the next week in the hospital while they ran a series of tests and tried different dosages of medication. They surmised that the estrogen, no matter how small of a dose, had rendered my beta blockers ineffective and left my heart to its own devices. "Super-metabolizer" strikes again. Therefore, the extra energy I was feeling was due to having no heart medication to slow my rate down. While it is wonderful to have extra energy, it came at a pretty high cost and didn't last long before my heart showed its true colors.

Dr. Rho raised my heart meds to the point where they were comfortable it would sustain me and allow us to continue with the current estrogen regiment without my heart meds being entirely metabolized by my body. Finally, I was discharged home, and based on the cycle synchronization schedule, I had two weeks to decide I if would go forward with the significant increase in estrogen that was required to harvest my eggs. Fear gripped every moment of my existence, rendering me unable to leave the house except for short trips accompanied by family or friends. Driving was no longer something I was able or wanted to do, rendering me dependent on others for simple, quick errands. Even after my car accident, I was able to drive again, albeit with a severe paranoia of approaching vehicles and an edginess that made me dangerously over-cautious.

In 2007, in an effort to calm my fear of "inappropriate" or unneeded shocks brought on by fast atrial rhythms, Dr. Rho had given me a magnet, capable of disabling the defibrillator mechanism of my device. Under careful instruction, he gave me permission to use it, if and only if, another person was present and I was sitting up. That way if I passed out, the magnet would fall out of my hand, enabling the device to fire. In my head, the consequences of having it fire unnecessarily (and always unexpectedly) without providing relief, was much worse than horrible rhythms that persisted unabated. However, I now knew that my heart had the capacity to create deadly rhythms, but even that didn't persuade me from constantly having the small rectangular magnet in my pants' pocket. My other source of comfort was a water bottle that never left my side, habitually sipping nervously to calm myself when I felt the slightest twinge in my chest. I knew that these behaviors were a symptom of the post-traumatic stress that I was suffering from, but I figured there were much worse habits for me to form in dealing with my fear.

God entered my thoughts and prayers a lot during those two weeks, but it's astounding how quickly I put up a wall, telling God He wasn't great enough to carry me through this new chapter, with all of its uncertainties. My clarity on His direction, made so clear only six months previously, was now starting to become blurry.

Although, my desire to have children was still very strong, I knew that in proceeding with the surrogacy process, I could be exposing myself to the risk of death. The process of harvesting was only supposed to last two weeks, but I knew they would potentially be the longest of my life, with anxiety of the next shock (or worse) lurking around every corner. If I couldn't handle 50 milligrams, what made me think I could handle 3,000? Was all of this worth it? Everything in my being wanted to pack it up and call it done.

Honestly, I had never before considered quitting a chosen path, and I prided myself on my bulldog stubbornness and determination to barrel through any obstacle or challenge. My physical limitations had never before been an excuse to avoid the pursuit of a passion or dream. Fear had never controlled me like I was now gripped. In my mind, this time was different. The real possibility of death clung like a hovering shadow that could not be ripped away. On multiple occasions, I broke down crying and announced to Ryan and Rachel that I could not and would not go on. Yet the truth was that death was not what I feared most, it was living in the in-between; caught between the barely alive, but not quite dead. Fear in the face of physical pain, as natural as the "fight or flight" response; fear that can only be quelled with the knowledge of God's merciful presence. Jesus' fear, from which tears of blood formed, came from excruciating pain and anxiety, like mine, except for one HUGE difference: He knew He would be separated from God's presence and I never was out of God's careful watch.

Although I had remembered the reasons we took the surrogacy route, adoption seemed like a viable, much safer option that was looking more and more attractive. Ironically, after all he'd been through with me, his own doubts and worries heavy in the air, Ryan was now encouraging me to remain positive and stay the course. He whole-heartedly believed that this direction was God's will and that He would protect me; it was just another step on the journey. I knew that fear shouldn't be the basis for long-term decisions, but it was blinding me. I needed to trust and let go.

Ryan challenged me to confront my fears, even playing devil's advocate with me, "Fine, if you want to quit, go right ahead. It'll eat you alive with regret, but it's your choice to make. If we decide not to go this direction, know that I'm not ready to jump into anything else for a while." He knew that I couldn't surrender and walk away from the opportunity of having my own flesh and blood children.

"But, I'm really scared. I've never been this scared." Just the thought of more shocks caused a physical trembling deep in my body.

"We can get through this together, just like we have everything else," he said as he put both arms around me, his gentleness and quiet confidence dissolved some of my panic, at least for the moment.

Although God has been my primary source of guidance, Ryan's wisdom and logical mind is the rock that's kept me grounded and safe when my impulsiveness and optimism got the better of me. For the first time, during this crisis, he was the glass-half-full person, while I was a quivering, emotional mess.

What finally convinced me was a personal phone call from Dr. Rho about a week after coming home from the hospital and just hours after the "fine, quit" conversation with Ryan. Although I assumed he was calling to tell us to stop the process, he was actually wanting to persuade me to move forward with the surrogacy, which he knew I was vacillating on. He explained that if he could get me admitted into the hospital for cardiac monitoring during the estrogen increase, he felt sure that I could make it through the retrieval safely. He had once again showed me that he felt a special stake in the lives of our family and our future. God had chosen Dr. Rho to lead such a critical role in our surrogacy path. Standing in the face of all reason and sobriety, I began to understand that I was called to see this obstacle through. I believed God had His hand in every aspect of the situation and was constantly revealing His providence.

God had provided us with myriad of blessings (known and unknown). First of all, He had placed Travis and Rachel in our lives, and put it on their hearts to actively pursue the surrogacy issue with us, despite our persistent reluctance. Next, He surrounded us with an army of friends and family who were constantly there with encouraging words and prayers. He also provided a friend, who happened to be going through the same fertility treatments, who was willing to give us thousands of dollars of free fertility medication to us that was not covered by our insurance. And finally, He placed Dr. Rho in our lives—someone who was willing to do everything in his power to help Ryan and me have the family we desired.

How could I say no when God was pounding on my door in so many obvious ways? So often in my faith life, I have asked God to give me a billboard to make His path clear. Most times I was either not paying attention or missed His subtle nudges along the way. This time He was not going to give me an excuse to say I didn't understand.

However, even after the decision was made to continue with the treatments, I was reminded that this process still wouldn't be easy. My heart rhythm remained unstable for the remaining time I spent at home prior to my hospital admission and the planned increase of the estrogen. I was having frequent panic attacks. The most serious attack landed me in the emergency room of a neighboring hospital, as we were traveling to attend a funeral.

The attacks masked themselves in the same symptoms as a heart episode with shortness of breath, palpitations, sweating, and low blood pressure. For the first time, I relied on anxiety medication to sleep at night and keep my panic at bay during the day. While bed/couch rest was nothing new, this was equal parts physical and mental imprisonment. Though my path was well-defined, my fear of shocks continued to plague me. Just being patted on the back would send my heart racing. I think soldiers call it shell-shock. No matter how much self-talk I tried, my rational brain was not controlling my physical reaction.

On April 19th, 2009, it was agreed that I would enter the hospital to begin the increases to my beta blocker levels to ensure that they kept pace with the estrogen increases. The doctors would have me on 24-hour heart monitoring so they would be able to track any rhythm issues, especially of a ventricular nature.

Several times a day, Ryan would give me (or sometimes, I would have to give myself), the fertility injections in the stomach; all the while, I was waiting for an arrhythmia to hit. Thanks to Dr. Rho's careful tracking and balancing the estrogen with my beta blockers, my heart never did anything too profound, a few short bursts, but nothing sustained. After a week or so of the shots, they started the daily ultrasounds to see how the follicles were progressing, in count and in size. Watching them slowly grow, magical thoughts of who these little ones might be one day danced inside my head. My estrogen levels were soaring, and I was on a massive dose of beta-blockers and anti-arrhythmia drugs; amounts that made all of the doctors scratch their heads and the nurses double or triple check the orders before administering them. No one had ever seen that much heart medication given to a patient, not since I was pregnant. As a super drug metabolizer, if they wanted to stay ahead of the estrogen, they'd have to trust my body to tolerate what it had previously.

The days dragged slowly along. I experienced a lot of boredom, but also some good time to reflect and pray. I had some fast runs for arrhythmia, but mainly exacerbated by adrenaline from the panic that would ensue during it. Nothing happened that the doctors couldn't control, which was definitely my greatest fear. Ryan's mother, Kathy, drove 30 miles to visit me nearly every day, especially when she knew Ryan wouldn't make it. We would talk about everything from the latest TV gossip to the most philosophical and spiritual dialogues. We had some great Bible studies, and she brought in scriptures that were impactful during her times of sorrow and confusion.

These talks kept my spirits up and reminded me of the life that still existed outside of the hospital, but mainly it kept my hope alive. I prayed on Psalm 139 nearly every day. It gave me great comfort that God knew me so intimately, even as I was being knit together in my mother's womb, and just as I now watched my eggs nestled snugly inside a body that ultimately could not nurture them. Yet I had hope that God already had plans for them, just as He had for me.

"O Lord, you have searched me and you know me.
You know when I sit and when I rise;
you perceive my thoughts from afar.
You discern my going out and my lying down;
you are familiar with all my ways.
Before a word is on my tongue you know it completely, O Lord.
You hem me in - behind and before;
you have laid your hand upon me.
Such knowledge is too wonderful for me,
too lofty for me to attain.
Where can I go from your Spirit?
Where can I flee from your presence?
If I go up to the heavens, you are there;
if I make my bed in the depths, you are there.
If I rise on the wings of the dawn,
if I settle on the far side of the sea,
even there your hand will guide me,

your right hand will hold me fast.
If I say, "Surely the darkness will hide me
even the darkness will not be dark to you;
the night will shine like the day,
for the darkness is a light to you.
For you created my inmost being;
you knit me together in my mother's womb.
I praise you because I am fearfully and wonderfully made;
your works are wonderful, I know that full well.
My frame was not hidden from you
when I was made in the secret place.
When I was woven together in the depths of the earth,
your eyes saw my unformed body.
All the days ordained for me were written in your book
before one of them came to be.
How precious to me are your thoughts, o God!
How vast the sum of them!
Were I to count them, they would outnumber
the grains of sand.
Search me, O God, and know my heart;
test me and know my anxious thoughts.
See if there is any offensive way in me,
and lead me in the way everlasting. "
Psalm 139:1-18, 23-24

God did not make a mistake when making me and ALL my parts. I trust in His plan for my family and that if this child is to be part of it, He would make it so. God is the creator of all life and nothing is hidden from Him.

12

On April 28th, the eggs were ready for harvest, and I was to be discharged for about four hours to at a neighboring hospital because no one at UW did the procedure. My mom, by God's fine craftsmanship, had a job interview to be a medical coder at UW (in the same building where I was admitted) the same day, having flown in from San Diego just the day before. She came to my room that morning, and we prayed together before Ryan picked me up.

It was weird having to get discharged from one hospital, driving 10 minutes to another, having a procedure, and then being readmitted back at the original hospital; all within a period of six hours. Although I was nervous about being out of their care and supervision during the short transportation time, I was still under Dr. Rho's watchful eye. God had even intricately woven Dr. Rho's wife, another cardiologist, into our lives by wrangling her into being available to monitor my condition while I was at *her* hospital.

The procedure went off without complication, carefully plucking the tiny follicles from my ovaries with a long needle while I snoozed. I was back in the safety of UW cardiac monitoring before the pain meds had worn off. When I awoke in the recovery room the nurses told me that they were able to get nine eggs. Once Ryan had provided the other necessary ingredient, it was a waiting game to see how many embryos would be made. Five embryos became fertilized, and the fertility doctor decided that we would transplant the embryos on the third day after harvesting. She explained that three days would provide adequate time to grade the quality of the embryos and because of our high chances of success, she didn't think we needed to wait until the fifth day as many couples do.

Rachel made her flight arrangements, and the transplantation was planned for May 1st. Rachel agreed that transferring two embryos was acceptable so as to give us an even better chance of success. The whole process was very expensive, and we were hoping not to repeat it.

Fortunately, the peak of the estrogen levels was quickly over and steadily declining, along with my need for the large heart medication dosages. Dr. Rho was feeling confident in my ability to carefully step my dosages down at home and wanted me to be able to attend the transfer with Rachel. So the morning of the transfer, I was discharged from my hospital bed to Ryan's waiting car, where I was met by a smiling and eager Rachel in the backseat. We drove to the fertility clinic together, and Ryan dropped us off at the patient entrance while he parked the car.

We were both giddy with anticipation. Like little school girls we giggled and joked as Rachel pushed me in a wheelchair through the lobby and into the elevator, as I was still too weak to walk short distances. The clinic staff escorted us into an exam room and told us they were going to display, by digital video camera from inside the lab, the two embryos chosen to be transferred. As we watched the flat screen panel on the wall, we observed two quivering multi-celled embryos (eight cells on day 3) placed in a petri dish inside an incubator. The embryologist came back into the room to confirm that we saw the amazing display of life from the adjacent lab. After we confirmed all of the paperwork officially matching parent to embryo, she ducked back into the lab, and we watched on the screen as she delicately sucked the embryos into a long, narrow syringe. As she entered back in from the adjacent lab, we looked each other in the eyes and simultaneously said, "This is it, no turning back now."

As Rachel and I held hands, the embryologist carefully injected the precious solution into Rachel's uterus. We could see on the screen a silvery puff of air as the embryos floated to their final destination. Rachel swears she saw each of the embryos settle, but I wasn't sure. Either way, we both knew the gravity of what had just happened. So exciting, but not terrifying as the last time we were pregnant. Rachel's body was strong and safe, fully capable of carrying a child; much stronger than I ever could be.

Rachel had to lay flat for 30 minutes before they would let her up from the table. When they finally let her sit up she sprinted to the nearest restroom. She had been instructed to come to the appointment with a full bladder to make the procedure more observable, but after lying flat, being poked, prodded and mashed on, you could see her eyes start to water in great desperation. While she found the restroom, I went back to the waiting room where Ryan was parked with a magazine. I relayed the magical experience as best I could, but I knew I didn't do it justice. It did seem a bit crazy that all of the past six months of madness culminated in a half hour office visit.

We drove home together nervously jabbering. It was surreal to think about what those two groups of cells were now doing. Were they making themselves at home, nestling in for the long haul or would we come up empty again? Only time would tell. I kept asking naively if she felt any different. Obviously, she didn't, except for the pain meds she took before the appointment were starting to wear off. Our at-home instructions had been for her to take it easy for at least two days. We sat dutifully putting puzzles together and chattering excitedly on the sofa, the anticipation and nervousness in the air was palpable. Travis had stayed home in Montana with the kids during the transfer, so it was only Rachel and I. We took advantage of the relative quiet and just enjoyed the special time together. Soon, she would be going back to her family and life in Montana, and I would start the recuperation time it took for the mega heart med doses to be normalized. I was still moving at the speed of a slug and was easily startled by every missed or hurried beat.

Two days after the transfer, we got a call from the embryologist telling us the good news that two of the three remaining embryos had made it to "blastocyst" stage (five days of cell division) and would be able to successfully be frozen. We decided to proceed with the freezing because we were yet unsure about the outcome of the IVF and wanted to at least have one more attempt if it failed.

On the third day after the transfer we saw Rachel off at the airport, as she was anxious to get home to her own family and reenter her normal routine of life; as best as she could under the new and exciting circumstances.

The waiting had begun again in earnest. Rachel was to take a pregnancy test no less than ten days after the implantation in order to prevent a false positive or negative. Although she had an official blood test scheduled for the Monday following Mother's Day, she could not wait to know for sure, as her body was already giving her signals. On Mother's Day, as we were walking into church, we received a text message from Travis. It contained a single image of a pregnancy test stick with two strong lines indicating "positive." Ryan and I started to cry and hugged each other tightly. Maybe there would be no more Mother's Days that I cried during church about my empty arms, looking longingly (and admittedly with jealousy) at the other mothers surrounded by their happy broods of children. I would cry this Sunday, but this time in hope that God was going to answer our prayers. Again, with God's sweet humor, His tender, guiding hand, and perfect timing, that morning's sermon was on Psalm 139, the scripture that I could now almost repeat verbatim, having meditated so much on it the last six months. Coincidence? I don't believe in them!

"Praise be to the Lord, for he has heard my cry for mercy. The Lord is my strength and my shield; my heart trusts in him, and I am helped. My heart leaps for joy and I will give thanks to him in song."
Psalm 28:6-7

Rachel's subsequent "official" pregnancy test confirmed what we already knew. She was indeed pregnant. The HCG hormone that they use as a marker for pregnancy came back incredibly high. A positive initial test normally averages about 100HCGs. Rachel's was in the 700s, indicating that the chances were good that she might be carrying multiples. We were prepared for two (as much as you ever can be), since that was the number of embryos transplanted. Rachel was praying that there were no more than that, which is possible if the embryos split after the transfer.

But even all of the excitement of Rachel's pregnancy could not take away the daily fear that I still carried with me, especially since I was no longer under the close eye of Dr. Rho. As I have learned from my innumerable hospital stays, they are really a mixed bag. Being poked and prodded, shocked and drugged, starved and sleep-deprived; and yet not wanting to leave the protective bubble of doctors, caregivers, and continuous monitoring. Going home means starting fresh each time, seeking a 'new normal' level of activity and energy, living cautiously, attempting to stay in rhythm by limiting exertion, hoping to recover enough confidence to stretch my boundaries. The readjustment to home is a daily process, mainly a mental exercise, to reassure myself that I can stay stable one day longer. The days stack up until I can string a week together, then the weeks strung together to make a month, until eventually I almost forget that my heart is unpredictable and start living 'normally.'

Yet all of the mental gymnastics could be lost in a few uncertain beats that snap me back to the reality of the situation. And then, I start the time string again, hoping the next period of quiet will last a bit longer. How long will it take to leave the house? How long will it take for me to feel comfortable enough to go grocery shopping? Take an energetic outing to a park or a museum? Leave the 30-mile radius of my hospital for a day trip? Or finally, leave the state or maybe, with God's grace, maybe even the country?

These are all decisions I've faced countless times, each time stretching the elastic of my comfort zone, knowing that it is not if, but when, the band will snap back to its original tight position. Hospitals enable me to allow others determine my mental or physical capacity. Consequently, leaving the place that monitors, treats, and tends to my needs is always unsettling. I know that it is an inevitable step and there is so much I miss by being in the hospital, but when I step out each time, I start anew with the same hopes and fears.

After the transfer, it took six weeks before the medication levels were back to pre-estrogen levels and I could go back to work. Always trying to help my peace of mind, Dr. Rho procured a monitor for me to send in information when I felt symptoms, allowing me to understand what was real and what anxiety was creating. With this knowledge, I hoped that I could rationally "tune" out the anxiety-driven symptoms better.

Unfortunately during the latest episodes of the egg retrieval process, I hadn't yet sought out formalized counseling to deal with my newly acquired PTSD and the fallout from the ventricular shocks. I needed someone who could assist me in coping with the fear and learning to enjoy life again. It took months, but a counselor helped me acquire the tools to anticipate those moments most likely to induce panic and plan solutions ahead of time for my most dreaded situations. I was eventually able to put my water bottle down and get behind the wheel again. The counselor agreed that it was acceptable to keep the magnet with me, as it did serve a functional role. Fortunately, in the end, my drive for freedom trumped my willingness to let fear enslave me.

One incident, in particular, became a turning point in my relationship with God and the consuming fear that threatened to steal my joy. During church one Sunday (the only place I would venture during the weeks immediately following the transfer), I left in the middle of the service to use the restroom. As I was sitting in the stall of the empty bathroom, my heart began to flutter. Although it was still relatively slow and only lasted a minute, it was enough to induce my panic and a flight response. My need to know someone was there overwhelmed me. I was a good hundred feet from the sanctuary and knew no one would hear me if I screamed, which was impossible anyway if I lacked the ability.

Although nowhere near a rhythm that would induce a shock, I realized that I was all alone, and my hands fumbled desperately to find the magnet in my purse. At that moment, I clearly heard God say, "But I am here, you are not alone." His voice stilled me immediately, and a smile filled my face. I finally recognized God's presence in those moments of panic, and He was asking me to trust Him with my mind, body, and spirit. I didn't get to stop trusting when the situation involved the possibility of pain and death. On the contrary, He was who I needed to seek first; even rational fear is not a free pass to tell God, "I don't believe you are present with me or want to calm my anxiety in this moment." He brought peace to my soul when I trusted that He would always be there, in my darkest, loneliest hour.

****

My parents' move to the Pacific NW occurred during the end of my recuperation time in mid-May. Both my dad and I were not in a position to be much help in the packing and moving process so it was decided that my dad would fly out to be with me. We needed to accomplish some important errands before the move and it would keep us out of the way of the heavy lifting. Chaya, Ryan, and his parents flew down to San Diego to help my mom with the last of the packing, and then drove the car and U-Haul north to Seattle.

During our few days alone, my dad shared some wonderful stories about his childhood, explained some of the family genealogy, and reflected on his summers spent on his grandparents' dairy farm. His grandparents would work him and his brother hard every day (except Sunday) bailing hay, milking cows, and feeding the animals, but evenings were spent playing in the hay loft, running through the corn fields, and listening to his grandfather tell stories about life on the farm. As everyone gathered for the evening meal, his grandfather, an elder in the local Methodist church, would pray and read from the family bible for an undetermined amount of time, the food frequently getting cold before they were permitted to start eating. However, the tangible lessons of discipline, hard work, family togetherness, and most importantly, reliance and thankfulness for God's blessings stayed with my father all his life, and I'd like to think into our generation too.

My dad always assumed the role as our family historian, as well as general knowledge keeper. He had an amazing memory that could pluck out names, dates, and places within seconds, even the most obscure details upon request. He rarely forgot a face or a name and could remember the name of the restaurants that we ate at during our trips to Michigan 15 years ago. I devoured my dad's storytelling like I was five again. Even the familiar stories I heard with different ears, especially knowing that I could one day be called upon to recite them. All of the rest of the stories would be lost forever.

It was our task to get Mom a good commuter car, as she had gotten the job at UW and needed a reliable car for the long commute (1-1/2 hours plus 20-minute ferry each way). We also needed to purchase a washer and dryer for the rental house. As efficiently as I could muster, we accomplished both tasks in 2-1/2 hours, including time for lunch. I buy houses and cars faster than some people can pick out an outfit. When I see something I want, I have no issue making a decision and very few I've ever regretted.

After setting up delivery of the appliances to Anderson Island and driving off the lot in our "new" used Toyota Camry, we knew we had the whole rest of the weekend to just enjoy each other's company. Dad could now relax, feeling a sense of helpfulness that he desired, and in his declining physical condition, this was rare.

I couldn't remember the last time I spent good quality time with just my dad. It was wonderful sharing my excitement and apprehensions about the potential for having children of our own. I blathered on endlessly about how I longed to hold them in my arms and smother them with kisses, rock them to sleep, experiencing new sights and sounds through their fresh eyes. I wanted to be a part of all their 'firsts' and guide them carefully through life's challenges. I'd teach them to build with fisher price toys and make crazy crafts. They would love books and have an insatiable desire to learn and explore. I aspired to be a kind, comforting parent, but also be purposeful and consistent in my discipline. My child would know how much they were loved, yet also know that they were not the center of the universe; a good self-image, balanced with an appreciation and empathy for all His children.

My father had been so supportive of our decision, and I knew how much it meant for him to be a grandfather. I yearned to give him the joy of being a grandparent, allowing him to experience another generation of his family. He had wanted Aiden so much and grieved deeply at our loss and his own. Initially, his pain turned into anger, physically yelling at God, pleading for an answer, and when none came, His bitterness kept him from praying for months. It took God audibly speaking for him to recognize His compassion in our pain and to embrace the grace and comfort He wanted to provide. I'm not sure what was said, but the peace was instantaneous and God reassured him that my mom, who struggled with the same anger and bitterness, would soon hear the same message. The next morning she awoke to tell my dad the amazing dream she just had. My dad just smiled, knowingly. Her healing had begun too.

The moving troupe arrived back safely three days later with my parents' belongings, including two dogs in tow. We filled the rental house with the acquired furniture and appliances (that stupid microwave that almost killed me died two weeks later!), and left Mom and Dad to get settled in. It was so exciting to have them finally in arm's reach of me, having been more than 1,200 miles apart for the last 12 years. Although I knew that my dad, if not my mom too, had a foot still left in California. Splitting their time between their two homes was reasonable to me, and with the summer fast approaching (by far the best season in the Puget Sound), it promised some opportunities to reconnect with picnics, outings, and simply enjoying rest together.

In the middle of June, with Rachel eight weeks along, Ryan and I flew to Kalispell, Montana for the first ultrasound. Travis, Ryan, and I had crammed into the corner of a small consultation room so the ultrasound tech could to squeeze in to examine Rachel's belly. When only two embryonic sacs appeared on the monitor, Rachel smiled and exhaled loudly, her anxiety finally relieved. Although cautiously optimistic, it nonetheless took Ryan's and my breath away. To think that we would double our family in one day was overwhelming. I admit to having many sleepless nights trying to figure out how I'd have enough energy to corral two spunky toddlers, not to mention pay for the new expenses with one less income. The sense of responsibility was ominous, knowing they were fully reliant on me, when I had a body that wasn't reliable. More importantly, I feared my own selfishness and impatience seeping through, exposing my own daily battle over sin. But God knew my heart and would provide the resources and strength necessary. He always did. He stands ready to provide before we even ask.

Immediately after the first ultrasound, Rachel and I drove to the bookstore to buy up as many "twin" books as possible.

"Who's having twins?" asked the cashier pleasantly as she rang up our purchase. "How very exciting."

Without thinking, we simultaneously blurted out, "We both are!" as we exchanged proud smiles.

"Oh, isn't that wonderful. I'm sure you'll make great parents," she said grinning playfully as if she was just privy to our secret.

Walking out, it struck us at the same time that the cashier thought we were a lesbian couple; pretty controversial for a conservative Montana town. We joke about it to this day. That night we had a huge celebration and toasted for the second time in seven months.

Ryan and I attempted to be at all of the subsequent ultrasounds, as twins are considered a high risk pregnancy and require much more monitoring. At our 13 week visit the tech made an observation that we appeared to be having two boys. My jaw dropped, and I looked frantically at Ryan for confirmation of what I heard. After a moment of stunned silence, the first word that I found was, "Noooo!" which was perfectly audible in the running video recorder. As sweat beads gathered on my forehead, I couldn't stop thinking about two rambunctious boys running circles around me. My late night sleeplessness about twins instantly multiplied. Ironically, my words would come back to haunt me when I realized that girls have just as much potential for chaos.

By the 18th week ultrasound, we were able to confirm that, actually, we had a boy and girl, a nice even balance. More specifically, we had a very assertive little girl and a brother, who at least in utero, was being pushed around. The technician couldn't even get an accurate size reading on him because she had her foot in his ribs.

"What a perfect family you are going to have. I bet you have a cute house with a white picket fence too," the ultrasound tech joked with us, completely unaware of the trials it took for this joy to be made real.

"Well actually…," I stammered, initially thinking of sharing but then deciding better of it. "Yeah, it's going to be wonderful," I said smiling gently. No point bursting his bubble.

Early in the first trimester, Rachel, always thoughtful, ordered a doppler device from Amazon just so that we could have frequent "communication" with our little ones. She was incredibly empathetic about maintaining our sense of connectedness to the babies since I didn't get to experience the day-to-day movement and sensations. Being 500 miles away in Kalispell, the ultrasound visits were the only opportunity I had to touch and see the babies within Rachel's belly. So, every week she would call us and put the babies "on the phone" one by one. She had been able to distinguish the personalities of each of the babies early on, so she could pretty accurately assess where each of them were inside her womb. We would get updates on all their recent activity and observations she made, and she kept a photo log of her belly growth every week of the pregnancy so we could see the subtle changes. What remarkable compassion!

During one of the weekends when my parents were over for a picnic, Rachel made one of her weekly calls and asked if they would like to meet their grandkids. Looking a little confused, we explained the technology that had allowed this miracle to be a tangible experience for us. Putting the doppler on her belly next to the phone, she first chased down Baby A, our daughter, with her signature fast heart rate and inability to stay in one place. After finding, losing, and finding her several times, Rachel went after Baby B, our son. He was much calmer than his sister and was content to let us hear him for a spell. The intensity of the heartbeat spoke to us clearer than words. I looked over at my parents, standing next to us at the kitchen counter, their mouths hanging open in disbelief and delight, a tear streaming down my dad's face. It is an image seared into my memory.

The role of the wooden statue my mother gave me during my pregnancy with Aiden began to make sense. It had said "Cherish" on its bottom, and now watching my babies grow inside someone else, it was clear to me that it was my pregnancy that I was to cherish. Watching Rachel's belly expand, I could relate to the movements she described and the challenges of even a normal pregnancy. I had been given the experience of carrying life, and now as I watched it happen again, this time through Rachel, I knew these two lives were as much a part of me as Aiden had been.

The first trimester was a real challenge for Rachel. She not only had horrible nausea brought on by an extra dose of hormones from carrying twins, and had to take painful progesterone injections every day until her backside was lumpy and sore, but early on she had some bleeding that caused everyone concern. The bleeding was upsetting at first, until it was explained to us that bleeding is very common in vitro fertilization (IVF) when the embryos attach themselves on the uterine wall. It rarely leads to anything serious.

Ironically, she had some odd food cravings that would be an interesting study in the genetics of pregnancy. One afternoon we came home to a phone message from Travis.

"Who is responsible for my wife craving Cool Ranch Doritos and KFC mashed potatoes? She would never choose these foods on her own, even during her first two pregnancies. I've had to take a half a dozen trips through the KFC drive-through because she NEEDED it." Click.

I had to fess up and admit that both of them were my vices. I called Rachel back to explain. "When I was pregnant with Aiden and couldn't keep food down, one of the things that seemed to consistently settle my stomach was KFC artificial mashed potatoes. Also, when I was young, on long summer days stuck at home by myself, I used to run across the road to a local convenience store just to buy Cool Ranch Doritos and seltzer water with any money I could find in jacket pockets and couch cushions."

Rachel replied, "How did you know I had bought seltzer water too?" Laughing ensued as I apologized for making her desire such horrible foods, totally foreign to her "natural and healthy" daily diet.

Through our giggles, she finished. "I still won't eat meat, but to appease Ryan, I will cook some of my food in bacon fat. I'd hate to be responsible for your vegetarian kids being tormented by a father who wants meat in each meal."

"Fair enough," I answered. What a crazy mystery.

Near the end of the first trimester and before Rachel started to show, Travis, Rachel, and the kids went to a large family reunion. Since they had not yet shared with most people the adventure they were on, an awkward situation arose when a distant family member attempted to engage their 4-year old son in small talk.

Innocently, he asked Jasper, "So, do you think you want your mommy and daddy to have more brothers and sisters to play with?"

"Actually, Mom already has cousins in her tummy," he stated matter-of-factly and walked away, leaving the gentleman's mouth hanging open. Travis, who was standing nearby and caught the tail end of the conversation quickly jumped in to provide a minimal amount of explanation.

"Actually, we haven't told many people this, but Rachel is carrying babies for my cousin, Ryan, and his wife, and she is in her first trimester." The response from the other people that overheard were surprisingly positive, but the general reaction was "oh, that's nice," with a lot of quite muttering. Remember this is small town Montana, with not much good gossip.

The summer flew by with the frequent trips to Montana and the novelty of outings with our newly-relocated family. It was delightful spending time with my parents and Ryan's. We could now have a Sunday brunch without having to take a vacation time. The weather cooperated all summer, one of the sunniest ones I can remember, and my parents felt comfortable with their new environment, although my dad always wanted it about 10 degrees warmer.

I was concerned about the upcoming fall and winter because I knew my dad was easily chilled due to the myriad of medications he took. From past trips to the Puget Sound during the colder months (anything outside of June-Sept), he didn't handle the cold and wet combination well (or should I say, even less well than any of us). Although it was their idea to move here, it was unfair to want them to stay here full time. Ever since I was pregnant with Aiden, I knew they wanted to be close to family. They were willing to make us a priority and find a way to live here despite the weather. San Diego was their dreamland, and they were sacrificing it for time with us. How I hoped they found our time together satisfying enough to justify the move and discomfort.

Despite my apprehensions about the coming winter, I knew magical things were happening in our lives and the lives of our family during the summer of 2009, all part of God's larger plan. God was using this time to remind us of the joy of His many blessings. It was a time of celebration, something the last few years greatly lacked, in both my health struggles and my father's. We had been through the valleys, and God was there. On the mountain, His presence was even more magnificent.

"Go eat your food with gladness, and drink you wine with a joyful heart, for it is now that God favors what you do."
Ecclesiastes 9:7

13

My dad, Paul, has always been a very special person in my life. As a daddy's girl, our relationship growing up was always extremely close. He could read my thoughts (for good and bad), and for the most part, I could do the same of him. Since the same heart condition plagued both of us, he was one of the only people that truly related to what I was experiencing when episodes occurred. We both faced fear and pain, and were constantly trying to find that next ray of sunshine.

While my heart episodes and hospital visits decreased after my AICD implantation in 1998, my father's cardiac situation grew steadily worse. It started with the atrial fibrillation growing more and more persistent, followed by a need for repeated cardioversions. His first AICD device was implanted, only weeks before my wedding. His condition remained somewhat quiet between 2001-2003, and then took off at a gallop. Even more cardioversions were necessary, and then finally in December 2004, it was decided to attempt an ablation surgery in order to diffuse the bad electrical activity. It was evident early on that the surgery had not been successful, and the atrial fibrillation continued unabated.

Attempting a second ablation, months later was even less successful, almost costing him his life. The surgical team accidentally punctured the side of his heart wall (an incident known as a tamponade), which sent blood pouring into his chest cavity, literally drowning him from the inside. In the weeks following this almost-tragic event, he described to me a near-death experience where the most beautiful and peace-filled white light was drawing him in. In his semi-conscious state, as he was getting ready to yield to his new home, the surgeon jammed a long needle into his heaving chest and began to extract the suffocating fluid. Despite the horror of his dramatic resuscitation, he survived to continue the painful battle. God must not have been ready for him, and his family definitely wasn't prepared to lose him so soon.

Through a series of horrible missteps, my dad endured a third ablation and two more AICD changes in the two months following his tamponade. In his third ablation, the doctors intentionally destroyed the AV node (the source of heartbeat function) in an attempt to manually control his rhythm with the pacemaker function of the AICD. The cardiac team then convinced him to change out his current AICD with one that had special programming touted to be beneficial for his specific type of rhythm issues. Immediately after it was installed, the doctors informed him that this particular model was under recall for failing to administer life-saving shocks. Since he no longer had his own heartbeat, they had no choice but to hastily replace the device with a more reliable unit.

Just as my heart was prone to atrial arrhythmias (upper chambers), all of the episodes in my dad's history thus far had been atrial related. However, in March of 2006, he received three shocks for ventricular tachycardia. These deadly rhythms appeared to be part of the insidious progression of the disease. He continued to try to work, but no longer had the endurance for the long walks around the hospital required of a chaplain. Holter monitor studies (portable recording devices) showed that the dangerous ventricular beats persisted, and the doctors told him that his work must end. By April 2007, he was on permanent disability, slowly deteriorating, emotionally and physically, at home. Unable to contribute monetarily and domestically to the household reduced his sense of worth and self-esteem. Fearful and depressed, he became a shell of his former self, spending most of his days reading and watching TV. My mom was now fully responsible for the financial and care-taking burden, but also became the object of his frustrated transference.

His ventricles, stiff and inflexible like mine, started becoming unable to pump the blood out, and consequently became thin and ineffective. His condition was now at the "burnout" phase, where congestive heart failure prevailed and simple activities were difficult due to shortness of breath, fatigue, and chest pressure. Despite his pain and inability to function normally, the last three years had taught him that he wanted to be near his family more than anything else. Watching from far away in California was no longer an option for him, and he knew his time to act was short. So much was happening in Washington, even if he couldn't be actively involved, he wanted to be present.

As our first summer together in Washington wound to an end, filled with reconnection and fun, it was now time for Ryan and me to get serious about preparing our home for two little ones. We were forced to steal our weekends back from family engagements and allow my parents to begin their life here in earnest. My parents were continuing to adjust to their rental house on Anderson Island, exploring the local amenities, and beginning to build friendships within their new church community. Not only did my mom's job in Seattle keep her busy, but I think she actually enjoyed the alone time while commuting two hours in Pacific NW sunshine with the top down on her convertible. With my mom gone 12-14 hours each day, my dad was grappling with long days alone, acutely aware there was no one there if any emergency arose. It made him extremely uncomfortable knowing that it would be quite an ordeal for him to get medical help in any sort of expedient manner. In an attempt to calm some of his fears, my parents made prior arrangements that during a non-life threatening heart episode, a speed boat would take him across the water, with an ambulance waiting on the other side, assuming the ferry schedule wasn't timely. The worst case scenario involved a helivac flight to the mainland; definitely not an ideal situation either way.

As part of my parents still having a foot still in California, my dad had maintained his cardiologists in San Diego and had not yet explored changing his medical team to Washington. Consequently, my dad and mom had a planned trip back to San Diego the second week of September in order to replace the old battery in his defibrillator. They intended to stay in their partially-filled home before the procedure and during recovery, and then fly back to Washington. Afterward, my father promised to switch his care to my trusted cardiology team at UW.

This procedure was routine for both of us; I've had three so far, and this would be number four for him. A defibrillator replacement is not a dangerous or complicated surgery and normally involves about a four-inch incision just below the collarbone and the reworking of the pectoral muscle to create a "pocket" for the device. The complication with my dad was that his AV node was ablated (destroyed), and the pacemaker part of the device was his only heartbeat. The doctors would have to maintain his rhythm until the device was back online. This obstacle was also not out of the ordinary for the surgical team, and just meant another layer of caution they needed to employ.

My parents were to leave on the 12th, right after my dad's 57th birthday, which fell on Labor Day weekend that year. Ryan, his parents, and I had spent the whole weekend working on preparing the nursery, and by Monday, I was exhausted. In anticipation of a strenuous weekend, I had told my mom beforehand that I was reasonably sure that we wouldn't be able to attend his party on Monday because I didn't expect to have any energy left. However, the night before, I called her to confirm that we were in fact coming, but not to tell my dad. In the days leading up to his birthday I had this overwhelming fear and knowledge that he would not make it out of surgery. A small voice kept telling me that I needed to be at his party and make the time count. I had never experienced these feelings before even though he had been through a lot worse procedures. The feeling was so strong about his imminent death that I actually brought a hand held tape recorder with me to the party (I didn't disclose my reasons to him, obviously, but I think he was gripped by the same sense of impending finality). I desperately wanted to capture a piece of him for myself and his soon-to-be grandchildren.

As we were pulling into the driveway for his party, I could see him standing at the kitchen window like a little kid, smiling from ear to ear. My sister was already there, and he was not expecting anyone else to come. When we got to the door he was standing there with tears in his eyes, and he hungrily threw his arms around us. After having spent the last three months together, seeing each other almost weekly, I didn't realize how important our presence was at this rather informal party. Guilt began to creep in that I was even thinking of missing his birthday.

The day was rainy and dreary, but no one seemed to notice. My sister and I baked his cake together, and Mom prepared one of his favorite meals. We laughed and joked about even the most mundane things; my dad had more energy than I had seen in years. As he opened up his presents, he had the exuberance of a kid, even putting on the Seattle Mariners sweatshirt that my sister had given him and taking a few phantom swings. He showed me the presents that his father had sent him; a memories journal and two children's books, one called, "I Can't Wait to be Your Grandfather," by Billy Crystal. Tape recorder in hand, I insisted that he read the book for his grandkids, and I told him I was going to play it for Rachel's tummy when she drove from Montana for the baby shower in two weeks. We went to the back bedroom and recorded both my mom and dad reading their respective books to the children. I was so elated to have this recording.

When it was time to leave that night, I held his hand at the door and gave him a hug that even then, I intentionally tried to burn into my memory. I can still feel the soft roll of his shoulders pressed to my chest and the tender grip of his hands on my back. He repeated over and over how much he appreciated us coming after a long weekend of work and how this had been the best birthday he'd ever had. Somehow I knew it would be his last.

My parents flew to San Diego on the following Saturday, in preparation for the Tuesday surgery. I didn't get to see them before they left because we had previously made plans with Ryan's parents. On the day of the surgery, I called my mom on my lunch hour to find out how the procedure went. She articulated some of the details and said the doctors assured her that there were no apparent complications and they anticipated releasing him as soon as his anesthesia wore off. My mom put him on the phone, but he was still pretty groggy and difficult to understand. When I called again from the bus stop on my way home from work, he was resting comfortably at home.

The And

It was so wonderful to talk to him and I just couldn't help but question why I was so worried in the first place. This procedure was routine, I told myself again. I must have just been paranoid and anxious from our earlier conversation at Christmas, coupled with all of the approaching changes in my own life. This reassurance didn't keep me from calling him several times on Wednesday. Although he was still in a lot of pain, we were able to talk openly and lightheartedly. Having the surgery complete, I now felt comfortable sharing my premonition of his death. To my surprise, he confided that he was grieved by the same prediction and had been deeply concerned. Laughing out loud, we celebrated together the blessing of his sustained life and a renewed future.

Although substantiated in the Bible, visions are a funny thing. Many people are prone to dismiss them as things from Bible times, or worse yet, a hoax our unstable brains produce. While I believe they need to be fully vetted by scripture, and their purpose might not always be clear, I know they still happen today. I think the natural inclination is to ignore or minimize them because if you tell people you've had one, they're likely to give you a smile and nod in a "you're crazy" kind of way. The difficulty is that my family has had too many visions validated, in very dramatic fashion. When my dad was in his late twenties, he had a dream the night before a business trip that his plane would crash. He woke up with a start and knew he could not go on the trip. He actually got up the gumption to call his boss and tell him that he was sick, unable to attend the meeting. That morning, the commuter flight he should have been on, crashed and killed all aboard.

Likewise, my sister dreamed one night that someone pulled a gun at her quiet suburban high school and proceeded to empty his gun amongst her friends. When she awoke she told my dad that she was worried about going to school. While dropping her off at the entrance of the school, my dad prayed with her, assuring her that everything would be fine--it was only a dream. She went to school, and by 10:00 a.m., the school was in lockdown with two people dead and 14 others injured. She was unharmed (at least physically), but her friends weren't. I don't think my dad ever forgave himself for not trusting her intuition, and I'd imagine he began to consider that the "gift" of premonition might be genetic. Sadly, I would also experience the "gift" on a couple of painful occasions.

Thursday, September 17th, was the final warranty walk through at Pioneer Middle School. Done one year after the school opened, the principal, the contractor's superintendent, the school district's representative, and I had a final "to do" list that needed to be reviewed for completeness to make sure the contractor had officially met his contractual obligations. About two hours into the walk-through, the district rep got a call on his cell and handed me his phone. Telling me that Ryan was on the phone, I knew right away that something bad had happened. Frustrated that my cell phone had been off, Ryan had called my office to try to locate me and was patched through to John, the district representative.

Calmly he told me that my mom had called that morning in hysterics, telling him that my father had passed away in his sleep Wednesday night, just hours after I spoke to him last. Being ever prepared to take control of an emergency, which unfortunately Ryan's had quite some practice at, he was in the process of getting us a flight to San Diego. All I needed to do was head home, pack a bag, and wait for further instruction.

The And

After sharing with my colleagues what had happened, I requested a moment to myself, and searched out the nearest classroom to futilely attempt to compose myself. My first reaction was shock as I sat quietly in a student desk, first reflecting on his birthday party last Saturday, and then reaching deep into my rich childhood memory bank; soon the tears started to well up in my eyes and quickly became an insuppressible flow. After a few minutes, the principal of the school came in to console me, and as I wiped the tears with my sleeve, she offered me a ride home so I didn't have to drive myself. Although I had my own car, she thought it would be best to let someone else drive my car and another of the team would caravan behind. I gave up trying to be the collected "professional" and just sobbed in her arms.

On the ride back, I kept playing back the last few days in my head. We were out of the danger zone after surgery. He had seemed to be just fine. What could have gone wrong? How could I have known that he wouldn't make it? Why did I let my guard down? Then again, why am I trying to figure out things that are beyond my comprehension and control?

When I arrived home, Ryan called to let me know he'd made flight arrangements for that afternoon, and my sister was on her way to our house in order to carpool to the airport. As I started to pack a bag, I realized my mental capacity to make a decision, about something as basic as selecting outfits, had vanished. Not knowing how long we'd be there or if they'd have the funeral in San Diego or Seattle left me stupefied, and consequently paralyzed me with uncertainty. Somehow, my bag got filled, but several times during our stay with my mom, I would look at the contents of the suitcase and be baffled by their inappropriateness or inadequacy.

As I was completing my only task, I remembered suddenly the tape recorder from a week ago, urgently digging through the clutter on my desk trying to find it. It was the only item that had any meaning left in my moment of crumbling. Exhausted, but successful in my pursuit, I found myself sitting in the middle of the hallway on the hardwood floor crying uncontrollably, playing the taped recording of my dad over and over. His voice echoing, "I can't wait to be your grandfather," only sent me sobbing again.

Our children, in Rachel's belly, were the whole reason he left his beautiful San Diego. He loved it and wanted to spend the rest of his days there. It was my dad's idea that they should keep their home in San Diego, even when they moved half of their belongings to Seattle. My dad could not give up the sunshine and would continually talk about the trips he was going to take when the rain got to be too much. Ironically, he never actually had to spend a rainy season here. I think the really stubborn side of him had said, "I am going to live the rest of my days in sunny San Diego," and God helped make it so. If I didn't know better, I'd think that they'd hatched a plan together.

14

Ryan, Chaya, and I flew out of Sea-Tac Airport that afternoon in silence. On the other side, my mother was waiting at the airport, accompanied by a friend of hers for support. It felt so surreal to be in a state of mourning in this beautiful place, which until this afternoon was where Ryan and I had vacationed and spent holidays with the family. It would be much more fitting if it was cold and rainy, but no – the sun was shining high in the sky and there were no signs of any clouds, just the way Dad loved it.

As we were driving to their home, Mom shared the details of finding Dad in bed after she had gotten up early, while it was still dark, to do some work. Surprised that he wasn't up by 9:00 a.m., since he was normally an early riser, she had gone in to check on him. She realized immediately that he was gone, probably for a few hours. Before she could gather herself to make the 911 call, she ran out of the house screaming. Living in a close-knit, town-home community, the neighbors knew that my parents were in town for a few days and responded to her cries instantly. Many of them, including the next door neighbor who arrived through the back gate, were aware of my dad's health situation so the explanation of what occurred was mercifully short. They stepped in right away, made the necessary calls, and waited with her until help arrived.

The ambulance arrived quickly, as well as a manufacturer's representative for his defibrillator, which is customary for obtaining the vital information recorded on the device. They informed my mom that the defibrillator had only shocked him once, indicating that it must have been a fatal rhythm which arrested the heart instantaneously, and not something the device sensed would be solved with repetitive treatment. We were comforted greatly that he had not looked pained, but extraordinarily peaceful in his death. We knew that getting shocked repeatedly and unsuccessfully was one of his greatest nightmares, something I can identify with closely.

The next morning, Friday, we went to the crematorium to discuss the details of their services. While they were very professional and tried to be considerate of the situation, I realized what a thriving business death is and how impersonal it becomes for the families involved. So many decisions… Buried or cremated? How would you like to receive the remains, ashes in a box or urn? Any clothes or items on the body you'd like retrieved? Would you like to watch him be cremated? Enough already! I understand better why preparation in advance, although not something any of us want to acknowledge, relieves painful choices of loved ones under duress.

My mother specifically asked that they remove his device and return it to us since it was suspicious that he died only days after receiving it. Rather questionably, this did not happen, and it was destroyed during cremation, leaving us to always wonder if it had functioned as programmed. We had decided not to pursue an autopsy for a variety of different reasons, mainly emotional. We were well aware that his heart would most likely be his end and dragging out the pain through an investigation delayed the healing process. The death certificate took much too long to be completed by his anxious, litigation-averse cardiologist, who labeled the cause of death as congestive heart failure, a result of the hypertrophic cardiomyopathy. The heart failure, however, had not shown up on the x-ray taken immediately preceding his device replacement, which made the doctor's diagnosis even more perplexing.

Looking back, there were so many unanswered questions that haunted me in my search for closure, many that had a direct impact to my own cardiac care. So often I was assured by my doctors that a defibrillator provides protection, but the truth is that they are not fail proof. My dad's heart failure was considered relatively mild, so how could it morph into a fatal condition in less than two days. My solace comes in knowing, even if we considered his death premature, it was part of God's much bigger plan, and His ultimate sovereignty reigns. My father no longer has to endure marginal living, but gets to live joyfully in the presence of a great and merciful God.

"Show me, O Lord, my life's end and the number of my days; let me know how fleeting is my life. You have made my days a mere handbreadth; the span of my years is as nothing before you. Each man's life is but a breath."
Psalm 39:4

My mom's sister, Kathy, joined us in San Diego not long after we arrived. She was a great source of comfort for my mom, having held vigil during the prolonged death of their brother, Tom, six months previous, and the death of their father, Grandpa Jack, in 2006. God's hand was at work in this reunion. The last three years had already played emotional havoc on my mom, and she was in no condition to face living alone. It was Kathy's intention to leave her unhappy marriage, and this situation provided a perfect opportunity to make a move. It was her plan to accompany my mom back to Washington and stay with her until they mutually decided to part ways. It was wonderful knowing that my mom would have a companion in the loneliness of widowhood, having been married 37 years and together with my dad since they were teenagers.

At my mother's request, the funeral was planned for Saturday, only three days after his passing, so that she could quickly head back to Washington and escape the memories of the home they had shared together for 12 years. We would leave as soon as the necessary insurance and other financial paperwork had been filed, under the idea that my mom would come back later to pack up the house, hopefully after she had a chance to digest everything that had transpired. I knew that the same pain would exist when she returned, having merely locked the physical reality behind a door, but I wanted her to be in control of the timing.

As we were preparing for the funeral, we found Dad's favorite Bible with a service already planned out in it, songs, scripture verses, everything. My mom had never seen the paper on which the service was written, and I suspect he may have prepared it right before he left Washington. Being a pastor and chaplain throughout his life, he had a large collection of Bibles from a variety of translations, most of which were still located in California; he had brought only a handful of his favorites to his new home during the move. However, during the short excursion for his surgery this week, he specifically brought the favorite Bible he used daily.

The only item that was left vague in the service he had arranged was a note that he wanted "selected poems" read. As we went through the poetry books on his shelf, we found a Garrison Keillor book with two bookmarks in them. When we read the poems, it was obvious that these were the "selected poems." Boy, was he prepared! To his family's chagrin, my belief was confirmed - that his desire to spend his last days in San Diego was met by God's answered prayer.

The funeral, without a doubt, was exactly how he envisioned. The sanctuary of their church home in San Diego was packed, and many people spoke about his amazing attributes. One of the most impactful I heard was a close male friend of Chaya's, who described my dad as the father he never had, someone always willing to talk and provide support, even after Chaya had left for college. My dad never had a boy, and had a special place in his heart for the young men who my sister hung around with. I was blessed to be given an opportunity to see different angles of a man I knew only as Dad.

My sister and I both spoke during the service, sharing the gift he was to us and the lessons he imparted. He loved people intensely, without restraint or judgement. Hurting people gravitated toward him as he was always ready with a kind word or encouragement. Even his face would become pained, his forehead crinkled tight as he allowed himself to feel your agony. The compassion that he had poured out in his life, was now being released back into the sanctuary by the grieving crowd. It was hard to maintain any composure, especially when most of the people in the crowd were letting the tears flow unrestrained. It was then that I realized how much he was loved by his community, his colleagues, and his church home, and that if he had passed away in Tacoma, he would only have had his family and the friends he had made in the short three months he lived there. The throng of people who filled every seat would have been deprived of a proper send off, and we would have missed this outpouring of love. Even during the reception line after the service, people continued to share stories of his generosity, gentle spirit, and overwhelming kindness, something I had intimately experienced my whole life.

When we returned from the funeral that afternoon, and while I was munching on the abundance of comfort food that had been delivered to our house, I noticed that there was an email waiting for us from Rachel and Travis. Attached in the email was a picture of her ultrasound from Friday. Once again, Rachel wanted to make sure we didn't miss anything. Ryan and I had a flight to Kalispell, Montana scheduled for the day after my father died and consequently were unable to attend the five-month ultrasound. A shiver ran down my spine when the picture materialized on the screen. My mom, who was standing behind me, breathed in deeply. The picture of baby B's face, my son, looked exactly like his grandfather Paul, pointed jawline and all. God's handiwork gloriously revealed, bringing tears and smiles to each of us.

If that wasn't enough, another providential surprise awaited us in the form of two priceless baby shower presents, tucked neatly in a gift bag and placed in the entry closet. My mom found them while rifling through the closet for important life insurance files. They were presents that she knew nothing about. I had to assume that Dad had bought them prior to the move in May, and left them here with the intention of bringing them back to Washington after his surgery. Inside each of the respective bags was a blue and pink pacifier with a stuffed horse attached to them; something special from the grandfather they would never know. Little did he know how much comfort he would bring two little ones and one sad mommy.

The day after the funeral was my sister's birthday. Her birthday would ever be marred by its proximity to Dad's death. She didn't want to go out to dinner or have any celebration whatsoever (not that any of us were really up to a party). A Starbuck's drink, with some ribbons on it, was brought to her by a friend, which I believe was the only present she accepted. As a newly-crowned only child at 10, her relationship with Dad had become extremely close after I moved away to college. He would listen to the difficult spiritual questions that she posed only to him, not always with answers, but with open ears and a non-judgmental heart. There is a hole that he left in her which I hope someday is filled with someone that can challenge her and love her as much as Dad.

We spent the next few days milling about the house, getting paperwork in order, and talking about Dad and the blessings of his incredible life and graciously peaceful death. During one of our emotional downloads, my mom shared with us that she too had a premonition about my dad's death. Trying not to lend credence to the premonition, she decided not shared it with him, although she became dreadfully concerned when he had shared his dream with her. She was afraid to speak it into existence.

While flipping through the newspaper during one of the mornings spent fitfully trying to allow our minds and emotions a break from the present reality, something caught my eye in the sports section, which my father read religiously. The Detroit Tigers had played a series against the Minnesota Twins the last three days, as their final meeting of the year before the playoffs. It jogged my memory of a story my dad had told, just before his passing, about a dream where he was in heaven, watching his favorite baseball team, the Minnesota Twins, with his twin brother, David. The day after my dad died, the Twins were playing the Detroit Tigers, his brother's favorite team. With smiles on our faces, it was hard not to imagine my father and his brother taking in the game, laughing and enjoying the view in the stands behind home plate, both with wholly restored hearts.

On Wednesday, we flew back together with my mother and aunt to Seattle. The crematorium had actually delivered my dad's still warm ashes to my mom by courier at 5 a.m, just hours before we were to leave. We all breathed a sigh of relief that they made it on time, so we could "all" go home together. Although we knew he was already home with Jesus, the rest of us still had a way to go before we found our peace.

During the flight home, despite my reservations, we made the decision to proceed with the baby shower that was scheduled to be on Saturday, September 26th, only four days away. My mom didn't want to cancel it because she wanted something to divert her attention in a positive direction and lift everyone's spirits. I didn't know if I was emotionally ready to move from deep sadness to what was supposed to be great joy. Chaya had designed and mailed out all of the invitations, put together the activities and goodie bags. The room was reserved and the food was ordered, but there was still a lot to prepare. However, I knew if we postponed it, not only would there be a million painful phone calls to make, but Rachel probably wouldn't be able to attend, which to me was a deal breaker. She was getting pretty far along in the pregnancy to endure an eight-hour car ride already, and I didn't want to push the limits of common sense.

Baby showers are supposed to be joyous events, right? I had such grand visions for my shower. This is the next event that little girls fantasize about, after they've completed the weddings plans to their handsome princes. To me, this was a celebration of life, and I wanted to share my joy with everyone who had been cheering for me on the sidelines. There had been so many people who touched my life and played integral roles in seeing my darkest time transformed into hope and renewal. However, the day before the shower, all I wanted to do was curl up in a ball and sit in a dark room alone. With a little coaxing, I realized that too much was done to walk away now; hell or high water, we were having a shower.

Everyone in the family put on a happy face, thoughtful toasts were made, fun activities were played, scrumptious food was devoured, and beautiful presents were unwrapped. What could be missing? My stomach was in my throat, and my heart on the floor in a mix of sadness for the loss of my father just a few months before my babies were to be born. Rachel put on a smile and tried hard to play the supporting role, in what I'm sure most people would think was an awkward party situation. She recognized that although I was the guest of honor, it was her belly that was playing the starring role.

My shower left me awestruck by the expressions of love by family and friends, but I was also gripped by the reality that I would never see my dad again, and my children would never experience his love for them. I will always remember my shower as a beautiful affair that just happened to be at a calamitous time.

That night I went home exhausted, emotionally and physically. It took a weekend to recoup, but I actually began feeling ready to pick up life where I'd left off. My job and baby preparation still needed to get done; life could not stop and wait for me to "feel" like participating again.

When I did go back to work the following Tuesday, almost two weeks after my father passed, it was refreshing. I had a lot of projects to catch up on, including a design deadline for a large high school remodel, and the intense distraction would do me good. While I was still grieving my dad's absence, the peace I received about how content he was now, gradually started to overtake my own sense of loss. There was no question that he loved his family and wanted to keep living as long as the Lord allowed, but in the last few years he had spent much thought dwelling on the scriptures pertaining to descriptions of heaven.

Knowing there was a much better existence awaiting him, helped soothe his anxious soul.

Having recognized the futility in holding on to the "what ifs" in my dad's death, I began focusing my mental energy on the future as it appeared now. What did it look like to become a stay-at-home mom of two children? After quitting the only job I ever loved and never having been "domestically" inclined, how would I adjust? Around the house I felt useless; I couldn't cook, hate cleaning, and managed to shrink or color 'alter' most laundry I touched. For the sake of having children, I was giving up a career I loved and was good at, and was replacing it with 'home management' that I sucked at, and raising kids I had the great potential for screwing up. Would I ever return to work? Did I want to? Would I ever feel "successful" again? What was "success" anyway?

Too many questions that only time would answer, I sought the faith to let God guide my footsteps, one by one. He promised to be a lamp unto my feet — a light to my path, not a lighthouse that illuminates the rocky coast for miles. Faith requires believing, when the sun has not yet risen, stumbling and trusting Him to catch you. The brokenness of this world threatened to overwhelm me, interjecting heartbreak after heartbreak into my story. However, as a new set of complexities were about to emerge, God's reminded me of His steadfast love and comforting presence. Despite the curveballs thrown into my life that sent me swinging at air, I was a valued character He had purposefully written into *His* story; a story that never lost sight of His ultimate end, the restoration of all His creation.

****

The And

From the beginning, Rachel's pregnancy was fraught with complications, which seemed par for the course in our lives. Besides the extreme nausea and dehydration she experienced her first trimester, which required rehydration at the hospital and anti-nausea medication, her cervix started shortening at 20 weeks and progressed to funneling at 24 weeks. Two weeks after my dad's death and baby shower, she was put on bed rest. As her funneling and contractions increased, her doctors in Montana decided that it was time for her to seek more specialized care at a facility that could accommodate the delicacies of babies born before 30 weeks.

This was incredibly disappointing to her, as she had expressed during our original discussions that it was her desire to remain in Montana throughout the entire pregnancy, unless absolutely necessary. There was no question that it was now necessary, and I made a phone call to my high-risk OB/GYN at University of Washington, and Dr. Easterling agreed to see Rachel right away. We arranged for her to fly out to Seattle two days later, 26 weeks along. Having promised her that I would help to take care of her family if she was put on bed rest, I quit my job of 10 years to take care of her. I had already warned my boss a few weeks earlier of the possibility that she might need my help and if that happened, I would need to leave without much notice.

My work threw me a baby shower at lunch on my last day. As I sat in the conference room opening presents, I was flooded with emotions. I was ecstatic about being a new mom, but apprehensive that it would end in heartbreak as it did before. The timing of Rachel's problems struck a painful chord, as this was nearly the same week in the pregnancy that I had lost Aiden. I was also leaving a career that I loved for an absolutely unknown outcome. Many of my long-standing professional and personal relationships were forged during lengthy, intense design deadlines, and I would miss them dearly. My friend Diana, who had been there holding my hand after my 1st defibrillator shock, was again there holding me as I cried in the building lobby. Was history going to repeat itself with my new babies? I was still sitting on the edge of a cliff from the loss of my father, and now I was getting ready to jump into a scary new life of motherhood, where my professional resume didn't matter and my skills had yet to be tested. To top it off, there was still a big "maybe" on the outcome; then again, isn't there always?

My architectural firm had made it clear I could come back at any point, but it still felt very final. If all worked out well, I would be taking, at minimum, a few years off or possibly not going back. But what was next if the pregnancy did not end with parenthood? Would I want to go back like I did after we lost Aiden, or would I start a new chapter? The firm had already taken me back multiple times after short-term medical leaves. Although reassured to the contrary, I felt like a drain on the company. Either way, it was time to prepare for motherhood by taking care of the woman who was growing my children within her. And my faith necessitated that I look to God exclusively at this moment. He was in control, regardless of the outcome, and He had never left my side before, so I had confidence that He would not abandon me now.

Rachel's time on bed rest was excruciating for her, and she missed her family profoundly, even spending her 10-year dating anniversary away from Travis. The pain was evident in her eyes, though she tried to put on a brave face. To lighten the mood, we spent most of our days on the couch together, talking, laughing, musing what these two crazy kids would be like, all the while fearful of a premature birth. I knew that she felt responsible to provide us with the healthy, full term baby she had offered, and I kept reassuring her that whatever happened was in God's hands. We would handle the outcome, good or bad, with His help.

At the first office visit, the day after she arrived in Washington, the doctor discussed the potential for admitting her for the remaining period of bed rest. Thankfully, after a few more appointments, it became clear that the labor progress had slowed, if not ceased. The children were growing beautifully, and they already weighed twice what Aiden had at birth. This was all thanks to Rachel's diligent effort to put on weight early in the pregnancy, before she lost space for her stomach to expand. While she stayed with us, she frequently laughed that her "capturers were trying to fatten her up" by supplying a steady stream of her favorite foods.

After a grueling two weeks without her family, Travis and the kids drove out from Montana to be with her. Her children, accustomed to having their mom with them all day, were having a difficult time with the separation. During their stay, they started to act out in normal ways for a two and four year old; crankiness, clinginess, and not to mention a few knock-down drag-out tantrums. Rachel was the target for much of their disobedience as they knew she's couldn't leave the couch to discipline them. Travis was equally struggling to be the single dad and work full time. Mercifully, both his parents and Rachel's were a tremendous blessing to us, stepping in to watch the kids while he worked. Additionally, Rachel's friends would bring in food and take the kids for afternoons. This was becoming a full family/community affair.

In a pathetic attempt at motivation, we had nailed a calendar to the wall with an official baby countdown; excitedly we would cross off each day, slowly getting closer to our stated birth goal of "AFTER 30 weeks." Finally, after four tediously boring and precarious weeks, watching home design/decorations shows ad nauseam; we made it. At Rachel's 30-week appointment, Dr. Easterling decided that it was okay for her to return to Montana, as the local hospital could now accommodate the babies in the NICU. He told us that he was confident that we would make it a few more weeks. We found out later that, while trying to stay positive for us, he was not at all certain because he had called the Montana hospital before we left Washington to tell them to expect us any day. Nonetheless, with an approval letter from the doctor, we flew back together the next day (yes, on another domestic flight) although she was already two centimeters dilated.

So for the time being, I was in charge of taking care of her children, the younger of which had caught head lice from a hat exhibit at the Children's Museum during her stay in Washington. The day after I arrived, I found myself holding their daughter with Travis over the kitchen sink doing multiple rounds of lice treatment and washing every toy, blanket, and clothing item around the house in an effort to keep it contained. Talk about baptism by fire in the parenting department! What a hoot!

While in Montana, there arose a rather somber episode in the premature labor fiasco, this time involving the legal wrangling required to make the children ours officially. In the original scenario where the children would be born in Montana, it was decided that we would draft the legal documents and file it with the courts there. The initial contract of legal custody was drafted, and we were waiting for the final copy to be mailed to us for signature. However, when she was flown out to Washington with the chance of delivery, we had to hurry and get new papers drafted in our home state because the state statutes are so different. Then, all of a sudden, we were back in Montana, and I couldn't, for the life of me, get in touch with our original lawyer to get the rest of the paperwork. We had found our Montana lawyer through extensive research, and at the time, he was the only one that had ever processed a surrogacy case in the state. Since no other lawyer had experience with surrogacy, we couldn't easily start over, and certainly didn't want to repeat the expense, but time was running out.

I called him over and over, leaving more and more agitated messages on his machine (he was a single proprietor and had no assistant). My final call went something like this:

"Hello, this is Erin Reichman *again*. I *need* you to call me back right away! I have called countless times now, and the situation is urgent. The babies could be born any day and we don't have the correct paperwork in place. Since Rachel is the official birth mother, the children will automatically be listed on the birth certificates as Travis and Rachels'. As you are *well* aware, we would then have to endure a *drawn-out* adoption process to be named the official parents, and you will be responsible for the costs! I'm sure you are *very* busy, but we are paying you good money to complete this work for us, and it is *unacceptable* to be ignored any longer! Call me back today. You have the number!"

After weeks of calls, I received a phone call from a rep from the Montana State Bar Association. He informed me that our lawyer had died suddenly three weeks ago, and when someone from the Bar was sent to close out his affairs, they found the voicemails from me on his machine. How mean and horrible I must have sounded, oblivious to the poor guy's circumstance.

In a panic, Travis asked a favor of one of his friends, a tax attorney who had never handled family law. He was happy to help, but didn't have a clue where to start. I gave him our draft documents, and he reworked them slightly, until he felt comfortable with the verbiage. Ryan and I signed them, and he took them immediately to a judge, who generously fit us into that day's docket, due to our time-sensitive situation. Thanks to the hard work of our "tax" lawyer and the compassion of a judge, the papers ended up being completed only one week before Rachel's delivery. Having been given a glimpse into the background of our story by Travis, they both conveyed how deeply touched they were to be a part of such a wonderful story.

They joined the multitude of people, integral to the execution of the direction we believed was from God, and in turn, they became personally invested in our story, and it became part of theirs. God has a beautiful way of orchestrating circumstances that bring people together under a united purpose. Some people call it a divine appointment, a special and life-changing meeting that would never have occurred without God's intervention. My story is filled with them; as are the stories of most people, if they look close enough. I believe that "coincidence" is what people call an event they can't explain and when they can't see it as a slice of a greater plan. Recognizing the innumerable plot lines He is entwining in the lives of all His creation makes you realize how incomprehensible God's sovereignty is; He is truly a master weaver - omnipresent and omnipotent.

15

Thanksgiving has always been a special celebration for our family, but each year it seems to become even more monumental. This year was no exception. In 2006, it was a dinner with Travis and Rachel, in which they offered for the first time to carry a child for us. In 2008, it was the toasting of our official decision to attempt surrogacy together. So, it was really no coincidence that Thanksgiving weekend of 2009 would once again be that reminder of why we are to give thanks.

Ryan had driven to Kalispell on Wednesday to spend the holiday with me and the rest of the Steindorf/Barrie clan. During the past six months, we had been able to spend a good deal of time with Travis' parents, David and Tam (Ryan's uncle and aunt), and Rachel's parents, Lloyd and Joanne, and her sister Elise. They had been there to watch their grandkids during our prenatal appointments and had been instrumental in caring for the family when Rachel was initially put on bed rest. They became second family to us while here in Montana.

Travis and Ryan had prepared two fabulous turkeys in the turkey fryer, giggling like school girls while injecting them with a concoction of mystery flavorings. Joanne hadn't been feeling well the last few months, so she and Rachel spent the day observing from the couch and nibbling on whatever food they could stomach. While Rachel tried so hard to stay positive and do everything she could to keep the babies intact for a few more weeks, being stuck on the couch was her prison. Watching everyone invade her kitchen, especially during special holiday meal preparation made her fidgety and a bit cranky. She is a fabulous cook who loves to plan, host, and spoil her guests with grand meals. I know it killed her to not be able to help. To make it worse, she was not able to eat more than a few bites because of the space the twins were taking up in her painfully, protruding abdomen. The previous two weeks her appetite had slowly been diminishing to multiple tiny snacks every few hours, and she was getting exceedingly uncomfortable.

We had been taking weekly trips to the doctor to monitor her cervical progression, including a trip on Monday, where it still appeared hopeful that she would be able to hold out delivery a few more weeks. We had been told by doctors in both Seattle and Montana that we should throw a big party if we made it past 32 weeks, a point in time where the lung development was stronger and the risk for many of the early gestational diseases are significantly decreased. Thanksgiving would be that party.

Ryan spent the whole weekend with us, enjoying good laughs and celebrating the milestone we had reached. Early Sunday morning, confident of Rachel's stable condition, he headed back on his nine-hour journey. He called that evening during dinner to let us know he arrived safely at home in Seattle and to say again how much fun he'd had. We both hated the separation, but knew it had a limited timeframe. Rachel and Travis had been away from each other at least as long while she was with us in Washington, and they weren't getting anything out of the deal. We could handle it a bit longer. Little did he know that the separation was about to end within hours.

Rachel knocked on the door of my room about 3 a.m. Monday morning. "I'm pretty sure that I'm in labor. The contractions started about midnight, and have gotten worse and more frequent."

Like an expectant father, I bounded out of bed in a stupor, searching frantically for clothes amongst my suitcases. I was acutely aware that her two children had been born very quickly, so I was relieved that they lived only half a mile from the hospital, especially since I couldn't put two thoughts together, let alone two socks.

Never wanting to take their hospitality for granted, I naively asked, "Do you want me to drive your car?" I've obviously never done the "pregnant lady run" to the hospital before.

"Yes, that would be best," she replied with a smirk. "I don't think I should be driving. Travis is upstairs in bed and is going to stay back with the kids until my parents come over to babysit." Miraculously, I was able to clear some cobwebs from my mind, and we left immediately.

Since she had already been two centimeters dilated at the last check-up, I knew we didn't have much further to go. When they checked her at the hospital she was now six centimeters. It is standard protocol to attempt to stop labor on babies this premature, but I suspected it was probably a futile attempt. Calling Ryan as soon as we arrived at the hospital, he was already prepared to come back, having never even unpacked his bags from the night before. An hour and half later they checked to see if the drugs had worked to stop dilation (which we knew it hadn't by Rachel's continued contractions). She was now eight and a half centimeters, and they prepared her for the operating room, where it is necessary to deliver twins.

Once more I called Ryan to give him an update. Assuming that she was delivering soon, he had already left. His parents had just left and were about an hour behind him. I think he resigned himself to the fact he would not see his children born (which I think was his hope to protect her modesty and not to mention his queasiness for anything surgical or bloody). Early in our discussions with Rachel and Travis about their wishes for the pregnancy and delivery, Rachel stated that she really wanted both of us to be as involved as possible, including with the birth. Selflessly, she wanted nothing to stand in our way of feeling like the rightful parents of our children. Ryan was insistent he would be fine not being at the birth, but I wanted him there, if only to support me.

It was still the plan for Rachel to try to deliver naturally, but she knew that a caesarian was possible if the second child became distressed or wouldn't turn properly. They had given her a spinal block and were in the process of inserting the epidural when Travis and I heard a loud pop and were spattered with liquid from 10 feet away. The doctor administering the epidural explained that sometimes the resistance in the vein causes the expulsion of the medication and that was what we'd just experienced. Not to be alarmed.

However, moments later, Rachel, who was sitting on the side of the bed, collapsed, and her eyes rolled to the back of her head. Travis, who just arrived minutes before and was in process of putting on his scrubs, was able catch her quickly and lie her down in the bed. The doctor grabbed the oxygen mask behind the bed and put it over her face without delay. The doctor again justified the situation saying that, on rare occurrences, the lidocaine gets into the blood stream and that giving her oxygen will remedy the problem. When she came to, she didn't remember passing out and fortunately within a few minutes she was largely restored to her previous laboring state, despite some lightheadedness. So much for the non-eventful, non-medical-intervention delivery that Rachel had hoped for.

We all walked into the surgical suite together, which by this time was alive with a well-organized troupe of nurses and staff, all running about with their respective tasks. Compared to Rachel's last delivery of her daughter quietly at home, this must have seemed like a three-ring circus. Rachel on the gurney, Travis at her head, myself at her feet, her OB doctor, a doctor and nurse for each of the children, the anesthesiologist, an ultrasound tech to guide the turning of Baby B (my son) and another doctor to do the turning, and at least three or four people whose task I couldn't exactly identify. Fifteen people in one small surgical suite. I just kept praying that the birth didn't turn into a caesarean section, which would have meant Rachel would be unconscious with gas because the epidural had failed. She wanted to be fully engaged and losing that opportunity would be heartbreaking for her.

Baby A, our girl, had been positioned head down from 4-5 months along and had never wavered in her desire to be first. Dr. Easterling had noted in one of his exams while we were still in Washington that he could literally poke her in the head, she was so ready. So, without much fanfare, after a half a dozen pushes, I watched our beautiful little girl emerge. Adeline Anina Reichman was born at 8:15 a.m., November 30th, 2009, weighing a full 4lbs, 12 oz., phenomenal for a baby just shy of 33 weeks. She screamed right away and continued to squirm vigorously while they were wiping her down, taking her measurements and assessing her condition. Adeline was a name that Ryan and I both loved, and it was the pair to the boy's name we had picked when I was pregnant with Aiden. Anina means "let my prayers be answered" in Aramaic, Jesus' native tongue. They definitely had been.

They handed her to me, and I just stared at her in awe and gratitude. A beautiful life created in His most perfect plan, and I got to call her mine. This moment had been five years in the making and it was difficult to wrap my arms around the enormity, and small, fragility of having a little baby (or two). This precious little girl looked up at me with squinted, puffy eyes—she too, trying to take in the shock of it all. I walked her into the Neonatal Intensive Care Unit (NICU) which would be home for the next four weeks. It was hard to let the nurses take her from me, but I was being urgently beckoned back to the operating room. This struggle to find the balance and time for both needy babies was now my new reality.

During my absence, the doctors had turned baby B from the outside and were struggling to get him to move his hand out of the way so that he could come head first. The doctors knew that they had one chance to get him out before a caesarean would be necessary and wanted me in there when they attempted the maneuver. If it failed, the shiny metal instruments were draped and prepared on an adjacent tray. In a superman move of her own, the OB doctor reached in and pushed his hand back, allowing the head to come into place. She shouted for Rachel to push now, and that's exactly what she did. Three pushes later, our son arrived into the world. Isaac Harrison Paul Reichman was born at 8:42 a.m., and weighed 4lbs, 5oz. He too, screamed right away and wiggled around in his slightly smaller frame, the skin hanging loosely round his arms and legs like a baby elephant; seven less ounces definitely made a difference.

Isaac was a name of great meaning to us due to its biblical reference. Isaac was the long hoped and prayed for son of elderly Abraham and Sarah. He represented to us, not a promise from God, as he did in the Bible, but a hope of things prayed for and a symbol of God's magnificent power to do the impossible. Harrison was a family name on both sides of Ryan's extended family, and Paul, well, having just lost my father, he needed a namesake. Definitely a mouthful, but so perfect for Ryan and me.

Although his Apgar score was very good, Isaac had some breathing issues when they were assessing him, and the oxygen mask next to him in the incubator didn't seem to be helping him in his struggle. Rachel had been given a steroid shot over a month ago to speed up lung development when they suspected the babies might come imminently, but the effects had diminished when they weren't born right away. The surfactant production (a natural chemical found in the lungs) needed to keep the lungs open did not yet meet the demand. His chest, with all his ribs protruding sharply, would compress down forcefully under great strain when he tried to breathe in. It was obvious that he needed more help than his sister. They whisked him off to the NICU to hook him up to a ventilator, a word that I had been frightened of from the start of our premature birth concerns. While they were performing the procedure to insert the tube, they shut down the whole NICU to all visitors, meaning I couldn't even see Adeline for the laborious hour and a half it took to complete the procedure.

With no access to the children, I took the opportunity to check on Rachel's condition. She was resting well, exhausted but in very good spirits in a postpartum room with Travis by her side. I assured her that both babies were doing fine, but that Isaac was getting some special care and telling her that the doctors had reiterated several times to me that a ventilator was very standard for preemies. This was not a sign of any long term issues. She had been so concerned for their health that the thought of them having issues because *she* couldn't keep them in utero pained her greatly. Ryan and I tried to comfort her countless times that, while we were so appreciative for all that she had done to keep them healthy and safe, in the end, God was in charge of the outcome.

Travis decided that everyone needed a good breakfast this morning and left to bring his starving wife back some good, non-hospital food. Excusing myself to let her get a shower and find some rest, I started the long string of calls to family and friends. Ryan had only made it to Moses Lake (about 190 miles) by the time Adeline was born, and Ritzville (about 235 miles) when Isaac was born, and still had many miles left to go when I called to tell him they were finally here. He was so excited to hear the descriptions of each of them, and I couldn't wait to have him here to share in the experience. It was God's providence that the roads were clear in all three mountain passes that the trip traversed. This is quite unusual during this time of the year, as the normal volume of snow and slick roads frequently preclude us from making the trip in the winter.

Next, I tried to call my Mom, but I only got her voicemail as she was busy driving back from San Diego, where she had completed some projects for her consulting business. Despite numerous attempts, I didn't actually reach her until 4:00 p.m. that day. Ryan's parents were driving to Montana, a few hours behind Ryan, when I contacted them.

The big surprise came when I called my Grandpa Howard, my paternal grandpa. Although Ryan and I had been out of touch since Rachel's bedrest started, I had heard from my mom at Thanksgiving that Amanda, his daughter from his marriage to Wendy (a younger woman he met after my grandmother died), was scheduled to be induced with her first child on Sunday, the day before.

When I reached him on his cell phone, he was in Texas waiting for the birth of his granddaughter, which had been postponed a day due to bed availability. So, Amanda was about to give birth in a matter of hours on the same day. He would become a grandfather to Piper and a great-grandfather to Adeline and Isaac on the same day. This was crazy, considering there had not been a birth in our family for over 25 years. He broke down crying in happiness. After a few moments of sniffling and failed attempts to keep talking, he handed the phone over to Wendy. The first and last time I had ever heard him cry was the day my dad had passed away.

His raw emotion was so filled with love and joy, it brought tears to my eyes. This day seemed to, at least in a small way, redeem some of the unfathomable pain he had endured watching both of his sons and his first wife slowly deteriorate and succumb to their ailing hearts, not to mention losing his first great grandson and knowing that his granddaughter might also beat him to the grave. Today was a day of celebration, and God had given it to him ten-fold.

Ryan finally arrived around 1:00 p.m., shaving nearly one and a half hours off a trip that normally takes nine hours. Good thing the traffic cops had taken Monday morning off after a long Thanksgiving weekend. By the time he arrived, we had been given access to the NICU again. Because Isaac was now hooked up to a ventilator and unable to be picked up, I had been holding Addie all morning when Ryan walked in. Rachel had gotten word that he had arrived and went to the NICU to meet him. She started crying when she saw us holding Addie together and told us that seeing us at that moment had made the last eight months' worth every bit of pain and discomfort. After Ryan held her, we passed her to Rachel. Watching her gently cradle Adeline, there was no jealousy that she might have a motherly attachment to her.

While she had deeply loved Addie and Isaac, and vowed to protect them as her own through the long, difficult pregnancy, there was no confusion that her real family was at home waiting for her. Undoubtedly, her relationship to the babies would always be special, and we have continued to foster that bond. Even now, the kids celebrate "Roo Day" (as in KangaROO), on her birthday, understanding that her "pouch" carried them. Generously, she had given all of herself for our joy and could share so intimately in it. However, she couldn't wait to be reunited with her own family and resume her normal life of wife and mother. She checked out of the hospital by 5 p.m. that evening, less than nine hours after she had delivered our twins.

We spent a good portion that first day staring at every part of their little bodies, from their fingers to their toes. Adeline's face was round and delicate with cute little lips and a tiny mouth, even then she exuded an air of joyfulness and spunk in her sweet grins and stretches. She had light hair and fair skin, which contrasted greatly from Isaac, who had dark hair and a more olive complexion. Both of them had enormous eyelashes, something the nurses commented on right away. We felt guilty giving Addie all the attention, but all I could do was gaze at Isaac and touch his delicate skin. We longed to hold him, but we were afraid we might hurt our fragile little son. Thankfully, even with an IV in his head, a breathing tube obscuring most of his tiny face, and a feeding tube snaked down his throat, he seemed to be sleeping comfortably. It was so frightening, but the staff kept reassuring us that the medical interventions were temporary, and he would gain lung strength quickly. He looked so tiny next to his "gigantic" sister. His skin hung loosely on his small bones, and his gaunt face emphasized his strong pointed chin, exactly the face staring at us in the ultrasound after my father died.

The nurses, from the beginning, got us actively involved in their care, from changing diapers to feeding and burping them, and introducing us to the three-hour cycle we would learn to embrace and depend on. By early evening the first day, Ryan's parents, Mike and Kathy had arrived, anxious to meet their grandchildren, cuddle and feed them, and breathe in their sweet scent. Although, the small NICU was already tight with the other babies and their families, the nurses graciously created a little nook for our family to be together, amongst the hustle and bustle of care providers.

16

We left the NICU that evening exhausted, mentally and emotionally. We had made previous arrangements with Rachel's parents to rent their "extra" house, which was across the street from Travis and Rachel. It was the most cozy, quaint two-bedroom home and was more than we could have hoped for. Knowing that we would be spending a lot of time at the hospital and needed a place to crash every night, this place was perfect and it was a lot more comfortable and affordable for our visiting family to stay in a home with a kitchen and amenities. Just as importantly, we could now give Rachel and Travis space to be a family again.

Although we spent little time there, it was a special place where we could unwind and ruminate about the rollercoaster of the kid's triumphs and setbacks. The living room was dimly lit with heavy curtains and big oversized, soft couches, which was a welcome escape from the snowy Montana winter that descended two days after the children were born. The soft, pillow-topped bed in a main floor bedroom beckoned our weary, swimming heads every night. Leaving by 7:00 a.m. every day to make the first morning feeding and returning after the evening feeding at 9:00 p.m., it was wonderful to have such relaxing accommodations. Every morning and evening I stopped over at Travis and Rachels' to pick up breast milk that she had pumped. She had decided to pump to help her body return to normalcy quicker and to assist the babies in their early development, and continued to pump for the entire month the babies were in the hospital. Her home was always open, with an invitation for a delicious, warm meal any time we tired of hospital cafeteria food. Her love for us never ended.

Furthermore, the hospital could not have been more accommodating during our long days in the NICU. They gave us a room to use across from the NICU, which wasn't just a place to put our belongings, but had a bed, chair, and TV for the time between feedings when we needed a rest. They allowed us to order food from the cafeteria, which they considered part of the care for the little ones because they weren't eating their "adult" share. This cut down on the expense of eating out and it was so difficult to leave the hospital for food and return on time for their next feeding. They ate every three hours, and frequently it would take an hour and a half to feed both kids. The hospital encouraged us to participate in every aspect of their care, as much as the babies' conditions allowed. They also knew we needed the family time to bond and acclimate to our new roles.

By midnight of the first day, Isaac had pulled his ventilation tube out and it never needed to be put back in. The day after they were born we started kangaroo care since both of them could now be held. This is where a baby is placed, with only a diaper on, inside your clothes and onto your bare chest (which was challenging with all of the leads, IV's, oxygen and feeding tubes). The skin-to-skin contact was so calming for both us and them that we watched the slowing of their heart rates and steadying of their breathing on the monitors. We did this two to three times a day after feedings, quietly talking to them and allowing them to fall asleep on our chests. Isaac reacted right away to dad's voice and would even turn to face him so he could hear it clearer. It was so relaxing that many times I found myself dozing as well.

As is very common for preemies, they were so young that they hadn't yet learned to suck so we began gavage feedings (breastmilk or formula fed through a nose tube). They each had a nose tube inserted that brought the food directly to their stomachs. Before each new feeding, the nurses would check their tummies to make sure all the food had been digested. If some food remained, that amount would be deducted from the next feeding to protect from overfeeding and spitting up. They both received additional nutrition through an IV solution in order to make up what they weren't digesting on their own. We gave the babies a pacifier during the feedings as a way of simulating the feeding process and so they would associate sucking with their tummies being filled.

The NICU had a very strict schedule that the nurses kept them on, and the twins adjusted well to it. Slowly, they began to put on weight. We were fortunate to both be there for all of the major milestones, first bath, first bowel movement (yes disgusting, but not when this is an important sign of digestive health), first temper tantrum, first time dressed in more than a diaper, responding to our voices, etc. Thankfully, Ryan's parents were also there to enjoy the first days with the children. My mom and sister took the train out the following weekend, and both Travis' and Rachel's moms came for a visit or two during the first few weeks. We were surrounded by immediate and extended family, and the hospital once again accommodated our odd situation and had let all four sets of grandparents into the NICU.

We had our first big setback at five days old when Isaac was diagnosed with RSV (Respiratory Syncytial Virus), a virus he caught in the nursery. While many adults get the virus without noticing anything but cold-like symptoms; in infants, especially preemies, it can be very dangerous to an already compromised immune and respiratory system. The virus is contagious so they had to isolate him with another infant in separate room away from the NICU. This required us to wear fresh scrubs and masks every time we went in for a feeding. It was painful to have the babies in different rooms and caused a lot of extra running around.

Emotionally we were spent; watching the illness steal away Isaac's lung improvements and vigilantly hoping that symptoms would not appear in Addie. Unfortunately, when Addie was diagnosed eight days later and moved to isolation, they suspected she was probably exposed days ago and was already at the peak of her infection. Both babies were now in the same room and we no longer had to move from room to room, ceremoniously dressing and disrobing. Thankfully, besides being extra tired and having a little pneumonia show up on the x-rays, they remained miraculously unscathed.

Isaac's diagnosis was ill-timed, as it was identified only a days before Ryan had to return to Tacoma. Ryan could only stay in Montana for their first couple weeks and then needed to return for a week to keep his office functioning back in Tacoma. During the time Ryan was away, my mom stayed with me and helped with feedings, diaper changes and baths. I needed the company during the long days at the hospital. It is a pretty lonely place, no matter how much activity there is constantly. Although the kids were doing really well, there were still scary moments, such as a breathing episode or momentary heart rate drop when it was good to have someone to provide encouragement.

I wasn't the only one who needed encouragement though. Rachel's mom, Joanne, who had still been feeling ill had finally agreed to be checked out by a doctor, and after running some tests, they determined that she would need to have surgery to remove her gallbladder. During the surgery, they made a horrible discovery. She had advanced gallbladder cancer that had spread extensively. The surgeon ended up rerouting her digestive system as a stopgap, and closed her abdomen without being able to take the root of the problem away. Her prognosis was very poor, and everyone knew it. She remained in the hospital for several weeks and didn't get discharged until a few days after the babies. Internet searches on the survival rates of gallbladder cancer patients did not provide much hope. With treatment, they were advised that she had not more than a year to live. A time of great joy for Rachel quickly became one of tremendous sadness.

Word had quickly gotten out in our small little town of the great blessing that had been provided by Rachel and Travis. We had several requests for interviews, print and radio, to share our story. On Christmas morning, our story made the front pages of both the Kalispell and Great Falls newspapers, and was featured on the local station of NPR. The media attention was fun and a good distraction from the intensity of NICU. Strangers approached us on the street inquiring about our miracle twins, but the sorrow of Joanne's illness put a damper on our excitement. In the nine years I've known Rachel, her parents had become good friends, full of support and kindness. After just losing my dad, I understood the pain of seeing a parent waste away and be gone forever.

After nearly three weeks, all the babies that had originally been diagnosed with RSV had returned to the main NICU, abandoning the makeshift isolation room that had housed them. Addie and Isaac were given a small room together, so when Ryan returned for the week of Christmas and New Year's, we had a private space with our family. It felt as close to home as a hospital could possibly be. They had nice soft lamps and rocking chairs, and by Christmas, we had both babies out of the isolettes and into open-air bassinettes that allowed us easy access to them. We even grabbed a few pictures of them both in the same bassinette, until we realized that Addie was trying to nurse on Isaac's ear.

We started our first family tradition by reading "The Night before Christmas" on Christmas Eve together, which had been my family's custom growing up. Getting to dress them in cute Christmas sleepers and hats, which had been donated to the NICU by previous patients' families, was so fun after weeks of only diapers. I had been so anxious to put on the preemie clothes I bought for them when I suspected they would arrive early, but now at three weeks old, they no longer fit them.

The first morning that we missed the 8:00 a.m. feeding was Christmas, which was spent at Travis and Rachels' home with her family. Her mom, Joanne, was notably absent. It was a somber occasion with a few smiles during the present exchange. Ironically, when we picked names at Thanksgiving for our Christmas exchange, I received Rachel's name, and she received mine, though neither of us disclosed our secret recipient.

Ryan and I were able to give back to Rachel just a little of the happiness that she had given us by providing some funds to be used on a trip; a trip that would be their last family vacation with their mother. It was Joanne's dream to return to the Florida coast where she had many great memories growing up. Although I had already received the most astonishing gift possible – two beautiful children, Rachel made for me a DVD with a picture slideshow of Addie and Isaacs' pre-birth lives set to Beatles music; pictures of the embryos prior to transfer, ultrasounds, shots of her belly every month, and culminating in a picture of the four of us together holding the children. What a treasure it is to watch, but always with a box of tissues!

Preparing to take the children home from the hospital, the time between Christmas and New Year's flew by. We had some painfully sore diaper rashes, with Addie going through four different formula types before we found one that didn't make her delicate little bottom bleed. Their acid reflux remained a problem, but nothing serious to keep them from going home. They both passed their car seat tests in which the nurses strap them in their chairs in the NICU for a few hours and monitor their breathing, heart rate, and temperature to make sure they could maintain their vitals for the long car ride home.

The final test for us, as parents, was what the hospital calls "rooming in" which is planned for two nights before discharge. The kids leave the close supervision of the NICU and spend the night with us in our room across the hall. The nurses check on us periodically and take vitals, but we are responsible for all feedings, diaper changes, and baths. They had prepared us well during the four weeks in the hospital, and we had done all of these tasks before, but we always had someone watching over our shoulder, and preemies with the potential for critical medical episodes can be rather intimidating. The "rooming in" provided us an opportunity to prove to ourselves that we could take care of these two little ones, despite the nerves of first-time parents.

In spite of an episode of hand-to-hand combat with projectile feces during Adeline's diaper change, it went relatively well. Needless to say, we were exhausted by morning. There was no sleep in a small hospital room with two kids, two adults, and one twin bed (which was pretty much useless when there is no quiet to be had). We were confident that things would go much better in our own home with separate sleeping and living areas, if we could get a sleeping and eating schedule established and get used to taking shifts.

Their final night in the NICU, the nurses sent us home early and told us to get as much sleep as possible in advance of our first night at home with the kids. Giddy from the anticipation and wanting to prepare our (temporary) house for their arrival, I foolishly neglected to follow their advice. Lying awake most of the night thinking about all the stuff I needed to do and all the ways I could screw up, I managed to work myself up. I've been waiting for the day that my home would be filled with a family for over four years, or perhaps since I was a little girl dressing up and feeding my dollies.

New Year's Eve was discharge day. Addie was now 6lbs 8oz, and Isaac was 5lbs, 13oz. As we were driving away from the hospital, I looked in the rear view mirror at the two bundles curled up in the back seat. Now I was really scared! What have we gotten ourselves into? This was really happening, no going back now. I sent a quick popcorn prayer up to God: "Please Lord, be present in my fumbling and inadequacies. I'm positive I will screw this up. Thank you in advance for your grace in each day."

With two new babies in the car we couldn't go much slower on the snowy, icy roads, our wheels crunching unhurriedly through the parking lot, fingers vice-gripped on the steering wheel. Your perspective changes when you are responsible for more than just yourself and you can't afford to be fearless or cavalier.

We drove to our temporary home and gingerly carried the babies inside. During the remaining part of the day they slept well and there were no spit-ups with their feedings, and I thought for a brief moment, what was I so worried about? Confidently, we wrapped them up tightly in matching Christmas blankets from Joanne and waddled through the slow and ice over to

Travis and Rachels' house for a small New Year's Eve get together.

It was wonderful being able to pass them around and share them with the many friends who had been helping Rachel and Travis during her challenging pregnancy. Rachel's kids were able to hold them for the first time, having seen the twins only once, when the nurses pushed Addie and Isaacs' incubators against the observation window. Jasper and Grace felt so attached to the "cousins" that were in mom's tummy, I couldn't wait to see them grow to be great friends like Travis and Ryan.

We headed home early from the party, keenly aware that we might have a long night ahead of us. The nurses had warned us that we shouldn't expect them to sleep in a dark, quiet room, the opposite of what they were used to in the NICU. Did we listen to them? No, of course not. We put both pack n' plays in our bedroom with us, climbed into bed, and shut off the light. Not surprisingly, this arrangement back-fired and we moved to plan B, trying the one parent, one child approach. This also didn't work because then we both didn't sleep. In the end, both kids ended up in their bouncy chairs, parked in front of a blaring television in the living room, with one parent standing guard. This allowed the other one to sleep in the bedroom for a few hours before trading places. Yep, our kids, despite all my aspirations, were introduced to TV on their first day home.

New Year's afternoon, Ryan's parents arrived to be our caravan home to Washington. Our plan was to leave early the next morning and be home for Ryan to start work on Monday. Again, we trucked across the road and spent our final evening with Travis and Rachel, but this time Joanne was there to see us off and hold our kids one more time. Her face was completely drained of energy and color, and her vibrant smile was muted.

But even in her illness, her presence made the room full of life; the completeness of a family.

The final night in Montana was as restless as the night before, but at least this time there were four people to rotate through baby duty. However, Kathy took most of the burden so the two main drivers, Michael and Ryan, were as refreshed as possible for the drive. In the morning, we packed and cleaned up the house, and marched across the street to say our final goodbyes.

The hugs were endless and filled with more vigor than normal, and it was impossible to contain the tears; a usually stoic Rachel was more emotional than I had ever seen her. Pulling away in the car, I kept thinking about how Rachel must be feeling. The euphoria of accomplishing the generous and rewarding task of carrying our children stood in stark contrast to the agony of refocusing her energy on the painful road ahead for her precious ailing mother. The distraction of her daily companions was gone, and they were taking their treasures home with them. Before we even left, I longed to go back to Montana soon, but I knew it was unrealistic with two little ones, Ryan's work demands, and countless new responsibilities.

After spending nearly every day together for the last three months, Ryan, Travis, Rachel, and I all recognized that each of our families needed to resume the "normal" lives that we had left to start this adventure, yet we also realized that life would look dramatically different. Ryan and I now had doubled our family and our responsibilities, and they were facing the gravity of Joanne's health journey with a potentially devastating conclusion. We would miss our daily time together and having each other for emotional support or just a good laugh. The miles that separated us were great, and we knew that we wouldn't see each other often. However, there was no question that our newly created bonds were special and rare, and would forge us together forever.

On the drive home, Ryan and I had decided to split up the kids between the two cars, so there was someone who could attend to them in the back seat. They were still a bit unpredictable with their breathing so I wanted to keep a close eye on them, especially Isaac, who would ride with me. Having left in the dark of morning, I was very tense until daylight because I couldn't see Isaac's chest moving in the blackness. Every minute or so, I would put my hand under his nose until I felt his gentle breath across my knuckles. Yes, I am an overly-worried mother. My trust that God will see them safely through has continued to grow, but needs constant renewal through prayer and devotion.

The nine-hour trip became closer to 11 hours because of the frequent stops for feeding and changing, which is not bad considering we had given ourselves two days to get home and managed to get home in one. My mom and Chaya were waiting at our house for us to arrive with a banner and balloons framing the front door. It was a wonderful homecoming and soothing to be back in my own home and bed for the first time in over two months. I felt like I had finally started the life that I had envisioned three and a half years ago when we moved into this house. In my mind, we had finally arrived, whatever that meant. As many new parents will attest, bringing your children home is just the launching point of a wildly entertaining, rollercoaster ride. Especially with twins, Ryan and I had not arrived; we had just left the station.

God had orchestrated an amazing miracle in our life. Not just the birth of long-awaited and prayed for children, but the abundant growth of a friendship that would forever be cemented by extraordinary circumstances. His sovereignty defies comprehension, but regardless of its mystery; it is undeniable. Within His beautiful creation, there exists a tremendously fragile cycle of life, precisely ordered and made complete by God's gracious gift of eternal life.

God, knowing how we are quick to forget His everlasting love for us, planted an ebenezer (or object of remembrance) in our lives many years beforehand in the form of the song, "Lightning Crashes," by Live. While to some, it might seem an odd, rather unromantic song, it held great meaning for us, and we used it for our first wedding dance together. More than a decade later, and we can now personally identify with many of the life experiences touched on in the song. Pain and joy are a natural part of this broken world, but everything that happens is meaningful and relevant to His purposes. God's hand in our lives cannot be minimized. God has used the song to help us grasp the significance and the reality of life, death, and rebirth in His greater plan. In my interpretation, the song even acknowledges the divine Spirit that God puts within each of His people, binding them to their Creator.

17

Someone told me while Rachel was pregnant, that it was a good thing that we had twins first because we wouldn't know how much easier one child at a time is. In short, you don't know how difficult you have it. Truthfully, while the first six months of newborn twins was rough, the help of our families was second to none. Dr. Rho had prepped the whole family by telling them that sleep deprivation would not be good on my heart so they needed to help eliminate the awful fate that accompanies new babies. Starting the first night we were home from Montana, our solution was to create a schedule where someone was assigned a shift of "baby duty" around 9:00 p.m. that lasted until 6:00 a.m.

I've had friends with young children gasp in jealously when I explained that at least 5-6 nights a week a family member would report to baby duty, allowing me to sleep 7-8 hours a night in preparation to care for them the remaining portion of the day. Additionally, everyone understood that Ryan, his clients, and the structural integrity of the buildings he designed would all benefit greatly from a decent night's sleep, so he was also granted reprieve on most weekday nights.

On Sunday nights, or any night where help wasn't available, Ryan would pull the 8 p.m.-2 a.m. shift, and I would handle the rest of the early morning and day. Every so often, while the assigned family member was pulling night duty, there was what we called the "two-alarm fire," where both babies would start crying simultaneously. The naturally occurring "mom ear," bestowed upon moms on the day of their first child's birth could laser focus in on the commotion even a floor away, listening to hear if it was going to resolve quickly or if my assistance was needed. Most of the time, a quick trip downstairs to triage the situation was all that was necessary. Adeline and Isaac were great sleepers and not prone to uncontrollable bouts of crying, despite a little reflux from prematurity and a nasty, recurrent diaper rash. When they did cry, they normally had a diagnosable reason and were easily satiated. Knowing what some of my friends have endured with colicky babies, having two very mild-mannered, happy kids was a true gift from God.

I fully realize how spoiled we were to receive this kind of help, and I couldn't be more grateful. Everyone in our family participated; even Ryan's dad, Michael, pulled weekly duty. He was impressive, especially knowing that while he loves children and is a great playmate, the unreciprocated care of a newborn was not naturally comfortable for him. What a trooper! Not only were we incredibly blessed to have to happy, healthy babies, but all of our immediate family was close by to enjoy them.

The first six months flew by and there was great joy and activity in our house. We lived quite communally, and there was rarely a time that it was just the four of us. When we did have those moments of relative quiet, when it was just Ryan and I holding our two beautiful children, we tried to stop and savor the precious minutes. Countless days were lost in the cold, rainy winter mornings, lying on the couch in front of a roaring fire with two little ones gently snoozing on my chest, gentle music in the background. It was mesmerizing watching their tiny bodies rise and fall with each breath, their big diaper butts rising skyward from their curled up bodies. Their sweet smell intoxicating, and their warm little bodies brought such peace to our hectic days.

Having multiples can sometimes feel like an assembly line for feeding, burping, playtime, and baths, but Ryan and I tried to not let it become robotic, enjoying the coos and smiles we would endlessly attempt to extract. With Adeline and Isaac, it was quite easy to garner the response we craved; as they were both happy and carefree little creatures. Addie, to this day, knows no strangers and smiles freely at anyone willing to pay a lick of attention to her (still working on teaching stranger caution). Even Isaac, who tends to be more reserved and cautious, was easy to break into a giggle.

They were growing so fast, trying to capture each smiley, drooly gurgle in my memory seemed impossible, and consequently, we took an embarrassing amount of pictures and videos. Thankfully, we rarely had difficulty telling them apart, not only did they not look alike, but to my initial dismay, they were frequently dressed in recognizably gender-specific clothes from the pink and blue shower presents. Being a female in a male-dominated profession and knowing the pressure to be defined by gender roles, I didn't want to introduce any stereotyping in attire and toys. Having a pretty pink princess was a frightful thought to me.

Keeping a very precise log of all the developmental milestones (new teeth, rolling over, giggling, etc.), we also tracked each medication administered, and every feeding and bowel movement. Some people would call it anal retentive; we called it "keeping sane." During the lengthy, tiring days, I didn't want to have to think about who had done what and when. This was especially helpful when there was a "shift" change, which in our fatigue, allowed for minimal download to take place; all of the previous day's activities were right at your fingertips.

Schedule and consistency are essential when it comes to multiples, especially when they are young. Feeding was every four hours at first, taking 45 minutes to an hour per child. If you didn't feed them at the same time or right after one another, there would not be time after they played to get anything else done (like feeding yourself). Their naps were the only break we had from constant activity, and if their nap times became staggered, life got a bit off kilter.

Caught up in the craziness and enchantment of parenting two beautiful newborns, the first six months ran together like a watercolor in the rain. Through a fog of baby-tending, one night stood out with great lucidity and contrast; wholly removed from my current activity, and changing my present reality. God's providence ruled supreme as always, but this time, He provided a warning of impending events so that we could prepare, at least minimally. The life jacket is best fastened when the seas get rough, not after you've already fallen overboard.

Early February, only a month after we had returned from Montana with the children, and five months after my father had passed away, I had a dream. I was sitting at the dining room table of the house I shared with my parents before leaving for college. Across the small, round table was my father, in flesh and bone.

Since his death, I had never dreamt about him, either in a past or present form. This saddened me because I missed him greatly and was deeply afraid of having my memories of him slowly fade away. Dreams of him from the past would have kept him alive in my mind, but I couldn't even will my mind to produce them. Having an unshakeable faith in the afterlife and knowing that God created a heaven for followers of Christ like my father, I fully admit there is much I do not understand. However, my belief is that there is a realm where the past, present, and future collide, where heaven and earth operate in the same plane. How? No idea, but nothing is impossible for the creator of the universe. So when my sister told me that he came to her in a dream, just days after his death, to comfort her and give her peace, I did not question that this was truly my dad, not some figment of her subconscious that desired to keep him alive. Knowing her intense bond with him, and his special role as her spiritual mentor, it seemed like a natural thing for him to do.

My dream, I understood immediately, was not intended for comfort, but for information. Even before he spoke, I knew he was not a passive character or apparition that would fade into a vapor; he wanted a fully interactive conversation.

When he finally spoke, it was abrupt, but with a sad, gentleness in his eyes, "You don't have much longer to live." No hello, no 'God and I were talking and...', no smoothing words of preemptive explanation.

Left speechless for a moment, I then started rationalizing and arguing with him. "You have to be wrong," I whined. "I have responsibilities now, like never before; two children that are counting on me to see them through to adulthood and a wonderful husband who I couldn't leave with the entire burden." As much as Ryan already shouldered for me, we were still a team, and he needed me.

"How could this be?" I demanded, beginning to get angry, first with him, and then with God. "The unfairness of all I had been through to have these amazing children, only to be taken hastily away from them, before they even knew me." In retrospect, the harsh reality was that God had gifted Adeline and Isaac to me, but they were still His children ultimately, and He had every right to take me out of the scene whenever He chose.

He continued to stay quiet, again looking at me with his sorrowful eyes and crinkled, distressed forehead that manifested when his empathy for someone overwhelmed him. After I calmed a bit, cautiously, yet doggedly I started asking questions.

"Will it be my heart?" I inquired, something I had assumed all of my adult life.

"No," he told me, "your heart is not involved. A tube will burst inside your body, and it will be a prolonged and painful death." My hope for a quick, nasty, fatal heart rhythm was dashed.

"When will this happen?" I requested.

"I don't know exactly, but soon," he whispered slowly, his voice cracking with affection.

I didn't ask him why God would allow this to happen with the beautiful new blessings of children still freshly imparted. It was if I knew that he didn't have the answer for me. After Aiden's death and the grieving journey God joined me on, I inherently understood that I could never fully comprehend His purposes. Trusting in His goodness and grace-filled sovereignty was my only option, regardless of the pain that my humanness induced. But why had God sent my father to relay such horrible news, not some stern angel or enigmatic parable. I can't be sure, but in our brief dialogue, I believed him the second I heard. Maybe that was why, because God knew I would take my father's implicit compassion and words solemnly.

And then it was over, as abruptly as it had begun. I woke up with a start, sitting straight up in bed and glancing around the room breathlessly. Through the darkness, everything appeared eerily normal and calm. The logical part of my brain got right to work, feverishly trying to dismiss what just occurred. I stood up gingerly and shuffled down the hall to the bathroom. Resting my hand on the cold porcelain to steady myself, with the other hand, I reached for the bathroom cup and threw some cold water on my face, attempting to shock myself back to my previous oblivion. Returning to bed, I laid awake, wide-eyed, staring at the ceiling in disbelief. It was only midnight, so I had been asleep only a couple of hours at this point. Looking at the clock for the last time around 4:00 a.m., I fell asleep shortly after that. Immediately, I was in the dining room with my father and repeating the same dramatic conversation as before, almost like a tape recorder had clicked on again.

This time when I woke up, I decided to wake Ryan too, which isn't an easy task or something I like to do without valid reason. He could tell by my tone that I was in a panic, so he swiftly changed his initial reaction of annoyance. Sharing my dream with him, I asked him if he thought there might be any truth in it. He wasn't sure, but he didn't brush it off as nonsense, especially knowing about the premonition I had of my father's death and our family history of dreams coming true.

Without talking to anyone else, we spent the next day or so analyzing what it meant, praying, studying His word, and pleading for discernment from God. I even spent time on the internet trying to deduce what "tube" could burst causing death; the only thing I could come up with was an aneurism of some kind. But in our bewilderment and searching, neither of us wanted to make a big deal out of something that could be purely a fear-fueled delusion. But we also didn't want to ignore the seriousness of a potentially dire warning.

"Do not put out the Spirit's fire; do not treat prophecies with contempt. Test everything. Hold on to the good. Avoid every kind of evil."
1 Thessalonians 5:19-22

The biggest question was whether the dream was true. If the answer was no, issue over, and I'd try like mad to forget the horrible nightmare. If it was true, what was the point of the forewarning? Did it necessitate action on our behalf? More importantly, could His plans be changed?

Although neither of us received clear direction, we were in no place to ignore the message. We felt that the forewarning might have been an opportunity to get our stuff together and make sure anything unsaid was resolved. At the same time, I didn't want to tell everyone for fear that I would worry people unnecessarily, and I never wanted to indulge in drama. Yet as the week drew on, it was obvious to everyone close to me that something was weighing heavily on me. Not wanting to be evasive to those who asked, Ryan and I decided it would be best to talk to each family member, making sure they knew how much I loved them. If they thought my emotional outpouring was odd, only then would I share a little of the dream and explain that, though I knew it could be incorrect, I didn't want to take a chance. Finally, I decided to write letters to Ryan and each of the kids expressing my overwhelming love for them, describing their most special attributes and relating my hopes for their futures. The letters remain sealed to this day.

Of all my family members, I was most afraid to talk to my mom, as she was still visibly tormented by my dad's passing and had expressed to me on multiple occasions that she was deeply fearful of my premature demise. The thought of losing her eldest daughter after she had lost her husband, father, grandchild, and brother in a matter of three short years might be too much for her to bear. After much deliberation and several sleepless nights, in the end, I resolved to share the heaviness of my heart with her; my love for her superseded my desire to stay quiet. I chose my timing carefully and purposefully took the babies to her house for a sleepover without Ryan. When it was finally quiet for the night I broached the issue warily.

"Mom, I'm not sure what it means," stopping to catch my breath, I reluctantly continued, "but I wanted you to know that I had a dream that dad told me I was going to die soon. It could be total hogwash, but either way, I wanted to tell you how much I love you and appreciate all you've done for me. Hopefully, this whole incident is nonsense and something to joke about years down the line." Her relaxed face had transformed from anticipating a tender mother daughter moment to a dumbfounded, searching stare.

She remained silent for a moment, but then spoke in a calm and subdued voice. "No, I think we need to take this seriously and start praying right away and ask God to reconsider His plan." My mom has always had an intimate and vivid prayer life with God. Her faith is so strong that she can rest, trusting His goodness and nurturing, confident that He is listening and will answer her with clarity.

I had already been praying quite a bit, begging for more time and cataloguing the responsibilities that demanded my presence. Yet I was afraid to be so bold with Him, lacking confidence that God would change an event He had already predestined. She firmly believed He could be persuaded through fervent prayer and intercession. Meanwhile, I had effectively chosen to surrender my will to Him, simultaneously praising Him for what he had already provided, and trying desperately not to be ungrateful by wanting more. Hindsight, I think there is room for both approaches; ask for Him to reconsider, but be content if God answers, "no." I'm not saying content is easy, FAR from it. Only through persistent prayer do we find the peace to accept the reality of this broken world, focusing instead on the beauty of an eternity with God.

The next morning, my mom told me that a scripture verse was given to her by God during the night. The scripture was Isaiah 38, where King Hezekiah was told by the prophet Isaiah that he would soon die of his current sickness and he was to get his house in order. King Hezekiah wept and pleaded with God to spare him so he could continue serving Him. His cries were heard by God.

"In those days Hezekiah became ill and was at the point of death. The prophet Isaiah, son of Amoz, went to him and said, "This is what the Lord says: 'Put your house in order, because you are going to die; you will not recover'."
"Hezekiah turned his face to the wall and prayed to the Lord, "Remember, O Lord, how I have walked before you faithfully and with wholehearted devotion and have done what is good in your eyes." And Hezekiah wept bitterly.
Then the word of the Lord came to Isaiah: "Go and tell Hezekiah, 'This is what the Lord, the God of your father David, says: I have heard your prayer and seen your tears; I will add fifteen years to your life. And I will deliver you and this city from the hand of the king of Assyria. I will defend this City'."
Isaiah 38:1-6

God does indeed listen to our prayers and can "change" his original plan. More philosophically, it could be asserted that God knew the prayers that Hezekiah would say upon the news of his impending death, and that an extended life was the final predestined outcome; all the glory given to our merciful God.

My mom believed with her soul that prayers were needed to solidify the final outcome that God desired to provide, the continuation of my life. I found out only later the magnitude of the prayer chain; starting with personal calls to friends who put me on a prayer chain at their respective churches, and individuals from those first churches who send out messages to their friends. Unbeknownst to me, the prayer chain had picked up momentum and hundreds of people, most of whom I had never met, pleaded with God for my life. Unlike hospital patients lying in their deathbeds, these were prayers to ward off an event that still had not occurred, and may never. I felt a bit foolish, with a "Chicken Little" complex, but this intense prayer crusade was indispensable in my mom's eyes. However, as the months unfolded, the reality of the dream came into full clarity, and the campaign my mom undertook seemed less and less frivolous.

18

One night in early March, only a month after my dream, I was awakened by excruciating pain radiating throughout my entire body. I couldn't actually pinpoint the source of the pain; it seemed to be from everywhere. My chest hurt, but not in the way that would indicate my heart. My back hurt, and I couldn't catch my breath. I flipped from side to side, and then tried lying on my back, but could not find a position that eliminated or even reduced my pain. I woke Ryan up because I didn't know what to do. He suggested I turn on the television and try to see if it would pass, distracting me with the mindless shows on at 2:00 a.m.

When I had heart episodes in the middle of the night, Ryan was always quick to respond, knowing the urgency of the situation. This time my condition was much more perplexing and non-descript, and he wasn't sure of the duration or severity, so he assumed it would abate on its own and went back to sleep. However, after about a half hour, I couldn't stand it anymore and was unsure when relief would come. I woke him up again to tell him that I wanted to go to the emergency room. He resisted at first, but when I started pulling on my pants, he realized he didn't have much of a choice and got dressed too.

We went downstairs about 3:00 a.m., and since it was a Saturday night, my mom was on duty with the kids. Seeing me cringing in pain, she knew we were heading to the hospital, but we couldn't tell her exactly why. She wished us well and reassured us that she would stay until we returned from the hospital. Since this wasn't a heart issue, we took a chance at one of our local Tacoma hospitals. Although they were busy handling a couple of belligerent drunks in the lobby, the triage staff brought me back to a room fairly quickly; my heart condition always puts me in the front of the line. Even though I felt fairly confident that my heart was not the culprit of my current pain, my medical history cast a shadow of doubt in their minds, and for liability sake, they couldn't take a chance of having me wait in lobby.

Unfortunately, as soon as they officially assessed through x-ray and EKG that I wasn't in cardiac distress, I got shoved to the back of the priority list. I must have looked like just another patient complaining of unverifiable pain, attempting to get some free pain meds. Even when I told them I was a nine on the pain chart (out of ten), they looked at me in disbelief. Finally, after what seemed like an eternity, they relented and gave me something to ease the pain. When they asked again where I was on the pain chart about half an hour later, I was about a four, still uncomfortable, but a lot saner.

Since I was now comfortable, they informed me that I was being discharged. They could do nothing more for me, including investigating the source of the problem. I went to my general practitioner to follow up, and they started treating me with acid reducers, claiming I had experienced a bad reflux event. However, they ran no further tests. For months I took the medication and had no further flare ups. Until one Friday night after I had some Chinese food.

I returned to the ER in late May, this time to the other local hospital. There was no way I was going back to the original hospital (come to find out later, they share the same ER doctor staff, so I guess the joke was on me). Complaining of exactly the same symptoms as before, but this time the pain was associated with nausea. I ended up running past the security check station, hand over my mouth, so I could throw up in the lobby restroom.

This time they admitted me for observation and prepped me for a colonoscopy planned for two days later. The test showed that I had some bowel irritation, which the doctors admitted could have been the cause of my problem or the result of a different problem; unhelpful, a waste of time and money, and no closer to a solution. After they got the ambiguous results, they pushed forward and scheduled me for another test, one that could determine if my gallbladder was functioning correctly.

In this test, I laid on my back while they did a CT scan of my abdomen. Drinking a fluid that would act as a dye as it moved through my digestive system, they were hoping to see how fast or slow it moved through my gallbladder. In the darkness of the room, lying on a cold, metal table with a giant x-ray-like machine slowly and repeatedly passing over my belly, the test went on and on. I could tell the technician was getting impatient, as well as a little worried about how long it was taking for the dye to appear. It never did. Finally, the doctor in the adjacent room, whose job it was to read the test, called me in to discuss the results. He told me that my gallbladder was completely obstructed, either by a gall stone or something else and that I should see my general practitioner as soon as possible. My GP informed me that a gallbladder removal was recommended and there really wasn't any other reliable option. It needed to be done right away before I had another, more serious attack.

I was really frustrated when I found out officially the source of my problem. My various medical teams had been speculating that this was probably my issue, but they wanted to rule everything else out before evaluating the gallbladder. Two months had been wasted, and I was scheduled to fly to Michigan the following week for a second memorial service for my father.

Raised in Michigan, where most of his extended family still lives, the additional service allowed them, including my grandfather and his family, to formally say their goodbyes. It was a trip that I couldn't fathom missing and had been planned months before I had my first gallbladder attack. As there were a handful of family members also flying in to attend the service, I wasn't in a position to request the service be rescheduled.

Additionally irritating was when I found out from my GP that the old test for gallbladder response, before the invention of the fancy gadget they used to diagnose me, was to send the patient home to eat a highly greasy meal like Chinese takeout (yes, she actually said Chinese) and see if there was a negative reaction. If that was the old standby test, why didn't the second ER hospital trip trigger an investigation for a potential gallbladder issue? Regardless, it was inevitable that surgery would be necessary; the question was whether I could stay healthy long enough for our important family trip.

We scheduled the surgery for the Tuesday, two days after we returned. I would have to be on my best behavior the entire trip and not eat anything that could trigger an attack, no fat or grease of any kind. If you've ever tried having a highly specialized diet while eating out for every meal, it is painful! Fortunately, the fear of repeating one of those nasty gallbladder attacks far exceeded my cravings for the cheeseburger at some roadside cafe.

Promising to be quite an adventure, this was also to be the first plane trip Ryan and I took with our now six-month-old twins in tow. Thankfully, my mom and sister would be accompanying us, and we had a bunch of extra hands on deck. We flew straight from Seattle to Detroit (relatively peacefully, as both kids slept most of the way), where we picked up a rental car and drove four hours north to Marlette, MI, my father's birth place and family homestead. My grandfather, his wife Wendy, and their son Hunter met us at the local, family-run motel, and we spent a relaxing evening together before the service the next morning.

This was the first time my grandfather was able to meet Adeline and Isaac, his first great grandchildren. As we sat in the booth of the restaurant having dinner, I handed my slobbering six-month-old son over the table to my grandfather, his teething biscuit hanging precariously out of his mouth. My heart was full, watching my usually stoic grandfather tear up as he carefully examined his new great grandbaby, who undoubtedly, looked remarkably like his own son, Paul. Given his age and recent inability to travel lately due to back issues, I wasn't sure this day would come, and I was extremely grateful. At the same time, a brief melancholy washed over me, imagining the demonstrative delight my father would have had their first meeting; my father's big heart forever worn on his sleeve.

Although my father was cremated, he was going to have a bronze grave marker set next to his twin brother and his mother in the family plot, stark reminders of the decimation of the family by this horrible disease. At the service, following a short message by his cousin, we played a couple of my dad's favorite songs, which had been part of his original service. Listening to "Bridge over Troubled Water" and "I'll Fly Away" was enough to bring fresh tears to my eyes nine months later. I saw relatives I hadn't seen since elementary school, and some family members that I had never met before. Everyone seemed to have a story about my dad and his brother during their childhood, which I soaked up like a dry sponge.

The absence of my father could not have been more obvious the rest of our family trip. I had never been to my parents' old stomping grounds without him narrating, and my mom painfully recognized the gaps in her recollection of their hometown (as well as how much had changed in the thirty-five years since they lived there). Actually, we left a part of him (in ash form) at each of the significant places we stopped on our pilgrimage to all of his old haunts, most notably Marquette in the Upper Peninsula, where he attended Northern Michigan University and had lived with my mom for the first three years of their marriage. I was deeply cognizant that this would probably be my last opportunity to experience this period of my dad's life.

My sister was deeply affected by this portion of the trip, as this was also her alma mater. She had made many wonderful memories of her own here after leaving the comfort our parents' house in California to step out on her own. Michigan had been where most of our family vacations had been growing up, so while it was distant territory, it was also a very familiar place to test her wings. Bittersweet reminiscences, which moving forward, would be hers as the new memory keeper of this special location.

Fortunately, having two squirmy, over-stimulated kids with us brought some comic relief to the rather somber journey. The kids constantly kept us laughing, and the continual care they required, especially out of their routine and normal environment, was a needed distraction. The trip was hard and painful on many levels, but many good memories came from it too. The kids got to experience a motel hot tub, something that brought deep belly giggles and more than a little paranoia about sharing a tub with unpleasant "floaties" (to be clear, this was in our room, not the public one). There were several emergency feedings in the back of the rented minivan alongside the busy county road. But to top it off was the diaper explosion of 2010 that required all hands on deck to remedy, as we had not yet checked into the hotel for the day. If they had known what lurked within Adeline's diaper and all her clothes, they may not have honored our reservation.

We flew home a week later, having the great fortune of staying clear of any hospital during our seven-day vacation. On the flight home, the kids were not as compliant as my gallbladder, and they slept very little during the painfully long five-hour flight. I'm so thankful there were four sets of hands to pass them around and attempt to keep them entertained, at least avoiding screaming and angering all the passengers. This expedition had been emotionally exhausting enough without the outstanding task of organ removal hanging over my head. I just wanted to be done and over with it. Oddly, the thoughts about my dream, now almost four months in the past, were pretty far out of my mind. A simple, routine gallbladder removal seemed pretty innocuous, certainly not something that would be life threatening; all the more reason to believe that the dream was harmless and not prophetic.

Tuesday couldn't come faster, and I marched into the hospital like a brave little soldier ready to take my licks and move forward with some culinary normalcy. Ryan and Chaya joined me in the day surgery waiting room, while I finished up the insurance and consent paperwork. I was scheduled to have my gallbladder removed laparoscopically (three small incisions around my navel) at 1:00 p.m., and the procedure would be done within an hour. Recovery, I was told varied by patient. I might be ready to go home by 5 p.m. or I could need to stay until morning.

The pre-surgery consultation for the procedure had been done before my vacation, and so the surgical team had the instructions for my specific cardiac needs prior to the procedure.

However, while speaking with the nurse responsible for prepping me in the pre/post room, I learned that they had not made two crucial phone calls. The first one should have been to my primary cardiologist to get specific direction about any potential situations they could encounter and how they should be handled. Just as importantly, it was required during surgery that a company representative of my pacemaker/defibrillator device to be present when the device was turned off and on. Huge oops. So I waited patiently for the situation to be resolved, which took an hour and a half for them to find a pacemaker rep, and get them through traffic from Seattle to Tacoma for this "emergency" situation. What is it that they say about "your procrastination does not my emergency make"?

The final red flag of the afternoon came in the form of a verbal fight between my admitting nurse and the procedure nurse. They outwardly showed their disdain for one another and complained about each other mistakes in front of me. I should have taken all of these indicators as forewarning about the care they would take with me, but naively (and regrettably) I didn't spring from my bed, screaming and running for the exit.

When I awoke from the anesthesia an hour later, around 4:30, I was quite uncomfortable, feeling as though my guts, had been rearranged, which they had. Although I felt nauseous and very light-headed, thankfully my blood pressure and pulse had remained stable during the procedure, which is not a given for me. However, I didn't feel in any shape to be escorted to the door, but that's what was about to happen. While they didn't say it out right, these nurses were ready to go home, as their job in a "day" surgery ward was primarily the normal day shift and over at 5 p.m.

After the doctor had come in to check on my condition, the nurse asked me if I could stand. Once I had delicately and agonizingly completed her compulsory exercise, they offered me some crackers, sat me down in the chair, and told me they would wait outside while I changed and got ready to leave. I told them I didn't feel well, but they assured me this was normal, and I should be feeling much better within two to three days. Ryan and I stared blankly at one another. We couldn't believe they were sending me home so quickly, despite my concerns. Inquiring about whether I should stay a little longer to get my bearings, they murmured something about the complications of switching my care to the night staff elsewhere in the hospital and how I would be just fine.

So by 5:30 p.m., I was out the door, pain meds in hand. This might be very normal operating procedure for them, but it didn't set well with me. Not just the discomfort I was feeling physically, but the uneasiness I felt about the procedure in general. So, it shouldn't have surprised me when seven days later, my guts were telling me something wasn't copacetic.

19

Still feeling pretty rotten, the following Tuesday I asked Lissa to come over to watch the kids while I went to see the doctor. I was in constant pain, and my nausea appeared to be getting worse. When I called the doctor's office, I found out that the doctor who had done the procedure was out for the day, but the nurse from his office would see me. My intuition was that it was urgent and that I should attempt to get an appointment right away, even if it meant that someone would have to watch the kids for a short time. As I was walking through the house with Lissa explaining what the kids needed for the next few hours, she stopped, turning to me, and looked at me, with deep concern on her face.

"How are you really feeling?" she said, looking at me with deep concern in her eyes. "You don't look so great. Your face has a yellow hue, and your eyes are the same horrid color."

"Yeah, I feel as bad as I look, constant pain and nausea. I've called a few times, and they just keep telling me that it is normal to be uncomfortable. When I called today I was fairly insistent. I know that I should be starting to feel better, but each day seems to be noticeably worse. I sure hope they can help." I said with a weak smile as my guts churned unrelentlessly.

"Don't worry about the kids. I'll stay as long as you need. Just give me a call when you know something."

"Thank you again for coming on such short notice. You're a life saver."

When I arrived at the doctor's office, they took some blood work and called upstairs to the lab so they could get a CT of my abdomen. After a horrible game of "let's see how many pokes it takes to get an IV in the vein," they decided to abandon the test. The IV placement was so poor that the fluid made my arm feel as if it was on fire. The doctor finally got the information they were looking for by doing an ultrasound. It was quickly determined that the bile ducts and the canals that go through the liver were blocked and had become irritated, indicating that there might have been an injury or occlusion of the common (main) bile duct from the gallbladder removal. I vividly remember the nurses telling me during the procedure work-up and consent form signing that injuring the main bile duct was a small possibility, like 1:1,000. I should have played the lottery that day.

To make matters worse, the bile that was consequently flowing into my abdomen had thrown off my INR results (indication of the blood thinner's effectiveness). Whereas, my INR should have been between 2-3, I was now sitting at 9! Spontaneous internal bleeding can occur at anything over four. As a huge bleeding risk and jaundice beyond belief, they had no choice but admit me into the hospital. They decided that immediate exploratory surgery was necessary to correct the bile leakage that was occurring. The problem was that they could not attempt surgery until my INR was under control or I could bleed out on the table.

The quickest way to accomplish that task was to administer frozen plasma intravenously until they achieved the desired INR result. This meant hours of lying in a hospital bed with an extremely cold substance coursing through my veins. More concerning was that the enormous volume of plasma needed to bring my INR down six points was making my fluid volume extremely uncomfortable. Not only did I become bloated, but my fluid overloaded was making it difficult to breathe, a noteworthy symptom of heart failure, something I had never before experienced. While their solution was to slow the IV speed, they never addressed the heart failure by administering Lasix, a diuretic that would have helped to remove excessive fluid around my heart.

As a consequence of the slower plasma intake, the surgery that was previously scheduled for 8:00 a.m. the next morning had to be delayed a few hours. By time I was "acceptable" for surgery, I felt like a stuffed goose ready for slaughter. I could hardly move because I became breathless just rolling over, and my skin was tight in my arms and legs.

The surgical plan was to try to laparoscopically explore the bile leak, and place a T-tube cholangiogram into my biliary ducts, allowing for drainage of the bile through a plastic tube to the outside of my body. My thoughts were now lost in my dream from five months ago, trying desperately to replay the scene for any missing clues that could speak to what was occurring. The same thoughts were obviously fresh in Ryan's mind as well. As they were taking me down to surgery, Ryan leaned over the rail of the gurney, and we began to pray.

"God, please keep Erin safe and give us peace today," Ryan prayed, "It is hard to believe that her work here is done, I beg you to give her more time. The kids and I need her here. Not my will, but yours, Lord"

"Not my will, but yours," I reiterated. "You are good and you love us. Help us to understand the purposes of this pain in our life and how it brings glory to you. Make your presence known to us now," I wept. Opening my eyes, I reached out for a hug from Ryan, "I love you and the kids more than words can say. If I don't make it, please remind Addie and Isaac how much mom loved them." Sadness was crushing my heart, the tears stuck in my throat. Laying my hand on top of Ryan's and squeezing gently, there was no more to say.

Clearly, I made it through the surgery. However, by the following day, it was obvious that the procedure had failed from my heightened pain level and the lack of successful drainage. So they tried again the next day (after another horrible round of plasma volume overload, and the same prayers with Ryan alongside the gurney), placing a stent to help the external drain. The T-tube was removed, and a new drain location was created to remove the excess bile. After the second surgery I had two drains in my abdomen (one active and one abandoned), both of which caused a new type of pain, much more intense and biting than the earlier aching and cramping; pain that now kept me from getting out of bed.

I feared even the slightest movement, especially getting up because it meant that bile, which is exceptionally caustic, would rub the open wounds at the drains sites and create an excruciating burning sensation. Seeing my distress, they installed a pain medication IV in a new PICC line they installed, one that I could control. Whenever the pain got to be too much, I could push my button once or, if it was really bad, twice. It would put me to sleep in seconds so I hated using it when I had visitors, but most times I found sleep was preferable to the pain. Despite my desire to be hospitable, most of the next week was spent unconscious.

During my hospitalization, the children were bounced between my mom's house and Ryan's parents, so that Ryan could continue working. It was difficult to see him so forlorn and dispirited, with long days at work and then spending all of his free time at the hospital with me, only to go home each night to an empty house. It was quite a change from the bustling house and life from before our trip. Both of us were as low as I ever remember being, each lost in our own sorrow and misery; him as a mourning spouse and frustrated caregiver, and myself crumbling on the inside with fear of losing my family. The situation seemed so hopeless, especially with the prophetic dream coming true right in front of our eyes. Indeed, a tube had burst, my pain was intense, and without an end in sight, only death was the remaining holdout.

God, what now? While I tried to remain expectant, I know that at least presently, I was not God-glorifying in my thoughts. All of the prayer warriors that had been mobilized after my dream, continued to fervently plead for my life. My mom shared during her visits about how her whole island was praying for me, as well as prayer circles from churches all over Washington, Colorado, Illinois, Montana, Michigan, Minnesota, and California. There were a bunch of people talking to God on my behalf, including friends that didn't even have a relationship with Him. Amazing how prayer touches not just the recipient, but also the requester.

Nevertheless, I still didn't believe in my heart that God would be willing to change His plan. "His will be done" was my only consolation, and these days it was much more somber and resigned. Praise for His power and dominion did not fill my lips. Shamefully, the redemption of my soul in His glorious plan seemed to bring me little comfort. While I was excited about reaching the heavenly realms and meeting my Lord and experiencing the great joy that awaited me, my mind could not fathom how God could restore joy to my family's hearts. Somehow, I trusted Him with my life, but not with my family's, still naively thinking that I held the key and kept it all from unraveling. All my spiritual growth in the last three years was hanging in the balance. My faith and trust had been so easily shattered. I felt jealousy that I might not get to watch my babies grow up, and anger that God would "take" them from me. Though He is the giver of all good things, my sense of entitlement was blinding me from thankfulness and seeing His goodness.

The highlight of my stay was when the grandparents brought Adeline and Isaac to visit. Wrapped in wires, IVs, and multiple tubes, their endless fidgeting was problematic in my fragile state, but I loved having them near me and nuzzling them in my bed. Isaac was content to sit for a spell, but Addie was constantly squirming, showing off her new found independence. They never stayed in one place long and ended up crawling on the dirty, disease-contaminated floors. So after seeing them in their fresh, adorable summer outfits (not yet soiled from the day's activities), smothering them with kisses and cuddles, and maybe helping with a bottle and diaper change, they were usually wheeled out of the room in a stroller, just in time to push my pain button and fall into a fitful slumber.

About six days into my hospitalization, they tried one last time to open the stricture (blocked/injured area) of my common bile duct by using a catheter, but the procedure caused a reopening of the duct and necessitated a new drainage site and a brand new six-inch scar from my just under the bra line to my navel; more pain, more meds, more prayers. The doctors were at a loss for how to fix me and they couldn't get my pain under control. The drains were discharging some bile, but not enough to take my discomfort away.

Fortunately, my heart rhythm stayed stable, despite the doctor's best efforts to thwart it by skipping some of my arrhythmia medications due to low blood pressure. Ryan, in a courageous act of assertiveness, got into the face of the attending physician and demanded that I be given my normal dosages. He recommended that they research my heart history with the doctors at UW so they could be assured that my pressures would stay low and that holding my meds could be detrimental, if not outright dangerous. Unconcerned about being labeled the squeaky wheel, I was going to get my correct heart medication dosages, hell or high water. They finally relented.

Equally scary, was the worsening pulmonary edema and congestive heart failure that I experienced during my 12-day stay. Though they noted in my medical record that I was experiencing both of these issues, they never treated me for them. This is how my uncle died, and the hospital didn't seem to take it very seriously.

Finally, after all their solutions were exhausted, the team suggested that I see a specialist at University of Washington (my preferred hospital) to evaluate me and see if he could resolve my problem. Dr. Park, a liver and cancer specialist, agreed to add me to his already packed schedule, but he insisted that I heal at home for four to six weeks before he would attempt surgery again. Even in my impatience, I realized that my body was not ready to withstand another surgery, and waiting would ensure that some of the inflammation that had occurred from the bile leakage and subsequent surgeries had time to dissipate. Once the inflammation was gone, Dr. Park stood a much better chance of successfully repairing the damaged bile duct. However, the "pre-surgery healing clock" couldn't start ticking until the Tacoma hospital got my current drainage and pain situation stabilized.

On Day 10, my nurse, a gal who deserves my deepest gratitude, was given a mandate from the attending doctor to "McGuyver" the drain to work better, and miraculously, she did. Over the course of a day and a few trials and errors, she managed to effectively begin draining my sites through an ingenious suction contraption she assembled using the everyday medical materials available to her. Immediately, I began to feel better, and by the next day, my pain was relieved enough to ask for a bath. The doctors could tell that I was now ready to fly the coop and move on to greener pastures, even in my broken state. I missed my children and family immensely, and couldn't wait to be with them more than the short visits I could tolerate while in the hospital. Excitedly, I was released to home the next day.

Waiting for the next surgery began in earnest. I was advised that in order for my incision to heal, I could not lift more than ten pounds, which meant I could not carry my own children during the recuperation time. Now, both the children and I needed to be cared for. Reluctantly, I accepted that I was utterly useless in their care, but I resolved to not miss any more of the summer with them, even if only watching from the sidelines. Admittedly less than ideal, Ryan and I devised a schedule where Ryan would pack all of us (with an enormous amount of baby gear) into the car, and drive us back and forth between his parents' house and my mother's house, spending a week or two at each place. This is how we spent the next six long weeks, with Ryan hauling us around, yet blessed to have the whole family together at least on the weekends. Ryan missed us all tremendously and was very lonely on the nights that he couldn't visit, but it was too hard for him to remain focused at work while living out of suitcases during weekdays. However, difficult as it was for our immediate family, and the family that was housing and caring for us, we agreed that this was the best solution.

Being with the kids during this long healing process was wonderful, but there was still a sense that many of the joys of motherhood that I had been anticipating were just outside my grasp. Everyone tried to include me in activities such as feeding a bottle, dressing them, and giving kisses before they went to bed, which allowed me to stay engaged in their lives. But most of the time, I didn't have the strength or stamina to keep up with two antsy pre-toddlers, forced instead to watch others do the more interactive parts like playing with them on the floor or having a spontaneous ticklefest.

While playtime on the floor and helping with bathtime were not possible for me, I happily became a valuable cheerleader from the couch, with Adeline and Isaac frequently seeking my affirmations and shimmying over on their bellies to visit me. We also attempted to develop routines that I could participate in, even in my limited capacity. Each night before bed, the kids got a bath and settled down with a bottle in front of the TV for "Veggie Tales – Silly Songs." The same show every night, with all the adults joyously singing along, and Addie and Isaac peacefully falling asleep. So simple, but a very special way to bring happiness into a tough time of life.

Addie and Isaac were making huge strides in coordination and grasping, rolling and crawling, communicating without crying, and understanding directions. They loved to giggle and it melted my heart each and every time. Their personalities were being revealed daily, and it was beautiful to see the "people" they were becoming. Addie is full of exuberance, curiosity, and daring, sometimes getting her into precarious spots, such as when she cornered a ticked off cat in the living room. But she has a real tender, affectionate side too, like when we went on a picnic and I watched her belly crawl through a field of wildflowers, gently touching and smelling each one, taking care to not damage the delicate petals. Unfortunately for Isaac, she lacks a sense of personal space (nothing has changed from the womb) and frequently would crawl right over him to reach a toy. Her assertive attitude combined with the "me first" of a toddler made for some tear-filled tug-of-wars.

Isaac, on the other hand, is more reserved and cautious; slower to step out and try new things, but when he gained confidence in a new skill, he was undeterred and masterful. While Addie walked right away, she did so with a lot of falls. Isaac waited a couple of more months, when he was more sure-footed and hardly ever took a tumble. He has a heart of gold, is nurturing beyond measure, and highly sensitive to others' feelings. He is constantly concerned about his sister's well-being. If she is crying, he would start crying as well; not so on the flip side. He is incredibly playful and always quick with a smile. As a toddler, he made a game of rolling up in his blanket on the floor until you could no longer see anything but a giggling lump on the carpet. You'd roll him out, and he'd be a burrito again within minutes.

I was thankful to be able to witness the many beautiful moments of the babies' growth in those long months, but I couldn't erase the nagging sense of being neglectful in my motherly duties, along with being irritated at the situation I found myself in. Recognizing how blessed we were to have family that so readily gave up their homes and the quiet of their lives to take my brood in, I felt guilt for my discontentment. This was nothing like what I had hoped motherhood would be; swimming in diapers, covered in slobber, and guiding little hands in the exploration of their new world. All my fears about not being strong enough to handle parenthood came crashing down. I wanted these children so badly, but now responsibility fell to someone else. In my head, I heard the whisper of a big fat "I told you so," even though I knew there was none.

After a month of constant nausea and discomfort, being tousled back and forth away from my home, watching my children grow from the sidelines, and seeing my husband for only short bursts of time, I was having a full blown pity party. My patience for the next surgery was wearing thin; I longed to start my final road to recovery. Having met with Dr. Park early on in the waiting period, I knew it would not be an easy procedure. He explained the Roux-En-Y procedure to me and described the potential risks, including the chance that it might not be successful. My most recent six-inch scar would be reopened and extended by another four inches into an "L" shaped configuration. The surgical team planned to go in to my abdomen and cut out a section of large intestine and use it to bypass the blocked portion of the common bile duct that was occluded, allowing the bile to make it through my digestive system. The blockage and leak in my common bile duct was in the upper portion, tight to the junction of the common duct and the cystic duct, and right next to my liver. This meant that they didn't have much duct length to work with, and therefore, they had one shot to attach the transplanted segment of my large intestine. I don't recall ever hearing their plan B.

Finally, the day of the procedure arrived. While I was nervous about how the surgery would go, I was more excited about being on the flip side and recovering once again. The surgeon had warned me that I would be very uncomfortable afterward and I needed to stay on top of the pain management doctors, who, ironically, tended to be rather complacent about ensuring pain relief. The reality of his statement turned out to be agonizingly true.

Once again, Ryan and I spent some time in prayer before I was taken back to be prepped. We gave the surgery and outcome over to God, and thanked Him for our time together, as we had done countless times in the last few months. We both knew that this was another surgery that could fulfill the prediction, yet regardless of how long we had to prepare, neither of us was ready for me to go. I was not ready to give up my place as Adeline and Isaacs' mother, and Ryan's wife. Likewise, Ryan had repeatedly faced losing me during our multiple attempts to have children and had still not come to peace with it.

God, I believe, had not prepared our hearts for me to leave. I know that in heaven we will be totally content, with no desire to look back on our earthly life, but on this earth our feeble human brains naturally cling to what we know to be precious and invaluable; for me, that is my family. They are the most magnificent gift from God, and only He can supernaturally release me from the desire to remain with them in this broken world.

The difficult reality that I must acknowledge is that my reluctance to accept my potential death could be just another example of my desire to be in control. It is an outright lie that I can take better care of my family than God can, and I repent of having those thoughts. God is great, and I am not. He knows what is best, and I do not. I pray that when the time of my passing is imminent that God, in His supreme graciousness, will wipe away my fear of letting my family down or leaving things undone, and tenderly remind me that in His sovereignty, things are never left incomplete or broken.

The Newsboys' song, "In Christ Alone" speaks so powerfully to my heart about the need to rest in His great plan and grasp the hope provided in the victory Christ won over death.

"No guilt in life, no fear in death
This is the power of Christ in me
From life's first cry to final breath,
Jesus commands my destiny
No power of hell, no scheme of man
Can ever pluck me from His hand
'til He returns or calls me home
Here in the power of Christ I'll stand."

After I was moved to the pre-op room, they started my IV, attached monitors, and placed an epidural in my back, meant to eliminate the pain between my chest and my pelvis. The numbing sensation came on immediately, and I felt confident my pain management would be under control. Beginning to relax, they wheeled me into the operating room. They told me I would feel a slight burning as the initial anesthesia was given through my IV, but I would be out soon. Counting from 10 down, I made it to 7; then blackness.

Once the surgery was complete, I was taken to the post-op ward for care until I was ready for a regular patient room. Although Dr. Park had discussed the surgery outcome with my family several hours earlier, he came in later that evening, after I had awoken, to explain to me how the procedure had gone. The team had been successful at connecting my main bile duct to the new bypass intestine and they were hopeful this would eliminate the stricture and leakage issues for good. However, the doctor was so concerned about someone going in later and "messing up" the delicate new digestive system he had reorganized, that he also removed my appendix since it looked as though it would need to be done sooner than later. Why not do it now and save an additional surgery? I got a two-for-one procedure. He advised me that the recovery would be slow and that I would need to take it easy for the next six to eight weeks. The summer that I had been so excited to share with my new family was already gone and the fall was about to be taken as well.

Upon regaining consciousness, I realized that my pain was no longer under control as I had earlier believed. I told Dr. Park about the horrible pain I was experiencing, and he made some phone calls to the pain management team. Already into the evening, it was time for him to leave so he promised to check on me tomorrow to see how I was progressing. Then he was off, feeling assured from his phone calls that my pain would be resolved shortly.

However, despite his request, they never came. Having spoken with the nurses on the phone during the night, they had decided my blood pressure wasn't high enough to administer any IV pain medications, so I waited and waited. The pain in my abdomen continued to be excruciating and it took me pleading with the nurses to have the pain management doctors finally come. They arrived as a herd of attending, fellow, and resident doctors at 11:00 a.m. the next morning, almost 15 hours later. I was in tears and begging them to do something to relieve the searing agony, making me physically shake. After a quick evaluation they determined that the epidural was no longer working as it should. "Really?!" I thought. It took seeing me writhe around and a combined 15 college degrees for you to assess this! I wasn't just in pain anymore, I was livid.

They wheeled me down to the original pre-op room and reinserted the epidural line in my back, which gave me nearly instant relief. Why couldn't they have done this last night so I didn't have to be tortured all night and my sleep stolen? The recovery was already difficult enough with the nasal-gastric tube continuously draining horrid tasting fluids through my esophagus and the metallic taste of the epidural to top it off. I was continually dry heaving because it felt as though there was something lodged in my throat that I had to clear. I knew it was the nasal tube, but it couldn't stop the urge to cough. My blood pressure was having difficulty stabilizing so they started holding my heart meds, including my anti-arrhythmia drugs. This caused my heart to feel fluttery, and I demanded that I see my electrophysiologist, Dr. Rho. After Dr. Rho spoke to the attending cardiologist, he finally relented and allowed me to get my correct dosages, over 12 hours late. The nurses were also given instructions about the authorized range of blood pressures deemed acceptable for them to administer my heart meds. Normal hospital protocol is that top number (systolic) must be over 90, but mine was dropped to 85, where I was hovering.

Fluids were off limits to me for three days, which meant that all medication was administered by IV, including the dreaded potassium and magnesium. While potassium and magnesium given by IV is the preferred method for quick absorption into the body, doctors do not understand that it is also the most painful. The second night of my stay I woke up with my arm burning like fire. No matter how much I rubbed or shook it, I could not extinguish the flames inside my veins. I pushed the nurse call light, and when she came to the room, I asked her what she had put in my IV while I was sleeping. Just as I had suspected–potassium. She explained that she could try to slow the speed of the IV and put on a heat pack to make the pain tolerable, but I didn't have much choice because my labs indicated I needed the extra potassium. These solutions helped dull the pain a bit, but only slightly, and I was condemned to another sleepless night. I couldn't wait until the NG (nasogastric) tube was gone and pills were an option.

Ice chips were allotted only to wet my lips, but this time, unlike my previous ablations, the nurses could not be persuaded to let me to swallow the chips. It was imperative to my healing that nothing went down my digestive track until they knew for sure that there was no bleeding or other problems with the new bypass. That meant they were waiting for my body to give them signals that normal function had returned, in a nut shell, I had to pass gas. Once I did, they would resume slowly weaning me from fluids to solid food. On the third day, after hours in the bathroom, I finally passed the gas they required. The whole family celebrated my crude bodily function with high-fives, whoops and excited phone calls to other family members, unable to be a part of this momentous day. Disgusting, albeit natural, yet one step closer to going home. Jell-O was my reward that night!!

On the fifth day they removed the NG tube because it was no longer draining any more fluid from my surgery. Having the tube gone made the rest of my hospital stay seem like pie. I no longer had any dietary restrictions and it was also one less thing strapped to me, making bathroom runs less challenging. The pain had steadily diminished through the week and had become tolerable, with only the healing of a scar remaining. Getting released on the seventh day was nothing short of thrilling. It was so exciting to start my final recovery period, although not in my own home, but back to the grandparent shuffle.

My appetite was improving with the bile out of my system and the digestive track righted. I had lost almost 20 pounds, which I could do without, but it would have been a more enjoyable loss under different circumstances. Although, I was told that there were foods I wouldn't be able to eat anymore, like dairy and greasy cheeseburgers, I was overjoyed at the idea that most of my food choices were appetizing again.

This new recovery period was a repeat performance of the last round. Shuffling back and forth between Ryan's parents' house and my mom's house allowed Ryan to visit on the evenings and weekends. I could see the finish line this time, whereas last time it was still so far in the distance. Everyone was getting moody by this point, and we all wanted it to end sooner than we knew it would. Adeline and Isaac were getting increasingly mobile and difficult to corral during the period of the second recovery. They were nearing the 10-month threshold, my daughter standing unassisted against the couch, and my son sitting up on his own. I longed to be on the floor playing with them and bringing them into my lap on the couch, but I tried to restrain myself. Sometimes I could not resist, getting graciously scolded, appreciative of my desire to interact with my children. Whatever I could do to be involved, that didn't involve lifting or straining, I did. It took a while to realize that what my kids needed most was my presence. That's what they would remember, if they had any memory of the past five months of craziness.

The greatest lesson I learned during the summer of 2010 was a renewed appreciation for life; the family and friends that surround me, the sunshine and the natural splendor of the outside, but most importantly, for every minute/hour/day of breath we are given. Patience was a close second, but my retention of that lesson is poor, finding myself endlessly backsliding. However, I seldom forget the special gift I was given to have more time on this earth.

I believe God granted me more time with my children and husband, possibly because of all the prayers lifted to Him on my behalf, but also for the story He gave me to share that gives Him praise and glory. I don't know why I was spared the fate of my premonition, but I am thankful and want to live purposefully for His sake, making every day count. Mercifully, God's only desire for reciprocation is to have me glorify Him the rest of my days, however many they may be, and that is what I intend to do.

I want people to know how incredible His love and grace is, and to seek it for themselves. In the absence of a miracle, which is definitely within God's ability, my damaged heart has an abbreviated life span. Long past when I'm gone, I want this book to be a reminder for my children who their provider and sustainer is. The other intention of telling my story is to share a small piece of myself with all who lack hope in their moments of suffering and pain. My life is a testimony that we have a God that comforts those who hurt and wants to speak to those who will listen. Although it may be hard to understand in the midst of pain, He has a purpose for the path you are enduring, not just for other's benefit, but also for you.

"But we have this treasure in jars of clay to show that this all-surpassing power is from God, and not from us. We are hard pressed on every side, but not crushed; perplexed, but not in despair; persecuted, but not abandoned; struck down, but not destroyed.
"Therefore, do not lose heart. Though outwardly we are wasting away, yet inwardly we are being renewed day by day. For light and momentary troubles are achieving for us an eternal glory that far outweighs them all. So we fix our eyes not on what is seen, but on what is unseen. For what is seen is temporary, but what is unseen is eternal."
2 Corinthians 4:7-9, 16-18

It is a mystery to me why I was given the warning of my impending demise, (something I might ask God about when I get the chance) but I do know the dream and its aftermath were meant to be shared and provided as a reminder of His endless compassion and love. The vision that God allowed my father to relay was accurate and specific right up to the very end, but the end was rewritten, not by God, for He knows the entire story down to the minute detail, but rewritten in my mind and my reality. I get to live in "THE AND" a bit longer in this beautiful, but broken world, and eternally in the magnificence that is to come. My prayer is that you will too. Praise be to God!

EPILOGUE

After the drama of 2010, my heart stabilized for over a year and a half before it begun to show its true colors again. However, even in the calm period, my energy has slowly dissipated and prompted us to change houses. Although we loved our first family home and dreamed of raising our children in it, the reality was that it no longer fit my physical capacity with multiple levels of steep stairs, a washer and dryer in the basement, and bedrooms on the top level.

We made the difficult decision in January of 2012 to find a ranch-style home where everything I needed was on one level. God graciously maneuvered this move during the bottom of the housing market by sending the new owners right to our door 24 hours after we decided to sell, without even putting it on the market. Our neighbors, who were renting the house next door and had become good friends over the last year, agreed to our asking price and we found a new home within days. The whole transaction took only three months.

During the middle of the move, which is inevitably stressful with two toddlers even in the best scenario, God brought a remarkable reminder of his continual desire to comfort. Having an unusually tense day of working with the mortgage company and their realtor, I began trying to understand why I wasn't receiving important closing-related phone calls. Having learned several years previous that while our phone was in use, all simultaneous calls were automatically sent to a voicemail separate from our normal answering machine, I started to dig through our office files looking for the phone provider's instructions to access this unattended answering service. Finally I found it and sat down at the kitchen table to decipher the manual.

After connecting to the service, the first message left me speechless. It was my father, calling to see how I was doing, expressing his concern that I might be pushing myself too hard and reminding me that he loved me, his voice cracking under his own breathlessness. The message must have been at least three years old, and based on the chronology of the initial phone system setup, it was no more than a month before his passing. I found myself crying tears of joy, having longed to hear his voice again. He seemed to be reaching out from Heaven to tell me he was checking in on me. Thank you God for knowing exactly what I needed at that moment. My spirit was calmed and lifted, my feet not touching the ground for days afterward.

Likewise, the timing of the move was entirely under His sovereignty, knowing that a new round of complications were on the way. By the end of the year, I started experiencing significant heart failure issues, including the inability to lay flat at night, oppressive breathlessness and fatigue, and arrhythmia induced by the increased fluid pressure. After increasing my diuretic dosage and changing my heart medications around with no improvement, the doctors decided to try a third ablation surgery. We hoped the surgery would prolong the need for the arrhythmia medication of last resort – Amiodarone, which is notoriously toxic with permanent side effects such as multiple organ damage. Unfortunately, the surgery was a failure and their efforts could not suppress my continued electrical disruption.

We simultaneously were forced to make the difficult decision to put the children in full time preschool because I was no longer able to care for them consistently. My health was erratic, and I was in the hospital almost every week. Ryan needed a long-term solution that would allow the kids to live at home when I wasn't there, and since he had the flexibility to work from home, he could schedule his day around pick-up and drop-off times. The solution alleviated the need to schlep the kids from one grandparent to another.

Consequently, my ego took a big hit. Not only could I not work a career I loved, but I couldn't reliably care for my children either, and they were now bearing the burden of long, tiring days at school. Feeling guilty that I was forcing Adeline and Isaac to grow up too quickly, I grew jealous of the families whose 3-year olds frolicked carefree at home. In my uselessness, most days I found myself home alone, reading and doing puzzles, longing for interaction with the outside world. I wasn't able to even grocery shop without someone to push the cart or carry the bags into the house. Whenever I had to walk a long distance, I rented a motorized cart so that I wouldn't tire or go out of rhythm. Eventually, as the childcare and medical bills piled up, I recognized that the situation wasn't changing anytime soon and accepted that I was officially disabled. It was a tough pill to swallow, but I believe it was the beginning of my move from resignation to contentment. I stopped struggling for solutions where there were none, and just let God plan out each of my days, one at a time. And this is where my joy was found. My hope had not been lost, only misplaced. My hope can't be in the anticipation of a fully healed body (although I don't believe you should ever stop praying for it). Hope can only be found in gratefully receiving God's blessings in each moment and the future promise of His unending kingdom, where there will be no infirmity- physical, mental, or spiritual.

However, I was cognizant that contentment with life does not mean complacency and I owed it to my family to try everything. God wanted me to be proactive in the health of my body, so we began the process of heart transplant evaluation. I prayed fervently that I could get on the wait list, but this too hit a dead end. The particular tests that they run in order to qualify you for a new heart are not evidenced in my disease. The tests are looking for big baggy hearts that have no squeeze capacity. My issue was that my heart has too much muscle and is unable to relax enough to fill efficiently.

My only hope for a transplant is to be classified as an "exception", which normally puts you on the bottom of the wait list. There is not much upward movement unless you become "critical" and by then, it can be too late. The evaluation team decided that I should try the last rhythm drug available, Amiodarone, even though it is never considered a long term solution. The doctors had little hope that it would work, but by God's grace, it has! Although my heart failure continues to progress, my atrial fibrillation/flutter has been eliminated for the last two years. God, once again, wrote another chapter for me and gave me more time to enjoy His many blessings.

****

Some of you may still be wondering, what happened to our two remaining frozen embryos? Well, that was another beautiful labyrinth that God took us on. While we initially froze them in case the first IVF attempt did not work, after the birth of Adeline and Isaac, we knew that we would not be having any more children. So what now? Although it had been Ryan's and my first inclination to donate them to science, for some reason, when the bi-yearly bill came for the frozen storage fee, neither of us were willing to make our decision final. We paid the bill and waited for the next one, each time telling ourselves that it was silly to keep prolonging the inevitable.

However, about three years ago, Ryan and I simultaneously had a revelation that God wanted us to give the embryos away to our close friends, Brian and Cindy. They were still struggling to have a family, having tragically lost yet another daughter, Emma, at four years old in 2010 to the same genetic disease that took Maggie. We knew the agony of having our dream of a family dwindle before your eyes, while still grieving the loss of what could have been, and in their case, an actual child they had grown to love. Although we were both still vacillating on the idea, we were obedient to the direction we were hearing, so we made the offer to them. But just as Rachel and Travis' initial offer came when we were not ready, so did ours. Thankfully, they chose to sit and ruminate on the offer, and we did likewise. God continued to work on our hearts and many nights of sleep were lost, fluctuating between completely positive of our decision and absolutely terrified of the consequences. Our friends were fully aware of the potential genetic condition, so that wasn't the reason for our hesitation; it was entirely based on our ability to let someone else raise our genetic offspring.

After months and months of painful soul-searching, God reminded us that these were His children, and not ours. This was the exact timing that our friends came back to us to ask if our offer still stood. The answer was an emphatic "Yes!" While I admit that part of me wanted to see who these two children would become, my greatest hope was to see our friends have the family they desired. I knew I could now fully release myself from needing to parent them. However, Ryan and I had two stipulations. The first was that they had to implant both embryos, and the second was that our children and theirs would know they were related at a mutually agreed upon time.

Sadly, while I have no doubt that it was God leading us down this path, the IVF attempt was not successful. All of us were crushed, even to the point of wondering why God would take us down this long, painful road that He didn't intend to bless (at least not in the way we imagined). Again, the same stupid argument I had with Him about Aiden, and again the same answer came to me; because it's not about the outcome, it's about the journey and our relationship with Him—Trust, obey, and have peace. Beautifully, our friendship and love for Brian and Cindy deepened even more than we thought possible, and the master weaver simultaneously gave us resolution on what He intended for us to do with our embryos. What amazing sovereignty!

Devastatingly, about two years after the IVF failure, Cindy passed away from acute pancreatitis. Her death was so sudden and unexpected that all her friends and family were left reeling. She was a young healthy women that was supposed to enjoy many more years with her husband, Brian. I was the sick one and had been preparing for years for my departure. It made absolutely no sense to me. God's plan, once again, left me mystified and speechless. While I looked with sorrow at her lifeless body, all I could see was myself in her place and wonder why, why? Why her, and not me? Why anyone? Death is so contrary to what God intended. Thank you God, that through Jesus' victory, this is not the end, only "The And." There is another chapter in Cindy's life, and I will get to share in it someday. I am comforted to know that she loved the Lord and will be with her children again, but my arms will continue to ache for her breath-stealing hugs.

As for my children, they continue to be the most marvelous blessing in our lives. There have been challenges and drama, especially with Addie, such as her pneumonia hospitalization, the time she drank half a bottle of Tylenol, and her predisposition for running headlong into stationary objects. But for all the stress, I wouldn't exchange all the hugs, smiles, and giggles for anything in the world. Isaac loves music and he can't keep his body from moving when there's a strong beat. He's in love with Legos and Lincoln Logs, and has a real aptitude for space and form. Addie can spend hours focused on creating beautifully expressive drawings, already able to draw in perspective. She loves people and makes friends at every possible opportunity. Every trip to the park ends with countless hugs and goodbyes from kids she met only minutes before.

They are masters at making us laugh, eliminating any chance of boredom. Cracking jokes, doing a funny dance, or making a blanket fort, they are constantly reminding us to not take ourselves or life too serious, to remember the joy of our own childhoods.

These are a few moments that are too good to forget:
- One Christmas we decided to teach the kids about giving to others in need, so we chose an aid organization and let them pick out farm animals to donate. After we sent in our order, Isaac's face crinkled up in concern, "But how do they wrap up the animals as a gift? I don't want them getting hurt."
- Helping them to memorize scripture also had mixed results. Isaiah 26:4 -"The Lord is the Rock eternal," when translated by Addie became "The Lord is the walking turtle."
- Their humor is really telling of their personalities. A couple years ago, we were at a parade that was throwing an excessive amount of candy. Isaac's

reaction – "Mom, I don't want them to throw any more candy. Tell them to stop." Addie's reaction (assuming she was being personally gifted) – "I don't know why people like me so much."
- Punchlines are still a little elusive. Isaac – "Dad, this is a serious one. Why did the Daddy cross the road? Because all the cars had stopped."
- And self-diagnosis is second rate. Addie – "Mom, I think my foot is broken. It hurts when I walk on it and when I shake it, it rattles."

They are no longer toddlers, but full-fledged little people with minds of their own and the ability to accomplish so many tasks without assistance. Even at three, they began to show me that my help is no longer needed. Sometimes it was wonderful to be relieved of the physical strain of certain duties that challenged my heart when they were small and helpless, but it also reminded that they will never be my babies again. I celebrate their milestones like toilet training, getting in the car and buckling by themselves, and most recently, taking showers on their own, but I will miss the little perks of the tasks- nuzzling while changing a diaper, dressing them in the clothes I want (and match), or toweling off a sweet smelling baby after a bath. Watching them experience the world with such happy, carefree demeanors brings me great joy. As Addie likes to say, "I'm not ready for bed yet, I need to dance." Adults forget to take time to dance; life gets way too serious sometimes. We worry too much about the problems that don't even exist yet. God wants us to simply trust that He's got it handled and to rest in the creation He meant for us to enjoy.

It is for this reason that Ryan and I have decided to put off getting them genetically tested. We are afraid that knowing the results of the test at an early age would unfairly sway how we parent them. I don't want to even unconsciously hinder their activities and aspirations until there is a valid physical reason to do so. When the appropriate time comes (probably about eight years old), we will have them tested so that if necessary restrictions on competitive sports or preventative care is needed, we can provide it in a proactive manner.

In their maturation, they are beginning to recognize my limitations, including my need for others to assist in the physical activities that I am unable to participate in. Seeing me constantly go to the doctor or inhaling handfuls of pills, they now understand that Mom is sick and gets worn out easily. It pains me when they ask for me to join in their game and I have to decline. Recently, they have started asking, "When are you going to get better?" or "Are you still sick, Momma?" or "Are you going to die?" These questions pierce me deeply. I would like to be well more than they can possibly imagine. I ache to chase them in the yard and climb the playground with them; God willing, maybe someday. However, dwelling on what I can't do is counter-productive and takes my focus off of the things I can do. My energy is best spent on savoring every moment, thanking God for the blessing of their existence, and seeking to honor God in the days that He has given me.

Obviously, we are still praying for both Adeline and Isaac to be released from this burden and free to live a normal life, but we trust that God is in control of either outcome. Knowing full-well the hardship that is possible with this disease, from their very conception, we handed over Addie and Isaac to His perfect care and design. Even without the challenge of a heart condition, life on this earth is painful and we have never been promised anything different. Yet, God's beauty, peace, and joy still reign supreme. It is His creation and His ultimate victory in this broken world that we get to be a part of.

I am truly grateful for God's constant reminder of my need for Him in every life-giving beat. My life is full of dualities and contradictions, emotionally and spiritually, that cause me to wander and question my faith much more than I'd like to admit. Mercifully, I know that with God at my core, He will work all things to His glory; and my soul, which is His main concern, will prosper.

In Scotland, He brought me from distant to personal relationship. During my TIA, my confusion and frustration was turned to trust and surrender. When we lost Aiden, it was His guidance that changed my anger and despair to acceptance and dependence on Him. The surrogacy was fraught with fear and nervous anticipation, but I received assurance in His palpable presence, and joy in the fruit of the journey. In my brush with death throughout the gallbladder disaster, He transformed my hopeless resignation into gratitude for each moment we get to enjoy His overwhelming gifts. And now, when the future is just as uncertain, I have a renewed hope in the victory of His ultimate plan, but also in the knowledge that He loves me without regard for my limitations or productivity. I am here just to delight in Him and give Him praise. These are my ebenezers, and irrespective of the times I question my faith, His plan, or even His goodness, He will never forsake me and loves me just the same.

It is my hope that my story resonates with those who are challenged with chronic or terminal conditions, genetic or otherwise, that threaten to sap the joy out of their families. As you struggle to make sense of past pains and future uncertainties, I can full-heartedly empathize with the difficulty of the journey, but I plead with you to stay strong and not let your hope be extinguished; to continue searching fervently for God's voice and bountiful blessings. Without a doubt, my condition is not a mistake by God, and it has helped to mold my character in many positive ways. Regardless of our restrictions, God created us all with a purpose. The greatest challenge is deciphering how God wants to use the gifts He's given you, and allowing His strength to help you accomplish it – all for His glory and praise.

I speak it to God: I don't really want more time; I just want enough time. Time to breathe deep and time to see real and time to laugh, time to give You glory and rest deep and sing joy...
Ann Voskamp, *One Thousand Gifts*

"I have revealed and saved and proclaimed - I, and not some foreign god among you. You are my witnesses," declares the Lord, "that I am God."
Isaiah 43:12

Despite the pain, confusion and sadness that I have endured, I consider myself blessed to share my hope-filled optimism with my family, friends, and anyone who is inspired to pursue God and Christ Jesus more personally because of my story. If you seek Him, God will shape and guide your life to overwhelming joy in this life and the next. THE AND.

Myself as a fearless five year old

Our 2nd date – Military Ball

The And

Our Wedding

Chaya and I

My Dad and Mom at his last birthday

My baby shower

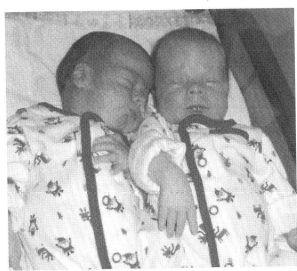

Isaac/Adeline in the NICU, Christmas 2009

Travis and Rachel in the NICU

Homecoming

Three months old

Halloween 2010

Rachel and Adeline

Ryan and Isaac

Brian and Cindy

First Day of School 2014

Christmas 2014

Made in the USA
San Bernardino, CA
02 August 2019